# POWER HEALING

Other books by John Wimber and Kevin Springer:

POWER EVANGELISM
POWER HEALING STUDY GUIDE


Books by Kevin Springer:

POWER ENCOUNTERS

# Power Healing

*John Wimber*
*with Kevin Springer*

 HarperSanFrancisco
*A Division of* HarperCollins*Publishers*

FIRST HARPERCOLLINS PAPERBACK EDITION PUBLISHED IN 1991.

---

**Library of Congress Cataloging-in-Publication Data**

Wimber, John.
   Power healing / John Wimber with Kevin Springer. — 1st
HarperCollins pbk. ed.
     p.   cm.
   Reprint. Originally published: San Francsico : Harper & Row, 1987.
   Includes bibliographical references.
   ISBN 0-06-069541-2 (alk. paper)
   1. Spiritual healing.  I. Springer, Kevin.  II. Title.
BT732.5.W55  1991
234'.13—dc20                           90-84440
                                                        CIP

---

In memory of David Watson.

*"Death has been swallowed up in victory."*

# Contents

# Acknowledgments

Our wives have made considerable sacrifices to see this book to completion. Carol Wimber read and offered valuable comments on each section and allowed many stories from her own life to be published. Suzanne Springer spent many long and late hours proofreading each draft, never complaining about the many changes that come during the writing of a book.

Kevin Perrotta, managing editor of *Pastoral Renewal* journal in Ann Arbor, Michigan, read every page of the early drafts and suggested changes that greatly improved the book. Dr. Peter Davids, adjunct professor of New Testament at Regent College, Vancouver, British Columbia, was particularly helpful in editing and improving the sections of New Testament commentary.

Roy M. Carlisle, our editor at Harper & Row, San Francisco, encouraged and supported us through each revision of the manuscript. Through our association with him during the writing of this and other books for Harper, Roy has become a friend as well as a professional colleague.

Several others read parts of the manuscript pertaining to areas in which they have training and experience, and their comments were helpful. They include Dr. John White, author and psychiatrist, Vancouver, British Columbia; Dr. Paul Reisser, physician and author, Thousand Oaks, California; Dr. John Carter, professor of psychology at the Rosemead School of Psychology, La Mirada, California; Dr. Russell P. Spittler, professor of New Testament at Fuller Theological Seminary, Pasadena, California; Dr. Alan Cole, Church Missionary Society of Australia, Sydney; Bishop David Pytches, vicar of St. Andrew's Anglican Church, Chorleywood, Hertfordshire, England; and Dr. C. Peter Wagner, professor of church growth,

School of World Mission, Fuller Theological Seminary, Pasadena, California.

There were others who encouraged us and made many helpful suggestions. In several instances they allowed stories from their own lives to be used as illustrations in the text. They include Sam Thompson, senior pastor of the Anaheim Vineyard Christian Fellowship; Dave Nodar, senior coordinator of The Lamb of God in Baltimore, Maryland; Fr. John Bertolucci, St. Francis Association for Catholic Evangelism in Steubenville, Ohio; and Anne Watson, York, England.

George Bernard Shaw once observed that the United States and Britain are two nations "separated by a common language." Keeping this in mind, we decided to write separate American and British editions to take into account idioms and language peculiar to each culture. In one case we reversed the order of two stories. Except for these minor concessions to cultural convention, there are no substantive differences between the editions.

All biblical quotes are taken from the New International Version (NIV) unless otherwise indicated.

John Wimber
Kevin Springer
September 1986
Yorba Linda, California

# Introduction

I thank God for *Power Healing*. I do not say this because I believe divine healing is the most important issue in Christian life and experience. **I don't**. Nor do I say this because it answers all the knotty problems that surround the issue of **healing. It doesn't**. No, I thank God for *Power Healing* because it reminds us that at the heart of God is the desire to give and to forgive. It encourages us to believe that God is good and that he longs to pour out his goodness into our hearts and lives. It warns us against locking God into a safe, distant past. It urges us to invite the winds of the Holy Spirit to blow freely—saving and healing, loving and forgiving.

Miracles and healings of all kinds and classes are simply part of what it means to live in the kingdom of God. They should be received gladly as one vital aspect of the normal Christian life. While these endowments are wonderful beyond the telling, nothing special needs to be made of them since simple goodness and daily obedience are far more central to our life with God. Understanding these matters is of supreme importance, for one of the greatest hindrances today to the free exercise of the ministry of divine healing is the tendency to view it as some sort of "big deal." Frankly, the religion of the "big deal" stands in opposition to the way of Christ. It is this spirit that can lead to the cruelest of excesses. But when we see divine healing as simply part of the normal life of the people of God, we are freed from elevating one ministry above another. Seen in this light, healing prayer is merely a way of showing love to people in need. Healing—physical and otherwise—is the natural outflow of compassion, God's and our's.

*Power Healing* exemplifies this spirit of compassion. Rather than exploiting the human lust for sensationalism it is a sane and thoughtful discussion of the place of divine healing in the contemporary Church. Its pages abound with examples of God's living power and love dwelling in the midst of his people. Reflecting on the content of *Power Healing*, several words immediately come to my mind.

The first is *boldness*. John Wimber always spoke with the confidence of one living out of the divine Center. Because of this he was able to face matters of intense controversy boldly, firmly, confidently. Prayer for the chronically ill, resurrections from the dead, the work of inner healing, and much more are all topics of frank discussion. The questions of demons and the "demonization" of individuals are faced with such candor that many people will have to gulp hard just to read about them.

The second word that comes to mind is *honesty*. John Wimber discusses with frankness the fact that some of those prayed for are not healed. He speaks candidly of his own illness. (And the conclusion of that moving, inspiring, and sad personal story is now a matter of public record.) In sharing some of the background of the Vineyard movement Wimber allows us to see the very human stumblings and fumblings that we all know so much about. He refuses to hide the warts, and for this we can be grateful.

A third way to characterize this book is with the word *biblical*. In saying this I am not suggesting that John Wimber was a biblicist who would scour the Bible for verses to proof-text every jot and tittle of life. No, he rather sought to allow a biblical world-view to inform all experience and teaching. All of life is scrutinized in the light of biblical revelation. Further, *Power Healing* is intently biblical in that it follows the scriptural path wherever it leads. John Wimber took divine healing seriously because the Bible takes it seriously. He took deliverance seriously because the Bible takes it seriously.

The fourth word is *teachable*. I find this aspect of the book particularly appealing. James reminds us that one of the marks of the wisdom from above is that it is "open to reason" (James 3:17). The moment we stop being teachable is the moment we become spiritually dangerous. In contrast, John Wimber's entire life stands as an icon of teachability, a continual openness to learn from others. The endnotes for *Power Healing* are a gold mine in this respect. The inclusion of a study on the signs and wonders manifestations by a social anthropologist from Oxford is further evidence of this spirit.

The wholesome humility here is genuinely refreshing.

The fifth thing that strikes me about this book is the emphasis upon *team effort*. The ministry of John Wimber was never a one-man show! I have discovered that the most effective prayer ministries—that is, those with lasting beneficial results—are those that are nurtured by a loving community and which emphasize teams of pray-ers. John Wimber and the varied ministries that grew up under his leadership have developed this concept extensively by carefully training prayer teams to minister to a needy world. In this book Wimber rightly stresses that the gifts of the Holy Spirit "are not primarily given to the individual but to the whole body and for the building up of the whole body." This healthy emphasis safeguards against any one person dominating a situation. It places the focus upon God who does the healing, rather than upon those who do the praying. This is a welcome emphasis for one clear sign that any movement is of God is that no single human being can (or should) control it.

Finally, allow me to share a personal note. In May of 1978 I was walking alone along a beautiful stretch of coastline in the Pacific Northwest, USA, when I had an unusual experience of the presence of God—an experience that lasted for perhaps an hour and a half. I was never the same again. One of the several instructions from that encounter was to pray for the rising up of new prophetic leaders who could gather the people of God into fresh, bold expressions of faithfulness and obedience. Since that day I (no doubt along with multiplied others) have been seeking God to raise up an incendiary company of Spirit-led, Spirit-ordained, Spirit-trained leaders . . . leaders who are,

> Lone like the Tishbite, like the Baptist, bold;
> Cast in a rare and apostolic mold.

I believe John Wimber to be one of that company.

Richard J. Foster

# A Personal Note from John Wimber

In October 1985 I* was in England for three weeks, teaching at conferences in London, Brighton, and Sheffield. Many people were healed. One was not—me.

During the previous two years I had suffered minor chest pains every four or five months. I suspected they had something to do with my heart but did nothing about them. Nobody, not even Carol, my wife, knew about my condition. But in England I could no longer hide it from her. On several occasions when we were walking I had to stop abruptly because of the chest pain. I was very tired for most of the trip. I had what doctors later suspected were a series of coronary attacks.

When we returned home to Yorba Linda, California, Carol insisted that I see a doctor. On November 3 I began a series of medical tests that culminated in a cardiologist's diagnosis that confirmed my worst fears: I had a damaged heart, possibly seriously damaged. Tests indicated that my heart was not functioning properly, a condition complicated and possibly caused by high blood pressure. These problems, combined with my being overweight and overworked, meant I could die at any time.

My doctor told me that I needed to control my blood pressure by taking medication and reducing my salt intake, to begin walking daily, and to lose weight. Furthermore, he said that if I went on living at the pace at which I had been for years (in 1985 alone I was away from home for over forty

---

*Unless otherwise noted, the "I" in the text is John Wimber.

weeks), I would most likely die from the results of stress. I complied with all of his directions.

But in my heart I did not comply with God's direction that I seek him for healing. People prayed for me, but I lacked faith to receive divine healing. These words may sound strange, but I in fact found it difficult to receive divine healing. Why? Because all of my life I have been a compulsive person, always working and eating more than I should, and I felt it was just that my body had finally started to break down. In other words, I felt subconsciously that I deserved my condition and that to pray for healing was to pray against what I deserved. I had eliminated the possibility of God's forgiveness and grace for healing in my life. This also meant that I found it easier to hear and follow doctors' orders than receive healing prayer, because I felt the medical treatment and regimen were discipline for my wrongdoing.

There was nothing rational or reasonable about the way I felt and believed. For years I had known and taught Romans 8:1–2: "Therefore, there is now no condemnation for those who are in Christ Jesus, because through Christ Jesus the law of the Spirit of life set me free from the law of sin and death." But knowing in the head is not the same as believing in the heart.

In December I attended a Palm Springs, California, gathering of about twenty key Vineyard Christian Fellowship pastors and their wives from around the United States and Canada. We were meeting for several days to discuss and pray about pastoral care in what by then had developed into over a hundred Vineyard congregations. My fellow pastors did not know much about my physical condition. I had no intention of talking about it—I did not want it to become the focal issue of our meeting. The third night I was awakened by the Lord. In my mind I sensed him asking me a simple question: "John, who is God—you or me?" He then told me that all of my life I had resisted his grace because of pride and independence, and as long as I insisted on making my own way, I could not receive his mercy. Then he showed me two areas of my life where I had resisted his grace.

The first area was my judgmental attitude toward Christians whose ministries made bold use of the media, especially for fund-raising. I had been (and still am) offended by many of the fund-raising practices used by television personalities. He said that my attitude toward these people was covering my deeper problem of pride and self-sufficiency. Furthermore, he said this created stress in me, because I felt personally responsible to raise money for the ministry rather than rely on him.

The second area that God spoke to me about was my health. He said that I had a choice—to die or to repent of my self-sufficient attitude and receive his grace. Here I was, a man who prayed for others' healing and trained thousands to pray for others' healing, and I was too proud to receive God's grace!

God also gave me a passage of Scripture and a promise. Romans 4:19–21 says:

Without weakening in his faith, he [Abraham] faced the fact that his body was as good as dead—since he was about a hundred years old—and that Sarah's womb was also dead. Yet he did not waver through unbelief regarding the promise of God, but was strengthened in his faith and gave glory to God, being fully persuaded that God had power to do what he had promised.

His promise to me was that in the same way that Abraham waited for his child I was to wait for my healing. In the meantime, he told me to follow my doctor's orders.

The next morning I told the other pastors about my condition and asked for healing prayer. I did not tell them at that time about the Romans passage. When they prayed over me for healing, Bob Craine, pastor of the San Luis Obispo (California) Vineyard Christian Fellowship, prophesied that "as I was with Abraham, so I am with you." I was greatly encouraged and sensed that God's healing power had already begun working on me.

In February 1986 I took a special stress test, and my heart responded normally. I still had high blood pressure and was overweight, but my condition was improving and the doctors were encouraged. I had cut back on my travel schedule; I watched my diet closely and made sure I got sufficient rest and exercise. I was confident that, like Abraham who believed and trusted God and eventually saw his son, as I trusted God I would be completely healed someday.

But then early one Sunday morning in June I was awakened with intense chest pains. I was admitted to the local hospital's intensive care ward, and during the next week I underwent extensive tests. The results of these tests were good and bad. My heart was not as badly damaged as my doctors had thought some months before; but they discovered I had ulcers. During my stay in the hospital the Lord comforted me during prayer and through the Scripture (especially Ps. 22). The doctors assured me that if I followed their instructions, particularly about cutting back on my schedule and getting plenty of exercise, I would live many more years. And the Lord again reassured me that he would heal me.

I wish I could write that at this time I am completely healed, that I no longer have physical problems. But if I did, it would not be true. Nevertheless, my story illustrates a principle that guides me in divine healing: obedience to God's word is the fundamental reason that I pray for the sick and receive prayer personally, even when I do not see healing as a result of those prayers. I decided long ago that if one hundred people receive prayer and only one is healed, it is better than if none receive prayer and no one is healed.

How do I know that Jesus wants us to pray for the sick? Scripture teaches that we are commissioned to do the will of God on earth, which is illustrated in the life and message of Jesus. Regarding the healing ministry, Jesus "healed many who had various diseases" (Mark 1:34); he gave the Twelve "power and authority . . . to cure diseases" (Luke 9:1); he commissioned the Seventy-two to "heal the sick . . . and tell them, 'The kingdom of God is near you'" (Luke 10:9); and, in a post-resurrection appearance, he said of those who followed him, "They will place their hands on sick people, and they will get well" (Mark 16:18).[1] So, in obedience to Jesus' life and message, I both pray for people's healing and receive prayer for healing.

The apostle John frequently writes that Jesus came to do the Father's bidding (John 4:34; 5:30; 6:38; 8:26; 9:4; 10:37–38; 12:49–50; 14:31; 15:10; 17:4). Further, Jesus did everything with excellence: "People were overwhelmed with amazement [that he healed a deaf and mute man]. 'He has done everything well,' they said" (Mark 7:37). Jesus instructed his disciples to pray, "Our Father in heaven, hallowed be your name, your kingdom come, your will be done on earth as it is in heaven . . . " (Matt. 6:9–10); Jesus wanted them to live as he did. When he gave up his spirit on the cross, Jesus cried out, "It is finished," indicating he had fulfilled that which the Father sent him to do (John 19:30). In Matthew 28:18–20, the great commission passage, Jesus told the disciples to "go and make disciples of all nations . . . *teaching them to obey everything I have commanded you.*" They were to carry out his ministry, which included praying for the sick.

Of course, our goal in praying for the sick is that they are healed and as a result the kingdom of God is advanced. Doug Coombs's story demonstrates this well. On February 10, 1985, Doug turned in his resignation to the church in Toronto, Ontario, for which he had served as pastor for fourteen years. That same day he and his wife, Mary, boarded an airplane for California; they needed a holiday and a time to try and make sense out of their current lives. "I was burned out spiritually and physically," Doug told me later. "I felt that I had been ministering in my own strength for so many years—I was fifty-four years old—and I didn't know if I could go on. I was full of anger and bitterness toward God and some people who had disappointed me. When I arrived in Los Angeles, my brother Wayne took one look at me and said, 'You look like you're going to die.'"

Wayne informed Doug and Mary that he had registered them all at a "Signs and Wonders and Church Growth" conference. I was to be the main speaker. They did not want to go, but they felt obligated since they were Wayne's guests. "I didn't even know what the conference organizers meant by 'signs and wonders,' but I *knew* I wouldn't like it," Doug says. "I had always been taught to be wary of anything supernatural, especially spiritual gifts.

"When I arrived at the conference I was immediately turned off by the 'praise' music and many of the folks who sang with their hands outstretched. For the first two days Mary and I were quite uncomfortable. We were observers, not participants. But we were also hurting terribly; we needed something to renew us spiritually and physically.

"Then on Thursday evening something strange happened. To this day I don't understand exactly how it happened. During the worship time suddenly I found the music a blessing. I felt a peace, even though I held my clenched fists to my side, determined to stay 'in control.' After John Wimber spoke he called all the pastors forward for prayer. [Out of the 3100 people in attendance there were about 1000 pastors from many different denominations.] Much to my surprise, I went forward. I don't know why; I was drawn up front. Then I heard John quietly pray a simple prayer: 'Come Holy Spirit and minister to your servants.'

"I was knocked over into the arms of a huge man who, I later learned, was a professional football player with the New York Giants. We had never met before. He said 'You are a pastor from Canada who has just resigned from your church. The Lord has called you to a new church, he will add many years to your life, and he will give you the gift of evangelism.' There was no way he could have known that I was a Canadian or that I had just resigned from my church. While he was speaking these things I felt a warmth going throughout my body and for the first time in several years I experienced the joy and peace of God. I was delivered that night of the anger, cynicism, and bitterness that I had allowed to take root deeply in my heart and that were holding me back in my walk with God. Physically I felt like a new man, as though years were added on to my life. All I could do was smile and thank God. I could hardly sleep that night, the joy and healing power of God were so real in my life.

"The only missing element in all this was the need for healing and renewal in my wife, Mary. The next morning, as we were walking into the church, she expressed the desire to experience what I had the previous evening. At that very moment, much to our surprise, up walked the New York Giants football player. He prayed for her, and she too was healed.

"That June I became pastor of Mississauga City Baptist Church, a congregation of about a hundred and twenty families on the outskirts of Toronto. My second day at the church I received a call from a man who, in broken English, asked if I could come to his home and explain how to become a Christian. During all my years of ministry I had never received such a request. When I arrived at what turned out to be a large apartment complex there were five other people, mostly Columbians, also in attendance. I gave a simple presentation of the gospel and the man who had asked me to come and his wife both committed their lives to Christ. The next week he invited me back, only this time we met in the complex's recreation room, which was full of people. Since that time there have been very few days in which I do not preach the gospel or pray for the sick.

"In one year the Mississauga City Baptist Church has more than doubled in size to where we have over six hundred people receiving pastoral care. This is all the more remarkable because we are in a multiracial neighborhood, which usually works against church growth. Our congregation is fifty percent white, thirty percent black, and twenty percent Asian."

This book is about divine healing, and it is best summed up in what has happened to Doug Coombs and to me. Both of us have experienced the healing heart of God: his love and compassion. For Doug that meant life and an expanded ministry. For me it has meant obedience and patience as I see others healed when I pray for them and as I continue to remain full of hope and faith for my own healing. For both of us it has meant reliance on God for the results.

As you read these pages I urge you to seek not formulas and methods for gaining a temporary reprieve from sickness and death; I urge you to seek the Lord and Lifegiver himself, Jesus Christ. That way, regardless of the visible results, your prayers will always have power for healing.

# PART I
# Why Does Jesus Heal?

# 1. The Long Struggle

One sunny afternoon in June 1964 my three-year-old son, Sean, wandered away from our home in Yorba Linda, California. When my wife, Carol, noticed Sean was missing she was not too concerned, because our neighborhood was quiet and well protected, being surrounded by eucalyptus trees and some of the many orange groves for which our county was named— Orange County. The groves also provided an ideal environment for honeybees. The backyards of most neighborhoods were dotted with white boxes that housed bee colonies and their bountiful honeycombs.

However, when Carol went out into the front yard looking for Sean, she heard screams coming from a backyard down the street. As only a mother can discern, Carol knew instantly that Sean was in serious trouble. She called out for my help, and we darted down the street.

Carol and I found little Sean walking aimlessly down the hill of a neighbor's backyard, terror stricken and waving at stinging bees. He had wandered into a neighbor's set of hives, inciting a swarm of bees.

We picked Sean up, brushed off the bees, and whisked him away toward home. On the way I could see ugly red welts forming all over him. My heart was racing as I ran across several yards, through our front door, and into our bedroom, where I laid Sean down on our bed. By now he had become quiet, perhaps because Carol and I were holding him, but more likely because he was in shock. When I took his shirt off I found more ugly red stings.

After the initial shock of seeing Sean in such a bad condition, I pulled myself together and began praying for his healing. But how, I thought, should I pray? I had only recently been warned by a pastor about what he called the dangers of charismatic gifts like healing and speaking in tongues. "They are divisive," he told me. "And the devil counterfeits them. It's best to stay away from them. What you need is sound doctrine, not excesses like these gifts." What was I to think? I was still a young Christian and did not want to fall into error.

But my son's present condition cut through his arguments. I began to pray for Sean's healing, but I did not know how to pray. I was desperately in need of words when I broke out into a language that I did not understand. My "tongues" were accented by intermittent salvos of "Heal him, Jesus, heal him." The longer I prayed, the more confidence and power welled up within me. I could feel faith for healing (though at that time I did not know what to call it) being released. As I prayed I could see Sean's welts go away. Within five minutes Sean was sleeping peacefully, and I was slightly confused about what had happened. When he awakened a few hours later, Sean had only one small red bump on his body. He was healed.

## CREEPING DOUBT

At first Carol and I were thrilled about Sean's healing. But soon afterward influences that came into our lives created doubts about divine healing. At the time it happened I believed God had miraculously healed him. But as I listened to teaching that denied God miraculously heals today, I lost confidence. I then became passive about the issue. I thought, "Who really knows? Perhaps there is healing, perhaps not. Perhaps Sean was healed. More likely he just got better naturally. Maybe he was immune to bee stings." (That thought was later discounted when Sean stepped on a bee and his foot swelled so much that his shoe no longer fit.)

About this time Carol and I were invited to attend a charismatic Bible study. Most of the people attending were members of mainline Protestant churches. At the Bible study someone spoke in tongues and brought an interpretation (see 1 Cor. 14:26–28). We did not know how to respond to this new experience. The interpretation began, "Thus says the Lord . . ." and was directed to the people in the meeting. Carol felt uncomfortable about it. (I cannot remember the specifics of the interpretation.)

Carol decided to investigate tongues and interpretations further. Something did not seem right to her. She looked up every Scripture passage regarding tongues and interpretation and discovered they were always praise to or about God, never God talking to the people, giving us instruction.[1] "The tongues and interpretation," Carol thought, "could not have been from the Lord." She concluded that we had been duped! There must be a powerful demon working in the charismatic movement, possibly even the Antichrist himself. She told me of her discovery, and I too became convinced that the meeting we had attended was not from God. We used that experience to evaluate *all* the charismatic gifts, including healing, concluding that we should be wary of them. As a result, we were no longer open to the charismatic gifts.

Looking back on our first charismatic prayer meeting, I realize now that we were guilty of drawing a hasty generalization. We assumed that if one doctrine or practice in a movement is wrong, the entire movement is wrong. Of course, there are instances where error in one doctrine, such as the resurrection or virgin birth, plunges an entire movement into heresy. But in this instance we equated tongues and interpretation with error in teaching on a doctrine such as the atonement! Further, we concluded that if tongues and interpretation were wrong, all charismatic gifts—including divine healing—were wrong.

What Carol and I experienced is an example of the struggle that many Christians have with accepting divine healing. Some of the many reasons for this deeply seated and pervasive resistance I explore in the rest of this chapter.

## COMING TO TERMS

Many Christians are hesitant about healing because they fear it might be associated with serious error and even occult practices. This concern is well founded. New Age movements like psychic healing and many aspects of holistic medicine have become quite popular in the West, and with them come heavy doses of Eastern religions, especially pantheism (that is, the belief that all creation is God).[2]

J. Sidlow Baxter, in his book *Divine Healing of the Body*, describes four terms normally associated with Christian healing: divine healing, miracle healing, faith healing, and supernatural healing. "Each of these is used ambiguously by one group or another," he observes, "with attendant confusion or sometimes hurtful delusion."

When describing Christian healing I find it most helpful to use the term "divine healing." What I mean by divine healing should not be confused with Mary Baker Eddy's teaching on healing. Christian Science rejects the idea of a *personal* God, whereas Christianity teaches that Christ is God, the Second Person of the Trinity—fully God and fully man. Jesus is neither like the impersonal "It" of Eastern religions nor the vague Moral Principal of many modern theologians. "For in Christ all the fullness of the Deity lives in bodily form," writes Paul in Colossians 2:9 (also see Heb. 1:2–4). "When we speak of 'divine healing,'" Baxter writes, "we always mean healing by direct intervention of the one and only true God, the living and *personal* God revealed in Holy Writ and crowningly so in our Lord Jesus Christ."[3]

The term "divine healing" is superior to:

*Miracle healing.* The weakness of this term is that miracles are also performed by Satan and demons (see Deut. 13:1–3; Acts 8:9–25; Rev. 13:13; 16:14; 19:20). So miracle healings may or may not be divine healings.

*Faith healing.* Readers of this term may infer that the source of healing is a person's faith and not Jesus. While faith is important for healing, I prefer a term like "divine healing" that emphasizes the centrality of God's action, not men's and women's responses.

*Supernatural healing.* Baxter says, "When we speak about

'supernatural healing,' we mean [a] scientifically inexplicable miracle. We may not always mean divine healing, for supernatural is not synonymous with divine. Satan and his auxiliary angels and demon accomplices are supernatural beings, and they can perform supernatural works."[4]

*Psychic healing.* Psychic healing includes such occult practices as psychometry (diagnosing by holding an object owned by the person), mediumistic or spiritistic diagnoses made through spirit guides, and clairvoyance. These practices are strictly forbidden in Scripture (Deut. 18:9–13).

Linda Coleman, in an article entitled "Christian Healing: Is It Real?" writes:

John Stott states that "*all* healing is divine healing, whether without the use of means or through the use of physical, psychological or surgical means." Although Stott's observation is valid in its context, we prefer to restrict the use of the term "divine healing" to cases in which God intervenes directly, bypassing the natural processes of the body and the skills of doctors and nurses.[5]

I understand Christian healing and specifically the term "divine healing" in the same way. I am writing about divine healing from a distinctly Christian perspective, one that encompasses a rich heritage from both Protestant and Catholic traditions.

Many groups deriving from Eastern religious thought—for example, Transcendental Meditation and Eckankar—report that they regularly heal the sick. Christians need not dismiss their claims out of hand; it is possible that in many instances people are healed. What should be rejected is the source of these healings, which is not God. In Scripture there are healings that were not from God. For example, see the magicians of Egypt in Exodus 7:8–13. My point is this: we can acknowledge that supernatural healings occur in non-Christian contexts without denying divine healing. But often both non-Christian *and* Christian claims of supernatural healing are rejected because Christians mistakenly assume, along with more secular skeptics, that miracles do not happen today. In the seventeenth century, Blaise Pascal, commenting on this problem, wrote:

It has appeared to me that the real cause [that there are so many false miracles, false revelations, etc.] is that there are true ones, for it would not be possible that there should be so many false miracles unless there were true, nor so many false religions unless there were one that is true. . . . Thus instead of concluding that there are no true miracles since there are so many false, we must on the contrary say that there are true miracles since there are so many false, and that false miracles exist only for the reason that there are true; so also that there are false religions only because there is one that is true.[6]

## TWO PHILOSOPHIES, ONE WORLDVIEW

Pascal's point raises another reason for many Christians' resistance to divine healing: the pervasive influence of a secularized Western worldview. While sincerely believing in Christ, many Christians' thinking is tainted by materialism and rationalism. These two philosophies, which together form the cornerstone of modern secularism, can be traced to the eighteenth-century French Enlightenment. Over the past two hundred years they have had a great deal of influence in shaping the Western mind.

A materialistic worldview assumes that nothing exists except matter and its movements and modifications, that there is no supernatural reference point in this life. Rationalism proposes that there is a rational explanation for everything, that for every human problem, there is a rational solution and that there is no room for divine providence.

Most Christians recognize the more obvious anti-Christian results of secularism: the preoccupation with acquiring and having material things and sexual promiscuity. While they may avoid these, they are nevertheless affected by secularism in other ways. One way is that they find it difficult to accept supernatural intervention, especially physical healing, in the material universe.[7]

Many Western Christians, though, would object to this analysis, claiming materialism and rationalism do not affect them, that they do not reject supernatural phenomena like the virgin birth, the deity of Christ, or the resurrection. But even for orthodox believers the subtle effects of secularization are there. While not creating outright rejection of the possibility of supernatural phenomena or the working of divine providence, especially events surrounding the first-century life of Christ, secularism *inclines* Christians to question modern reports of the supernatural.

I see the influence of secularism in theological works, even those found in evangelical seminaries. For example, several years ago an associate of mine asked the librarian of a large and prestigious evangelical seminary in the United States to provide him with a list of the library's most frequently used reference works, especially books used by first-year seminarians. The librarian produced a list that included twenty-seven works, mostly multivolume works including dictionaries like *The New Dictionary of New Testament Theology* and encyclopedias like *The New Catholic Encyclopedia*. My associate then carefully analyzed each volume, tallying the pages devoted to healing, miracles, and signs and wonders. Out of a possible 87,125 pages reviewed, here are the total pages (and percent of the whole) devoted to healings, miracles, and signs and wonders:

|  | Pages | Percentage |
|---|---|---|
| Healings: | 71 | .08 |
| Miracles: | 131.5 | .15 |
| Signs and wonders: | 85 | .10 |

When the high number of verses devoted to healings, miracles, and signs and wonders in the New Testament (especially in the Gospels) is compared with the low number of pages written on the same topics in modern literature, it is reasonable to assume modern secularism has influenced Christian scholars.

Of course, not all skepticism is unhealthy. I am not saying

we should be credulous. The problem is with what we exclude from our field of attention, with what we give no prominence to in our thinking. Many claims of healing are false, the fantastic fabrications of Elmer Gantrys, men and women out for material gain at the expense of the faithful, and many claims come from self-deluded but sincere folk. The Roman Catholic church has stringent criteria regarding miracles, introduced to ensure the authenticity of miracles, especially healing. Healing is one of the requirements for canonization as a saint. The ability to heal is an important confirmation of a saint's life, a supernatural seal of approval.

So, many Christians, caught in the web of Western secularism—and few of us are not affected in some way—have a formidable barrier to cross before they can pray for the sick. That barrier is the belief or suspicion that supernatural healing is impossible today.

## THEOLOGICAL CROSSCURRENTS

There is a long tradition of theological thinking that believes miracles no longer happen. Most supporters of this tradition propose that Scripture teaches the cessation of healing in the early church. Depending on which theologian one reads, they say healing (and signs and wonders in general) ceased after the authority of the apostles was established (the end of the apostolic age) or after the church was widely established and officially sanctioned. (Regarding the latter, the purpose of signs and wonders was to validate the authenticity of the Christian message. They were not needed after the church was officially and widely established, many theologians claim, after the Council of Carthage in A.D. 397, where bishops gathered and clearly defined the contents of the New Testament.)

Dispensationalists, Christians who emphasize different "dispensations" or eras of God's working in history, are the most ardent defenders of the cessation position. The Scofield Reference Bible, in which dispensational theology is laced throughout Scripture in hundreds of footnotes, has popularized the cessation theory among millions of English-speaking fundamentalists and evangelicals.

Many Reformed and Lutheran Christians also teach the cessation theory of the gifts.[8] Both Calvin and Luther (the latter changing his position in later life) thought the charismatic gifts ceased after the first century. (Calvin and Luther lived some two hundred years before the Enlightenment. They denied divine healing both because they rejected the Catholic veneration of saints and because they accepted a Catholic theology of suffering.)

Calvin writes in his *Institutes of the Christian Religion:*

[The] gift of healing, like the rest of the miracles, which the Lord willed to be brought forth for a time, has vanished away in order to make the preaching of the gospel marvelous forever. . . . [Healing] now has nothing to do with us, to whom the administering of such powers has not been committed.[9]

Luther, in his early *Sermons on the Gospel of St. John,* writes that the day of miracles was confined to the early church and that "the apostles have preached the Word and have given their writings, and nothing more than what they have written remains to be revealed, no new and special revelation or miracle is necessary."[10] It should be noted that in his later writings Luther confirmed a belief in contemporary miracles.

In contrast with many Protestant theologies, Roman Catholic theology asserts the possibility of modern miracles. Francis MacNutt writes:

In fact, healing is probably easier for Catholics to understand than for most Protestants, since we have grown up with a tradition of saints blessed with extraordinary gifts, including healing, the one that is still used as a test for canonization. Consequently, most traditional Catholics have little difficulty in believing in divine healing. What is difficult is to believe that healing can be an ordinary, common activity of Christian life.[11]

Evangelical Christians who deny divine healing are biblical

in one sense: they zealously defend Christ's healing ministry even though for theological reasons they deny modern signs and wonders. In this regard their beliefs lead them to view signs and wonders more as modern rationalists and materialists would than as historic Christians. They teach that faith in Christ based on a contemporary miracle or healing experience is no longer needed since we have the New Testament. Their theology is in part motivated by accommodation to materialism and rationalism, though they deny this on theological grounds.

Some Christians actually see miracles as *dangerous*, because Jesus warned: "False Christs and false prophets will appear and perform signs and miracles to deceive the elect—if that were possible. So be on your guard" (Mark 13:22–23). They interpret this passage as a warning about all miracles! This understanding of healing—that it served its purpose in the early church and can only mislead Christians today—has a chilling effect on Christians' openness to praying for the sick.

Most Christians who deny divine healing misunderstand its purpose, which they usually limit to authenticating the gospel and the witness of the first-century messengers. Once the Christian church was established, they say, there no longer remained any need for healing and other miracles, so God withdrew the charismatic gifts.[12] While authenticating the gospel and establishing the church were (and still are) two of the purposes of divine healing, there are others. They include:

- Demonstrating Christ's compassion and mercy (Matt. 14:14; 20:34; Mark 1:41);
- Bearing witness to the truth of Christ's claims about himself (Matt. 8:14–17; Luke 5:18–26);
- Demonstrating that God's kingdom has arrived (Matt. 4:23);
- Showing Jesus is the One who was promised by the Father (Matt. 11:1–6);
- Illustrating on the physical plane what God wants to do for us spiritually (Matt. 9:1–8);
- Bringing people to repentance (Luke 10:8–12); and

• Showing that the gospel is intended for the Gentiles as well as the Jews (Luke 7:1–10).

Most Christians who oppose divine healing on theological grounds, though, do make two valid points regarding miracles. First, both the Old and New Testaments teach that *miracles have a limited usefulness*. Because of the hardness of men's and women's hearts, miracles do not always create faith in the witnesses. For example, time and again Christ performed miracles in front of the Pharisees only to see them harden their hearts (Luke 6:6–11; Matt. 12:9–14). In one instance he refused to perform a miracle for them, because they were a "wicked and adulterous generation" (Matt. 16:1–4). Second, *miracles are subordinate and inferior to faith in Christ*. They point to Christ but are not themselves faith. Thus modern miracles are helpful to faith in Christ, though not necessary.[13]

## WHAT ABOUT SUFFERING?

The idea that all suffering is sent by God for our good is another major reason many Christians are resistant to divine healing. According to this thinking, when we pray for the sick we are actually opposing God's will. So healing is thought to deny Christians the opportunity to suffer with Christ, thereby letting them miss out on opportunities to mature in Christ.

*It is not the release from pain and sickness that is the primary goal of healing, it is the release from the guilt of sin.* C. S. Lewis, commenting on how God uses pain and sickness to break us of our rebellious self (a process that theologians call "mortification"), writes:

Pain is not only immediately recognizable evil, but evil impossible to ignore. . . . But pain insists upon being attended to. God whispers to us in our pleasures, speaks in our conscience, but shouts in our pains: it is his megaphone to rouse a deaf world.[14]

If pain is what rouses, divine healing is often what directs us to the cross of Jesus Christ, where we are released from the source of all sickness: sin. Like sickness, divine healing can be an occasion for sanctification, for through it we experience God's compassion and mercy. God sometimes chooses to allow suffering to draw people to himself, but that does not mean we have to accept it passively.

An evangelical theologian was recently asked, "Isn't a healing emphasis a good thing, especially for some churches where it is virtually nonexistent?" His response was to warn that divine healing is dangerous, because it may undermine the Holy Spirit's work of character formation (sanctification) in us by working against suffering. Further, he equated sickness with the biblical idea of Christians entering into Christ's sufferings and rooted his argument in interpreting Paul's "thorn in the flesh" as a physical ailment (2 Cor. 12). His concern was not that divine healing has ceased (in fact, later in the discussion he affirmed that divine healing is possible today); he was concerned that divine healing might undermine God's work of sanctification.[15]

My response to these kinds of concerns is that seeking and experiencing healing does not make life easy for the person praying or for the person who is healed. In fact, my experience has been quite the opposite: praying for the sick introduced difficulty in my life that was not there before. The actual process of learning to pray for the sick was accompanied by God purging me of pride and self-sufficiency. For the first ten months I prayed for the sick, for ten months I failed. During this time I was ridiculed and slandered, but still I chose to pray for the sick. I became angry with God many times. But he chose to heal through me only when I exhausted my personal resources and acknowledged I could do nothing apart from him. And that process has continued: just when I think I have it all he purges me again. So there is nothing incompatible between praying for the sick and growth through hardship. Neither are people who experience healing automatically put beyond all hardships in life. Instead, they are able to serve

God more wholly. They are still required to lay their lives down for Christ.

Suffering in sickness plays a part in spiritual growth. In any evil circumstance God blesses us when we trust and rely on him. Divine healing and the discipline of suffering are not mutually exclusive; we are not forced to choose one or the other. However, this is not always clear to some people.

Shortly after World War II, in his novel *The Plague*, the French intellectual Albert Camus addressed the question of what to do about suffering.[16] The story was set in the pre–World War II Algerian port of Oran, where bubonic plague brought by rats cuts the city off from the outside world. Oran becomes the stage for a morality play in which Camus forces readers to choose between two philosophies (as he defines them): humanitarianism and theism. Humanitarianism is symbolized by a doctor who fights the plague, theism by a priest who does not fight the plague and accepts it as God's will.

Camus makes it clear that if readers join the doctor and fight the plague, they fight against the God who sent it. But if readers join the priest and resist fighting the plague, they are antihumanitarian. Camus's conclusion is that humanitarianism is right and Christianity is wrong.

But there is a flaw in Camus's reasoning: his premise that to fight the plague is to fight the God who sent it. Traditional Christian doctrine has always held that illness is the result of original sin and its origins are in the kingdom of Satan. That is, illness is abnormal, not of God, and something Christ came to eradicate. It will have no place in the age to come. God may (and does) allow illness as a means of turning us to him and purifying our faith, but he is not the primary cause of illness. So to the extent that Christians hold Camus's position, they hold a non-Christian view of how God relates to the universe. Camus ends up attributing all good and evil to God, a position that would make God the cause of evil!

Jesus understood sickness as an enemy of men and women. Its source was evil and from Satan's kingdom. The deepest sickness is sin, and all other consequences of sin, including physical sickness and poverty, are subordinated to that. This does not mean that every sick person who is prayed for will be healed in this life; but it does mean that forgiveness of sins is available to all, and for many there will be physical healing. In the age to come, there will be complete healing of all who turn to Christ: the eradication of all disease and poverty, hatred and sin.

But the fact remains that some type of suffering is a mark of the Christian life. Paul writes in Romans 8:17, "If we are children [of God], then we are heirs—heirs of God and co-heirs with Christ, if indeed we share in his sufferings in order that we may also share in his glory." Paul and other New Testament writers teach that suffering is prerequisite to glory. Christ is our example of this: "In bringing many sons to glory," the writer of Hebrews says, "it was fitting that God . . . should make the author of their salvation perfect through suffering" (2:10). Paul says that "the sufferings of Christ flow over into our lives" (2 Cor. 1:5) and even goes so far as to say that he wants to know "the fellowship of sharing in his sufferings, becoming like him in his death" (Phil. 3:10). In 1 Peter 4:1, Peter writes, "Therefore, since Christ suffered in his body, arm yourselves also with the same attitude, because he who has suffered in his body is done with sin." Peter continues: "Do not be surprised at the painful trial you are suffering, as though something strange were happening to you. But rejoice that you participate in the sufferings of Christ . . . " (4:12–13).

So how are we to reconcile human suffering with divine healing? I believe the key is found in a correct understanding of God's nature, that praying for healing and growth through suffering are not mutually exclusive concepts. Here is how my argument works:

1. God does not directly will evil.
2. God does directly remove evil.

3. God sometimes overcomes evil not by removing it directly but by accomplishing his purposes through it. He frustrates evil and turns it to his good intentions.

4. What this means in practice is that there are many kinds of evil we experience that we do not approach passively.

Before applying these four points to sickness, it might be helpful to first apply them to persecution. Very few Christians would argue that we should pray for persecution; we do pray for deliverance, protection, peace, and release from oppressors. Christianity is a religion of life and victory over the world, the flesh, and the devil; it is not a religion of death and suffering. Yet at the same time we know that God works through persecution and even triumphs through it. "The blood of the martyrs," wrote a third-century bishop, "is the seed of the church" (also see Rev. 6.9–11).

The same argument may be made about sickness. Christians do not pray for sickness; we are called to pray for healing. Yet at the same time we know that God works through our sicknesses. My point is quite simple: just because we recognize God works through evils does not mean we react passively to them. Further, whether or not someone believes sickness is included in our sharing in the sufferings of Christ, the general principle still applies: God can use illness, but we do not have to be passive about it.

Still, there remains for some a question about what the New Testament writers mean when they speak of "entering into Christ's sufferings." Sometimes we forget that Christ's entire life was suffering: he was the sinless One in daily association with the world, the devil, and sinners. His sufferings were unique because none were for his own sake. His death on the cross and the events surrounding it were the culmination of his sufferings (Rom. 5:6–11). Like Christ, Christians suffer as they live in a world full of sin, the flesh, and the devil; unlike Christ, we suffer as sinners. Demonic and fleshly temptations are a form of suffering because the life of Christ dwells in us.

And, yes, there is a sense that illness is suffering, for our hope is the fullness of the new age—the kingdom of God or, as it is called in the book of Revelation, the new Jerusalem. In this city God will dwell with men and women and he will "wipe every tear from their eyes, [and] there will be no more death or mourning or crying or pain . . . " (Rev. 21:4).

But the New Testament writers are not primarily thinking of illness and temptation when they call us to enter into Christ's sufferings. Peter writes that we should "participate in the sufferings of Christ" as opposed to suffering as a result of our own wrongdoing. "If you are insulted because of the name of Christ," he writes, "you are blessed, for the Spirit of glory and of God rests on you. If you suffer, it should not be as a murderer or thief or any other kind of criminal, or even as a meddler. However, if you suffer as a Christian, do not be ashamed, but praise God that you bear that name" (1 Pet. 4:14–16; see also Matt. 5:11–12; John 15:18–20). In other words, when New Testament writers discuss suffering, they are referring to persecution.

There are several sources that Christians should expect persecution from. The first is from religious leaders, friends, and co-workers. In John 1:11 we read, "He came to that which was his own [people], but his own did not receive him." Jesus' greatest opposition came from the religious leaders of Israel, and Jesus constantly warned his disciples about religious opposition (Matt. 16:6–12; 23:1–39). Paul, as Saul, persecuted the church because of his religious scruples. The Sanhedrin, the supreme Jewish court in Jerusalem, had the apostles flogged. But the apostles left prison rejoicing "because they had been counted worthy of suffering disgrace for the Name" (Acts 5:41).

Jesus faced family opposition soon after beginning his public ministry. After healing the sick and casting out many evil spirits, his family "went to take charge of him, for they said, 'He is out of his mind'" (Mark 3:21). Even Mary, whom the angel Gabriel had told would give birth to "the Son of the Most

High . . . [whose] kingdom will never end" (Luke 1:32–33), came to Capernaum to take charge of Jesus. But Jesus was not surprised by their opposition. When he was told that his "mothers and brothers [were] outside looking for [him]," Jesus said, "Who are my mother and my brothers? . . . Here are my mother and my brothers! Whoever does God's will is my brother and sister and mother" (Mark 3:32–35). Jesus must have suffered deep hurt and loneliness when those whom he loved came against him, but he did not allow that hurt to impede him from doing his Father's will.

Paul instructs Christians married to unbelieving spouses to remain married (1 Cor. 7:12–15). Though he does not use the term "suffering" in regard to these relationships, the question is raised because of the many problems that arise in mixed marriages. He also uses the problems of living with nonbelievers as a springboard to discuss employee-employer relationships. "Each one should remain in the situation which he was in when God called him," he writes (1 Cor. 7:20). In many cases this meant remaining a slave and suffering at the hands of a cruel master (see also 1 Pet. 2:18). The whole of 1 Peter is about suffering and 3:1–7 gives Christians explicit instructions about how to live with non-Christians.[17]

Another source of persecution is people in the world. Peter warned, "Dear friends, do not be surprised at the painful trial you are suffering, as though something strange were happening to you" (1 Pet. 4:12). Yet all too often when Western Christians encounter opposition they are surprised. They are surprised because they are unaccustomed to suffering in this way and they do not think persecution happens in "Christian America" or "Christian Europe." They are wrong.

I recently talked with a friend who told me of his experience in a small New England town during the late 1960s. He and his young wife were high-school teachers, and through a Bible study they evangelized many of their students. Soon word of the students' conversions spread throughout the town, along with many rumors and lies about the meetings. Most of the town belonged to one of two denominations, and when the pastors heard their young people were studying Scripture and becoming "religious," they denounced the movement from their pulpits. (Neither of the pastors spoke directly with the young couple.) This further inflamed the townsfolk. The couple were forced to hold their Bible study off the high-school campus and their car was pushed over a small cliff. Finally late one night a band of thugs came by their house and placed a black cross and black garland on their front lawn. Of course, all of this opposition *increased* the young people's interest in the gospel—they had never seen their parents so upset. Yes, opposition to the gospel will come.

Except for John, all the apostles died in violent ways as a result of persecution. All great reformers in church history—from Augustine to Francis of Assisi to John Wesley—have been misunderstood, slandered, persecuted, and rejected by their contemporaries. Twentieth-century Christians now equate suffering almost exclusively with illness because they are not proclaiming and demonstrating the gospel effectively (or reaping the bitter harvest of suffering for the gospel).

## MODELS

Another reason that many Christians resist divine healing is their exposure to poor models. Few people can avoid seeing television faith healers. The most popular television healer in the 1960s was Kathryn Kuhlman. To me she seemed affected in speech, flamboyant in dress, theatrical in presentation, and mystical in demeanor. I could not understand her at all. I remember thinking her show had to be a fake, an elaborate production to mislead the masses. Whenever she would come on television, I would angrily change the channel and in disgusted terms ask Carol how the networks could sell air time to her. (On one occasion, though, I did not turn the channel fast enough; I was moved and puzzled when I heard her clear preaching of the gospel.) Her *style* led me away from rather than toward seeing God's works. Although many people were healed as a result of her efforts, I could not believe the healings were genuine.

(This is not to belittle Kathryn Kuhlman's ministry. Since that time I have come to appreciate and learn from her. I read her book *I Believe in Miracles* and discovered preaching "the Word of God [was] the foundation on which she . . . built her ministry, and she [was] definite in her belief that if one hews [i.e., conforms] to the Word, there will be *power* without fanaticism."[18] She never claimed healings came from herself; she always gave God the glory. Also, she never let people leave her meetings disappointed or feeling guilty because they were not healed, because her focus was on preaching the work Christ performed on the cross.)

Carol and I also visited several healing meetings (not Kathryn Kuhlman's) and became angry with what appeared to be the manipulation of people for the material gains of the faith healer. Even when it appeared that some people were healed, we were unable to accept it as being from God; Jesus, we thought, would never make such a spectacle! Dressing like sideshow barkers, pushing people over and calling it the power of God, and money—they were always asking for more, leading people to believe that if they gave they would be healed.

My reaction to the faith healers was more than culture shock. I never saw anyone practice healing in a way that *I* would want to do it. A good deal of the responsibility for not being able to understand or accept contemporary healers was my commitment to trying to be "cool," though I never measured up to my own standards of "cool-ness." ("Cool-ness" is a jazz musician's euphemism for pride.) I wanted to be socially acceptable, highly regarded in the community, sophisticated. Most of the contemporary healers appeared foolish, weird, or bizarre. But God has a way of using foolish things to confound the wise, of using imperfect but *willing* people to manifest his glory.[19]

Each generation, each person, may have a different reason

for skepticism regarding reports of healing. In my case, I did not see mature Christians who practiced the ministry of healing and I was influenced by an antisupernatural theology. Note that I did not *see* convincing models; they might have been there, but I never ran across them. These two elements—bad theology and bad models—fed on each other, consuming me in the process. The more I heard that God does not heal today, the more I criticized faith healers; the more I saw bizarre faith healers, the more open I was to an antisupernatural theology.

# 2. An Unlikely Healer

After my experience of praying for Sean's healing, I turned my attention to personal evangelism. I concluded that healing and tongues lead only to controversy and division. Better to do what I know is clearly taught in Scripture, I thought, than to become paralyzed by questions and fears involving controversial practices.

Between 1964 and 1970 Carol and I helped hundreds of people make Christian conversions. By 1970 I was leading several Bible studies a week, with over five hundred people involved. Many of them joined the same church that we were attending, which contributed to its rapid growth. This was a rich time of personal growth and ministry.

In 1970 I joined the staff of the Yorba Linda Friends Church. While efforts at both church work and personal evangelism were successful, I began to lose the kind of joy and peace that I thought would accompany such success. I was dissatisfied with my life and did not understand why. It was a disquieting and confusing time.

When I joined the church staff I also started attending nearby Azusa Pacific University. I eventually earned a degree in biblical studies. Bible school reinforced my acceptance of the supernatural foundations of Christianity: the virgin birth, miracles of Jesus, his literal resurrection and ascension, and so on. But it also unintentionally contributed to a more materialistic understanding of Christianity in the twentieth century. This influence was subtle, more the result of *not* teaching certain truths than outright disregard for the supernatural.

This is best illustrated by what I observed in our church circles about how God was thought to lead Christians today. As a young Christian I was taught that God leads through four means. In the first God gives one a burden to do or not to do something. Burdens are feelings or senses that are subjective, though circumstances frequently reinforce burdens. These feelings may be quite compelling. I was open to being led by "burdens" because I believed the Holy Spirit produced these feelings. I was taught that burdens were always suspect, because they were subjective feelings in need of objective verification. A second means through which God leads is Scripture, usually by the Holy Spirit highlighting a verse or passage that applies to a situation. Because this leading is rooted in Scripture, we thought it was always reliable. Unfortunately, application of this principle to individual situations can be quite subjective. A third way of leading is through the counsel of elders and friends. From time to time I received direction from friends that was quite beneficial, though occasionally it was not helpful. The last means of leading is through circumstances. Circumstances, I suspect, are the most frequent yet least reliable means of direction for Western Christians. That is, Christians tend to rely uncritically on circumstances for leading in their lives.

All four of these are valid criteria for knowing God's direction. But, except for the first, they all emphasize the empirical; they are easy to understand and accept within our rationalistic Western culture. Even the sense of burden, though highly subjective, is more often understood as a feeling than as a supernatural unction. (Being "in touch with our feelings" is a preoccupation in Western society, perhaps foisted on us by modern psychology, a reaction to suffocating materialism and an impersonal mass culture.)

Scripture, however, describes additional means of God's leading his people. For example, the Old and New Testaments are full of stories about dreams, visions, prophecies, and messenger angels. Though in Scripture these are acceptable methods of God's leading, for years I refused to accept them as valid for today. I relegated them to another era of church history, to a different dispensation of God's working. I became convinced that people who claimed these kinds of experiences were misled by the devil or suffered from psychological disorders. Natural means, rational and empirical, fit my Western worldview; anything that exceeded my ability to understand rationally was dangerous. Dreams and visions, I thought, were not compatible with sound doctrine.

## PUZZLING EXPERIENCES

But even after I accepted the arguments supporting the fact that the supernatural is not for today, I occasionally experienced supernatural leadings. Usually this happened during personal evangelism encounters.

For example, once after a Bible school class a student talking with the professor caught my eye. The student's name was Francisco. We were the oldest students in the class, he forty and I thirty-eight. I prayed, asking God what was going on in Francisco's life. He answered by giving me an impression in my mind: "That's my Spirit on him, and I am calling him to salvation." I assumed that the professor was going to evangelize Francisco, but he did not. I do not believe the professor recognized the opportunity to talk with Francisco.

I approached Francisco and tried speaking with him. But he was agitated and did not want to talk; he abruptly left me. So I prayed for him, remembering that we had the next class together.

During the next class period I continued praying for Francisco. About halfway into the hour, I sensed the Spirit of God again speaking to my heart: "It's going to be all right. Relax." I suddenly felt at peace and that God would answer my prayers for Francisco.

After the class ended, everyone left the classroom except Francisco and me. As I walked toward him, his head fell into his arms, and he began weeping. Then he looked up at me and asked what I wanted, why I was continuing to pursue a conversation with him. I took a deep breath and said, "I think God sent me, and he wants you to come to him."

Francisco stared at me for a moment, then began telling why he could not turn to God. "I cannot live the life. I'm not good enough." He went on like that for thirty-five minutes. He had hardened his heart to the gospel. I had no idea about what to say. As he continued talking, I became desperate for words. Then a strange thought came. "Francisco," I said, "do you know what a midwife is?"

"Yes," he answered.

"Do you know what a breech birth is?"

"Yes."

"That's what's wrong with you. You're breech. I'm trying to get you turned around so you can get born again."

"Do whatever you have to do," was his emphatic response. For some reason, his attitude instantly changed. Instead of fighting my words, he listened. When we finally prayed together, he went on for over forty minutes with one of the most eloquent prayers of faith that I have ever heard.

After praying and crying and praying and crying, he asked, "How did you know?"

"Know what?"

"How did you know that I was a male nurse?"

I did not know that. He had been an army nurse for twenty years. During that time he delivered hundreds of babies, many of them breech. When I likened his condition to that of a breech baby's, he knew God was speaking to him.

Later, when I told colleagues and friends about this experience, they rejoiced over Francisco's salvation. But they were also puzzled by the means I used. One colleague even cautioned me not to repeat the story. What else could they say? At that time, there was no room in our theology for these kinds of phenomena.

## "GOD, WHAT'S WRONG WITH ME?"

Despite my underlying personal dissatisfaction, over the next four years the Yorba Linda Friends Church grew rapidly, so much so that we had to build a larger facility. Our congregation grew to be one of the largest in the denomination. I was involved in planting other churches. I was very proud of my church, the congregation and facility, and my growing reputation among other pastors. But all that changed quickly.

One Sunday in 1974 I was walking along a corridor when I met a young man who had been attending the church irregularly. He confessed to me a serious personal problem and asked for help. My solution was to rebuke him for not attending church regularly. "You know," I said, "you wouldn't have this problem if you were in church more often. You need to be here and you need to learn to give more and get more involved. You need to be here if you're going to get your problem solved." I told him all these things with sincerity of heart, preaching at him.

When I finished my little homily, I walked away from him feeling pretty good about what I had said. Then the Lord spoke to my heart. I sensed him ask me a very simple question: "John, would you go to this church if you weren't paid to?"

As I considered the question I began walking slower and slower. This was *my* church. I had helped design the building and implement many of the programs and policies. I had personally evangelized many of the members. My fingerprints were all over the organization. But in that instant I knew my answer to the Lord's question. My problem was not the institution or the people—they were lovely Christians and God was working in the church. The problem was *in me*. I had allowed the church to replace God. I looked to the church for security, identity, financial provision—everything. Therefore, my answer was no.

This was a moment of deep personal revelation. I had been sincerely following what I had thought a pastor should do, and at that moment I realized that it did not work because of a problem in me. The thought was staggering and caught me by surprise. I rushed off to my office, sat down, and began asking myself what was wrong. I looked down and said, "God, what's wrong with me?"

God responded quickly to my prayer. He showed me how I had gotten caught up in administration and organizational machinery. I was more concerned with building bigger budgets and buildings than actually caring for people. I was mechanical and manipulative in my relationships, using people to gain my own ends, which revolved around building a large church and being recognized as a successful pastor. I was angry and frustrated with people who would not fulfill my expectations for them in the church. I would regularly lecture them on their obligation to support and build the church, but I rarely asked how they were doing or prayed for them. I had reached a place where I loved the institution more than I loved the body of Christ. In a sense I *was* a successful pastor; but my institutional success could no longer hide the fact that there was something wrong inside of me. What God showed me was not a pretty picture. I prayed, "God, how did I get this way?"

God again wasted no time in answering my prayers. He showed me how I had turned away and resisted the Spirit of God again and again. He recalled times that the Holy Spirit had spoken to me, and instead of listening and obeying I turned from him and went after the things that I thought were logical and orderly and that fit easily into the institution. I had encouraged people who had experienced any charismatic gift and who tried to tell others about it to leave the church. I was unwilling to listen to any discussions about the supernatural intervention of the Holy Spirit. I had characterized all those who prayed for the sick as charlatans out to rob the body of Christ. I was ineffective in helping people overcome serious problems like drug addiction and homosexuality, so I was harsh with them, driving them away from the church. A progressive hardening had gone on in my heart, a process in which I had lost all sensitivity to the Holy Spirit. I always took the easy road, the way that made the fewest waves, and the way in which I could always maintain control of the situation. He showed me how I had given myself over to things not of God but things that were like God and "for" God. And in doing that I had in my heart replaced God with my ministry.

I was crushed, broken in my inner man. I had been in that church as a member or pastor for thirteen years. God was leading me to see something wrong in myself, but the solution to my inner turmoil was not yet in hand. I was confused about what to do. All I could conclude was that I had to leave the pastorate so I could work through my problems. A few weeks later I was offered a position as the founding director of the Department of Church Growth at what is now called the Charles E. Fuller Institute of Evangelism and Church Growth. My skills at church growth had not gone unnoticed. I accepted the position, thinking Fuller would be a better environment in which to work through my problems. (My family and I remained members of the Yorba Linda Friends Church.)

Just before leaving the church a close friend and member of the congregation was stricken with brain cancer. The doctors gave her only a short time to live. I studied Scripture, especially the James 5:13–16 passage that describes elders anointing members for healing. I thought that if God does still heal today, he gives pastors the authority to lay hands on people and fully expect them to be healed. So in faith I followed the instruction of the passage and prayed over my friend, but she died. Once again all the old objections to divine healing came flooding back in.

During the next four years I introduced several thousand pastors to church growth principles, traveling across America and visiting dozens of denominations. Through seminars and consultations I taught about church growth. During this time, along with others like Winn Arn, C. Peter Wagner, and, later on, Carl George, I developed applications of the research from the church growth movement, especially that of Donald Mc-Gavran and C. Peter Wagner. I developed a talent for successfully applying this research in specific situations. In many congregations my suggestions led to dramatic growth.

At Fuller's School of World Mission (I was an adjunct faculty member there) I met professors like Donald McGavran, Chuck Kraft, Paul Hiebert, and the School of Theology's Russell Spittler. Their courses and reports of signs and wonders from the Third World once again softened my heart toward the Holy Spirit and divine healing. I was especially impressed by the relationship between charismatic gifts like healing and church growth in Third World countries. Not only was there numerical growth, there was vitality and integrity in many Third World churches.

This influence came at a key time when I was open to reexamining many of my beliefs about the Holy Spirit. I had been going through the motions of maintaining a relationship with God for several years—rarely praying and never reading Scripture devotionally. I was quite aware that I lacked a personal experience of God such as that described in Scripture and by many of the great saints down through church history. Also during these years on the Fuller Evangelistic Association staff I experienced a family crisis with one of my children, brought on in part by my extended absences from the home due to travel. This personal crisis brought me to the end of my tether emotionally and spiritually.

## A PERSONALITY MELTDOWN

Shortly after this, in January 1977, I was used by God to heal Carol. Notice that I write in the passive voice—"I was used by God"—rather than in the active voice—"I prayed for someone and they were healed." My part was passive, secondary in fact—I did not even know it happened until it was over. Let me explain.

During my time at the Fuller Evangelistic Association, unknown to me, God was altering Carol's attitude toward the charismatic gifts. Up to that time she was hostile, more hostile than I, to anything supernatural, especially healing. In fact, in women's Bible study groups around Orange County, Carol taught against divine healing. As an elder in our local church she had been responsible for driving out several members who were praying for others' healing and speaking in tongues. Also, her strong feelings against divine healing had always influenced me greatly.

But around this time she started pleading with God to change some of the people around her. She saw that I had been unhappy for several years and was praying that I would work through my problems. One night, through a dream, she was filled with the Holy Spirit. In the dream she saw herself preaching a seven-point sermon on why tongues are not for today. There was nothing unusual about that; she knew the script quite well, except for one change at the seventh point— she woke up speaking in tongues! After this she repented of her attitude toward the supernatural, weeping on and off for three weeks, away in our bedroom, anguishing before God. She opened herself to God; she learned what that meant as time went on. Her prayers for change in me were answered through change in her.

She described her experience later as a "personality meltdown." As a result she began to doubt much of what she had been taught about how God works, especially about divine healing. Through the dream she recognized that she had wounded the heart of God with her attitude, prejudices, and resistance to the Holy Spirit. Further, she thought that over the years she had been responsible for hardening me to the work of the Holy Spirit, robbing me of the ministry that God had called me to. Carol's first response to her dream and subsequent repentance was to visit over thirty people, one by one, asking them to forgive her for words and actions of past wrongdoing. Soon many of these people—and others (mostly people we had led to Christ)—joined in an informal home fellowship. These people worshiped God, prayed, and studied Scripture and, while they were not involved in the charismatic renewal, they had an openness to God that included an openness to spiritual gifts.

One day during a time of prayer in which Carol was praying for me, she remembered the incident some fourteen years earlier in which Sean had been healed of bee stings. She concluded that I might have the gift of healing, despite my hostility toward anything charismatic.

Carol then reasoned that if God had filled her with the Holy Spirit while sleeping, he could work the same way in me. To test her theory, she devised a careful plan, using painful rheumatoid arthritis in one of her shoulders as the test case. One night when we were at a cabin in the mountains, she waited until I fell asleep and placed one of my hands on her shoulder. She then said, "Okay, Lord, now do it." A surge of heat and energy came into her shoulder, and the pain disappeared. She was healed. I awakened wondering why my hand was hot. Carol told me what happened. I was puzzled about the healing, though glad that her pain was gone. Still, even this did not sway me toward practicing divine healing.

By March of 1977 Carol's prayer group had grown to over fifty adults. For most of the people the prayer group was becoming their church. They worshiped God, received teaching, prayed for each other, and formed supportive relationships. All that was missing was a pastor. I did not attend the prayer group meetings and had no desire to lead any congregation, especially an overgrown home group. But the Lord, with some help from Carol, had different ideas for me.

## BROKEN DOWN IN DETROIT

A short time after Carol's encounter with the Holy Spirit the currents of my personal despair and hope for spiritual renewal collided during a ministry trip to Detroit, Michigan. On the airplane I began crying out to God. It was a familiar prayer, only with a greater sense of urgency. "Oh God," I prayed in my heart, "what's the matter, what's wrong with me? I'm tired. The doctors say I'm eating myself into the grave. My blood pressure's too high; my head throbs constantly. I'm worn out from lecturing long hours. I'm tired of talking to people, and I lack your purpose."

My heart sank lower and lower. I sat there with my head against the window and said, "God, here I am, feeling as though I'm going to die soon. I still have young children living at home, and I don't have time to know them. I've tried so hard to lose weight, vowing many times I would control my eating. Many times I've tried to straighten myself out, and there's been no change. I'm so sick of me, and I don't even like you right now. This is the first time I've prayed in a long time and I don't think you're even listening to me."

I was still crying as we landed. When I disembarked, no one was there to greet me because of a flight mix-up. Outside a snowstorm was raging; I was stranded for the night at Detroit Metropolitan Airport. So I took a room at the airport hotel. But I could not sleep.

For the first time in several years I opened my Bible to read it for myself, as opposed to studying it for teaching preparation. I opened the pages to Psalm 61:

Hear my cry, O God;
   listen to my prayer.
From the ends of the earth I call to you,
   I call as my heart grows faint;
   lead me to the rock that is higher than I.
For you have been my refuge,
   a strong tower against the foe.
I long to dwell in your tent forever
   and take refuge in the shelter of your wings.
For you have heard my vows, O God;
   you have given me the heritage of those who fear your name.
Increase the days of the king's life,

his years for many generations.
May he be enthroned in God's presence forever;
  appoint your love and faithfulness to protect him.
Then will I ever sing praise to your name
  and fulfill my vows day after day.

In the words of the psalmist I saw my life and desires, every-thing I had just prayed about on the airplane. I realized how desperate my spiritual condition was, so I knelt down by the bed and asked God to show me what was wrong with my life. Before he could answer, I fell asleep. After a while, I grew physically uncomfortable, woke up, crawled into bed, and fell back asleep.

In the middle of the night I woke up; God was speaking to my heart. He said, "John, I've seen *your* ministry, and now I'm going to show you *mine*."

I began weeping again. "Oh, Lord," I said, "that's all I've ever wanted." I do not understand all that happened to me that evening, but it marked a turning point in my relationship with God.

As I looked back over the events of those fours I realized that God was bringing me to a place where I was open to his supernatural work in my life. I was beginning to see that there were reasons that he could heal today. In the remainder of this chapter I discuss some of these reasons.

## HEALING IN THE OLD TESTAMENT

In the Old Testament we see that God was concerned about Israel's health. The rule under the old covenant was that those who obeyed could expect health, while those who sinned could expect sickness. And there was no question that God could and did heal.

In the Old Testament God dealt with the people of Israel as a group. Thus, individual experience of God's blessings and discipline was in many cases determined by God's dealings with the nation of Israel. What happened to the individual was secondary; that is, frequently good individuals suffered because they were members of a disobedient nation.[1] Gentiles, who were not members of Israel, were "excluded from citizenship in Israel and foreigners to the convenants of promise, without hope . . . " (Eph. 2:12)—though a few Gentiles, for example Rahab and Ruth, could and did get in. This community identity affected individuals' health.

During their Egyptian captivity, God told Israel:

If you listen carefully to the voice of the Lord your God and do what is right in his eyes, if you pay attention to his commands and keep all his decrees, I will not bring on you any of the diseases I brought on the Egyptians, for *I am the Lord, who heals you*. (Exod. 15:26)

When the nation refused to listen to God's words and disobeyed him, he allowed Satan to send plagues and sickness. When the nation listened, believed, and obeyed him, God sent good health as a reward. Consequently the state of the nation's physical health was a reflection of their spiritual condition (also see Prov. 4:20–21).[2]

This way of God's relating to the nation as a whole was carried on through the three major Old Testament convenants—the Abrahamic Covenant (Gen. 12:2–3; 15:1–21; 17:1–27); the Mosaic Convenant (Exod. 20; Deut. 28); and the Davidic Covenant (2 Sam. 7). These covenants, similar in form to Near Eastern vassal treaties (especially those made by the Hittites between themselves and conquered peoples in the fourteenth and thirteenth centuries B.C.) contained a section of stipulations, terms that the Lord expected his people to meet. If they were loyal and obedient, blessings like good health and prosperity followed. If they were disloyal and disobedient, curses like illness and poverty were promised.[3]

Almost every illness recorded in the Old Testament was a result of sin and disobedience. An example is Saul's insanity, which was caused by his unrighteousness (see 1 Sam. 17–23, 31). For this reason, the problem of the suffering of the righteous rarely arises in the Old Testament. Instead, the Old Testament is more concerned with why at times the wicked prosper.

In the few cases where there is no clear link between sin

and sickness, the event is reported only to record God's intervention with healing (for example, see the healing of Hezekiah in 2 Kings 20:1–11). Job is the one exception. It should be noted that most of his suffering was not sickness, but loss of family, property, and reputation. The book of Job raises the question in the minds of readers of the nature of the relationship between disobedience and sickness. Job was a precursor of the full revelation that was to come in Christ, thus his story is an indication that the link between disobedience and sickness is not absolute.

A name used for God in the Old Testament is *Jehovah-Rapha*, which is translated in the New International Version "I am the Lord, who heals you." C. F. Keil and F. Delitzsch, commenting on Exodus 15:26, write, "All that is clear and undoubted is [that] . . . Jehovah made himself known to the people of Israel as their Physician."[4] His name points to the hope of the new covenant in which the coming of Jesus brings the fullness of God's mercy and healing power.[5] (For a complete listing of Scripture references to healing in the Old Testament, see Appendix C.)

## HEALING IN THE NEW TESTAMENT

In the New Testament Jesus always combined healing with proclaiming the kingdom of God. Through healing the sick Jesus defeated Satan and demonstrated his rule.

More individual healings occurred in the New Testament than in the Old Testament. With Jesus' coming there was an outflow of God's mercy and compassion in healing, and health and sickness were no longer exclusively reward for obedience or judgment for sin. In the New Testament, sickness is seen as an extension and effect of sin and is therefore evil in origin, representing the kingdom of Satan. (This does not contradict the Old Testament; God is still understood as being over all of creation, including the devil, although God himself does not tempt anyone with evil. The New Testament clarifies—not contradicts—the Old Testament. It shows a more complex picture, revealing the role of Satan.)

At the beginning of his public ministry, Jesus announced that the kingdom of God was near (Mark 1:15) and immediately began healing the sick and casting out demons. When he healed a demon-possessed man who was blind and mute, he told the Pharisees, "If I drive out demons by the Spirit of God, then the kingdom of God has come upon you" (Matt. 12:28). In Luke 17:21 he proclaimed that the kingdom of God, his rule, was within us, and in 1 Corinthians 10:11 Paul writes that "the fulfillment of the ages has come" to us. So Jesus brought the age to come into our "present evil age" (Gal. 1:4; Eph. 1:21), though as yet we only taste "the powers of the coming age" (Heb. 6:5), not the fullness of that age.

But what will the fullness of this coming age look like? One element will be perfect health:

He will wipe every tear from their eyes. There will be no more death or mourning or crying or pain, for the old order of things has passed away. (Rev. 21:4)

Men and women who love Jesus will be completely whole—physically, emotionally, and spiritually. The good news is that Christians can taste this now: "Therefore, if anyone is in Christ, he is a new creation; the old has gone, the new has come!" (2 Cor. 5:17). Even today we can experience wholeness in Christ, which includes the healing of our bodies, emotions, minds, and spirits. But because the fullness of the kingdom has not yet come, the healing ministry is partial, already present in this age but not yet completed.

## EVERY ASPECT OF LIFE

The New Testament also teaches that divine healing concerns more than merely physical or spiritual wholeness; it touches every aspect of human life that can come under the power or influence of Satan. Divine healing means:

- Forgiveness of sin;
- Restoration from sickness;
- Breaking the hold of poverty and oppressive social structures;
- Deliverance from demonic power and influence; and
- Raising the dead.

The idea of wholeness is the root meaning of *iaomai*, one of the five New Testament Greek verbs translated as "heal." This word is used of physical treatment twenty-two times (for example, see Matt. 15:28); it is used figuratively of spiritual healing five times (see Matt. 13:15); and, in James 5:16 ("confess your sins to each other and pray for each other so that you may be healed") *iaomai* may refer to both physical and inner healing.

Another Greek verb for "healing," *sōzō* (and its intensive form, *diasōzō*), is used in stories of healing by Jesus sixteen times. What is interesting about *sōzō*, which is taken from an Aramaic term, is that it has the twofold meaning of "to make alive" and "to make healthy." In Mark 3:4, Jesus, on the occasion of healing on the Sabbath a man with a shriveled hand, asked the Pharisees, "Which is lawful on the Sabbath: to do good or to do evil, to save life or to kill?" The phrase "to save life"—*psuchēn sōzai*—implies spiritual as well as physical salvation.[6] Regarding this twofold meaning, John Wilkinson writes:

It is clear that its [*sōzō's*] wide application in the Gospels indicates that the Christian concept of healing and the Christian concept of salvation overlap to a degree which varies in different situations, but are never completely separable. Healing of the body is never purely physical, and the salvation of the soul is never purely spiritual, but both are combined in the total deliverance of the whole man, a deliverance which is foreshadowed and illustrated in the healing miracles of Jesus in the Gospels.[7]

Other Greek verbs used in the New Testament give a fuller meaning of healing there. *Therapeuō*, the most frequently used word, indicates that divine healing is "immediate and complete restoration to health . . . [in need of] no more attention."[8] The remaining verb, *apokathistēmi*, means "to restore to a former condition of health."[9]

Healing is comprehensive because the kingdom of God has come to create a new order, a new creation. Healings are signs of the presence and power of God's kingdom. This is why when John the Baptist sent messengers to ask Jesus if he were the Messiah, Jesus answered:

Go back and report to John what you have seen and heard: The blind receive sight, the lame walk, those who have leprosy are cured, the deaf hear, the dead are raised, and the good news is preached to the poor. Blessed is the man who does not fall away on account of me. (Luke 7:22–23)

## CONFLICT WITH SATAN

The New Testament shows that healing is associated with repentance from sin and conflict with Satan. Health is frequently determined by individual righteousness or sin (Mark 2:1–12; John 5:1–11, 14; James 5:14–16). There also are verses in the New Testament indicating, as under the old covenant, that corporate disobedience and sin open us to weakness, sickness, and death (Acts 5:1–11; 1 Cor. 11:27–32). Western Christians live in an individualistic, fragmented society. Few people think sin committed by one person can affect the wellbeing, even the health, of an entire group. In this regard, private sin has corporate implications. The purpose of corporate disciplinary work, like that for the individual, is that we might repent of our sins and grow in grace.

Unlike in the Old Testament, the minority of all illnesses in the New Testament are the direct result of habitual sin in the individual. So while sickness *may* be caused by our own sinfulness, not *all* sickness is caused by it. Much sickness is caused by Satan. Jesus makes explicit the teaching of the book of Job—that the link between disobedience and sickness is not absolute—when, on the occasion of healing a man blind from birth, he says, "Neither this man nor his parents sinned, but this happened so that the work of God might be displayed in his life" (John 9:3). The rule in the New Testament is that the *righteous* suffer the majority of all recorded satanic attacks. As I pointed out in Chapter 1, Jesus himself was an innocent sufferer, all the disciples (except John) died violently, and the entire book of 1 Peter is about suffering for Christ.

This raises the question of why the righteous suffer. The answer to this in part is that we have been thrust into a war with Satan and, as in any war, there are casualties. At any time during the conflict the Lord may decide that we are needed on the front lines.[10]

## JESUS' EXAMPLE

One of the most compelling reasons to pray for the sick is that Jesus healed many. If he is our model of faith and practice, we cannot ignore his healing ministry. From the beginning, Christians have reflected on Christ's miracles and drawn great benefit from them. Their attitude indicates to us what Christian ministry is supposed to be like. Jesus never saw benefits in illness for sick people; he healed people wherever he went. The Gospels record forty-one instances of physical and mental healing by Jesus. This by no means represents the total number of individual healings, for many of these instances are summaries of the healings of large numbers of people. The individual accounts are descriptions of the more dramatic healings. In summarizing Jesus' ministry, John writes:

Jesus did many other miraculous signs in the presence of his disciples, which are not recorded in this book. But these are written that you may believe that Jesus is the Christ, the Son of God, and that by believing you may have life in his name. . . . Jesus did many other things as well. If every one of them were written down, I suppose that even the whole world would not have room for the books that would be written. (John 20:30–31; 21:25)

Out of 3,774 verses in the four Gospels, 484 relate specifically to the healing of physical and mental illness and the resurrection of the dead. More impressive, of the 1,257 narrative verses in the Gospels, 484 verses—38.5 percent!—are devoted to describing Jesus' healing miracles. Except for discussion of miracles in general, the attention devoted to the healing ministry of Jesus is far greater than that devoted to any other kind of experience.[11] (Appendix D is an overview of the healing ministry of Jesus from the Gospels in which I include Scripture references and descriptions of each recorded healing.)

Jesus embodied the kingdom of God, saving and healing people. He also equipped the disciples to heal, that they might effectively advance the kingdom of God. He trained and sent the Twelve and Seventy-two (Luke 9:1–9; 10:1–24); he included healing in the great commission (Mark 16:14–20); and throughout the book of Acts the disciples healed the sick. (Appendix E is a summary of the healing ministry of others, as recorded in the Gospels of Matthew, Mark, Luke, and the book of Acts.)

## CHURCH HISTORY

Although Christians have taken different views about the significance of divine healing throughout church history, examples in church history itself bear out my interpretation of Scripture. When I investigated healing in church history, I was surprised to find numerous accounts of the sick being healed. During the first hundred years of the church, what is called the apostolic era, healing was a common activity in Christian life. In fact, healings (and other miraculous phenomena) help explain the remarkable growth of Christianity during this period.

Typical of the second-century reports is this one from Irenaeus (ca. 125–202) in his *Against Heresies*, Book 1:

For some do certainly and truly drive out devils, so that those who have thus been cleansed from evil spirits frequently both believe [in Christ] and join themselves to the Church. Others have foreknowledge of things to come: they see visions, and utter prophetic expressions. Others still heal the sick by laying their hands upon them, and they are made whole. Yea, moreover, as I have said, the dead even have been raised up and remained among us for many years. And what shall I more say? It is not possible to name the number of the gifts which the Church, [scattered] throughout the world, has received from God, in the name of Jesus Christ, who was crucified under Pontius Pilate, and which she exerts day by day for the benefit of the Gentiles, neither practicing deception upon any, nor taking any reward from them [on account of such miraculous interpositions]. For as she has received freely from God, freely does she also minister [to others].[12]

The historical record from every century of church history contains reports similar to Irenaeus's testimony.

According to extant historical documents it appears that during the first four centuries of church history healings were frequent. Throughout the Middle Ages and up to the Reformation the reports of healings slacken, though there still are many interesting stories. From the Reformation up to today there is a steady increase in the reports of healings, with the twentieth century reporting remarkable numbers. (The abundance of twentieth-century reports may be accounted for in part by modern reporting methods.)

## POWER EVANGELISM

Another reason for praying for the sick is that healing aids evangelism. It is a "gospel advancer." I learned this from the Third World students who were enrolled in the School of World Mission at Fuller Theological Seminary. While their reports of individual healings were interesting, the resulting church growth and spiritual maturity were staggering. The Third World students at Fuller claimed it is easier to pray for people's healing than to tell them about Christ. In fact, they said, it is very easy to tell people about Christ *after* they have been healed. Scripture verifies this; notice how Christ frequently first healed the sick, then proclaimed the gospel of the kingdom of God.[13]

## COMMON SENSE

A final reason for divine healing is a common sense inference about what Scripture teaches us about God: he is all-loving, all-powerful, and all-healing. Most men and women do not believe God is evil, that he deliberately inflicts calamity on the world and enjoys observing people suffer. For the Christian, God is all-loving, all-knowing, all-powerful—he "takes delight in his people; he crowns the humble with salvation" (Ps. 149:4). In other words, God is kind, preferring that people be healthy rather than sick. Saying God is kind and wants to heal is not denying his sovereignty or dictating his behavior—he is still the God of the universe whose reign should not be questioned. Rather, I am describing God's nature, the way he has always demonstrated his love to men and women—especially in Jesus, who perfectly revealed him.

Most people prefer to be healthy and take practical steps to stay healthy. Further, good people want their friends well. Jesus is more than a good friend; his kindness is deeper than any we can experience. He died for us. He took on the suffering of the world. How could he not be committed to good health for us? It takes more faith to believe complex theological arguments that deny divine healing is for today than to believe God works now as he did in the first century.

By 1977 my attitude toward divine healing had changed from skepticism to openness; my belief that God could heal the sick today changed from denial to acceptance. But changed attitudes and beliefs did not ensure that I would actually do it. In fact, even after the night that Carol placed my hand on her shoulder and asked God to heal her, I refrained from praying for the sick. I still faced a much larger problem: how does God want to build spiritually equipped, healthy, and mature congregations? Little did I know that part of the answer to that question would lead me to divine healing. That story is the topic of the next chapter.

# 3. A Vision of God's Compassion and Mercy

By 1977 I believed God could heal the sick today. There were many factors that contributed to the evolution of my thinking and attitude about divine healing: new knowledge gained from Scripture study and prayer; my experience with the healing of Carol's arthritis; and the Holy Spirit's continual prodding, probing, and disciplining. Nevertheless, I did not believe the possibility that God could heal meant I had to actually pray for the sick. Certainly I did not realize how these lines of influence would converge and lead me into a healing ministry.

Shortly after returning from Detroit, Carol urged me to attend one of her home meetings. The little fellowship met in a small house without air-conditioning. The people worshiped God, sang, read Scripture, and sweated. Every now and then someone would lift his or her hands, something I was not used to. "Oh no," I thought, "what has Carol gotten me into?" But, despite my reservations, there was something I could not deny although I did not understand it: everyone seemed so happy and full of joy. Could God want his people packed in a hot room, singing and sweating late into the night? I was spiritually blind to what God was doing in the group.

After the meeting Carol and I went out for a hamburger. I was already in an irritable mood (because of the meeting) when Carol started telling me how her life was changing. The main source of her change came from Ralph C. Martin's book *Hungry for God*.[1] She said that what he wrote about the close nature of our relationship with Christ had been a vehicle for her opening her life more fully to the power the Holy Spirit. I said, "I suppose next you're going to tell me that you speak in tongues."

"Yep," she said. I was too shocked to respond.

She then questioned me about the prayer meeting. She asked, "Well, what do you think about the meeting?"

"It's not going anywhere," I answered. "There's no leadership. There's no direction. It won't last."

Carol hesitated, then turned to me and said, "John, I've always said that I didn't want you to be a pastor again, but if God should ever speak to you about that I want you to know that I'm for it."

During the next two and a half months God indicated his desire for me to return to the pastorate. For example, once when I was flying in an airplane with C. Peter Wagner, he turned to me and said, "John, why don't you go home and start a church in Yorba Linda?" A few days after this I was in New York City conducting a church growth seminar when a Lutheran pastor came to me and said, "I feel awkward about this, because I have never experienced anything like it before. But God gave me a message for you. I wrote it down. Here it is. I do not understand it." I took the message and he walked away. I opened the scrap of paper and read these words: "Go home." The Lord's direction was clear, so I obeyed him and returned to the pastorate.

On Mother's Day in May of 1977, I preached my first sermon as pastor of what is now called the Vineyard Christian Fellowship. (I was still working full-time as a church growth consultant.) I spoke from the Gospel of Luke, and for the next ten months I continued to teach from Luke.

## THE GOSPEL OF LUKE

In going back to be a pastor of Carol's home group I had formulated few thoughts about healing the sick. My concern was for the church. I wanted to see what God could do with a body of people who would listen to him and obey his commands, a group who could mature to where all were equipped, trained, and functioning in ministry.

At first we were by outward appearance a typical Bible

church, emphasizing teaching from the word of God, worship, prayer, and fellowship. The only apparent difference was we did not sing traditional hymns; we sang more contemporary songs and even wrote some of our own music. I did many of the things that I had learned earlier as a pastor, with one significant difference: I was now looking for God to shape my ministry, because in Detroit he promised me that he would "show me his ministry." I knew that I had to let God be in charge, allowing him to direct us . . . regardless of what I thought. So I was very flexible and open to new ideas and direction from God, but this was not easy for me.

We experienced the presence of God in our meetings. The key to our spiritual renewal was worship. We would sing and worship God for hours, and his refreshing presence always came.

While I was preaching from Luke on Sunday mornings, John Amstutz, a professor at Life Bible College in Los Angeles, taught about spiritual gifts at our Wednesday evening gatherings. Through John's teaching, a few members of the congregation began to show interest in the charismatic gifts, especially healing. Because my job still required much travel, I missed many of these Wednesday evening gatherings. Consequently, many of the people were ahead of me in their interest and desire to pray for the sick.

Because the Gospel of Luke is full of accounts of the healing ministry of Jesus, I was forced to begin some kind of teaching on the subject. My reason for being open to healing came out of a concern for the life and vitality of the church. When I began preaching on healing, I was surprised to see a few members immediately pray for the sick. In fact, they were praying for the sick long before I was!

By August of 1977 (four months into the Luke teaching) I was asking God if healing the sick was supposed to be a vital element of church life. I had seen there was a place for healing in the church and Luke was bringing it to the center of my attention. At that time the Holy Spirit conceived the healing ministry in my heart. This was the culmination of many years of his softening my heart toward the supernatural. He did it during one of the few Wednesday evening Bible studies I was able to attend.

While John Amstutz taught, I became distracted by thoughts about my Sunday teaching. So I quietly prayed, and God brought to my mind Matthew 9:1–8, the passage where Jesus heals a paralytic. I looked it up and read it to myself:

Jesus stepped into a boat, crossed over and came to his own town [Capernaum]. Some men brought to him a paralytic, lying on a mat. When Jesus saw their faith, he said to the paralytic, "Take heart, son; your sins are forgiven."

At this, some of the teachers of the law said to themselves, "This fellow is blaspheming!"

Knowing their thoughts, Jesus said, "Why do you entertain evil thoughts in your hearts? Which is easier: to say, 'Your sins are forgiven,' or to say, 'Get up and walk'? But so that you may know that the Son of Man has authority on earth to forgive sins. . . . " Then he said to the paralytic, "Get up, take your mat and go home." And the man got up and went home. When the crowd said this, they were filled with awe; and they praised God, who had given such authority to men.

As I prayed about this passage, many questions were raised in my mind. First, I asked God if my attitude about praying for the sick was supposed to be like my attitude toward personal evangelism. In this passage Jesus acted as though preaching and healing were both regular activities of the kingdom. I sensed God saying to me, "Yes, Christians are called to heal the sick in the same way as they are called to evangelize." In Matthew 9, Jesus regarded healing as no more difficult than forgiving sins ("Which is easier . . . "). In fact, from his words one may infer that healing the sick is *easier* than forgiving sins.

This then raised a second question. "Lord," I asked, "are most people (myself included) afraid to pray for the sick because their understanding of your nature—who you are and how you work—inhibits them?" Again, I sensed him saying, "Yes, most people are hesitant, even fearful, to pray for others' healing because they misunderstand my compassion and mercy. They know about me, but they do not always know me."

In Matthew 9, Jesus asked the teachers why they entertained evil thoughts in their hearts. The teachers knew doctrine, but their hearts were clouded with pride. They did not know God. Consequently, they could not recognize God when he healed the sick. In that moment I knew that, although for years I had refrained from praying for the sick because of a theology that denied God could heal today, my doctoral stand was a facade for the evil of unbelief and skepticism in my heart.

Finally, I asked, "Do you mean that we are supposed to pray for the sick?" God answered, "Yes. Just as I give authority to preach the gospel of forgiveness of sins, in a similar way I give authority to heal the sick." In the Matthew 9 passage, the crowd was in awe that Jesus could heal the paralytic and forgive his sins. In response they praised God "who had given such authority to men." The implications of this passage seemed clear to me: Christians are commissioned by God to heal the sick. *I* am commissioned to heal the sick.

## ALTAR CALLS

After conception comes gestation, the period of nurturing and developing. The gestation period for a divine healing ministry in me started the next Sunday and went on for some six months. During this time, almost every sermon I preached was about divine healing. Only a few weeks into this period, God spoke to me about having an altar call after every sermon to pray for the sick. I did not want to have altar calls, but in obedience to God the next Sunday I called the sick forward and we prayed for them.

At the first altar call no one was healed. In fact, a few of us who prayed caught the illnesses of the sick! We caught the flu, colds, even headaches! It was a humiliating experience. On the way home from that meeting I prayed, "Lord, never again will I humiliate myself like that."

But the next Sunday he again told me to have an altar call at both the morning and evening services. I obeyed, more fearful of the consequences of disobedience than of embarrassment. I repeated the altar call the following Sunday and thereafter for eight or nine weeks—but still not one person was healed.

During this time I became hurt and frustrated. Some people left the church; they felt they could not be involved in such foolishness. (I could not blame them.) Many of these people were not offended by the *theory* of divine healing; it was the actual *practice* of healing prayer that offended them.

I was not entirely surprised by their reaction. As a church consultant I often saw a discrepancy between what Christians believed and what they practiced. For example, I consulted at many churches whose pastors said they believed in evangelism, but when I measured their churches for growth I discovered very few new members. Evangelism in practice was not a priority for them: they had no staff, budget, or programs devoted to evangelism! I realized that my belief in the validity of healing for today was like my belief in the command to evangelize: it created an imperative to actually do it. Altar calls were a method of providing a place for prayer for the sick.

## "PREACH MY WORD"

But as the barren weeks rolled on, I became despondent. One day as I was studying, preparing for my Sunday sermon, I became so angry that I closed by Bible and said, "I will not teach about healing anymore." Then God spoke to me clearly. He said, "Either preach my word or get out."

"Get out?" I asked fearfully. "What do you mean 'get out'?"

Ignoring my question, the Lord spoke to my heart: "Preach my word, not your experience." Like a chastened schoolboy, I took the Lord's admonition seriously. So I continued to teach about Christ's example of praying for the sick and the need that we continue to do as he did.

We continued praying for the sick and through our failures became painfully aware of how little knowledge we had about *how* to pray. I began searching Scripture to understand more about healing, especially in Jesus' ministry. I also read every Christian book about healing that I could find. I read Francis MacNutt's book *Healing*,[2] an intelligent argument for the healing ministry. My motive was not only to learn how *I* could effectively pray for the sick, but to learn how I could train and equip *every member* of my congregation to pray for the sick. Looking back now, I realize how foolish it was to be concerned about equipping people to pray for the sick when we had not yet seen *one* person healed!

I also began to seek out others who were praying effectively for the sick, men with whom I could build a relationship and from whom I could learn. Noel Weiss, who was then a pastor at Melodyland Christian Center in Anaheim, was a Christian through whom God healed many. I found Noel easy to talk to, perhaps because before becoming a Christian he was—as I had been—a jazz musician. His method of praying for people was gentle and in no way manipulative. My knowledge of and faith for healing the sick were increased greatly through watching and talking with Noel Weiss and others with effective healing ministries.

But after ten months of unsuccessful prayer, I had my greatest defeat. By this time our church was meeting in a high-school gymnasium that had a curtain stretched across the stage. At the completion of each service we invited people behind the curtain to receive prayer. The gymnasium was not air-conditioned; the room was unusually hot and humid. On this occasion several men and I prayed for another man (I cannot remember what his condition was). We prayed for two hours, praying every prayer that we knew, desperate to see the man healed. Finally, in despair, we stopped. I was so disconcerted that I threw myself on the floor and began weeping. "It's not fair!" I screamed. "You tell us to teach what your book says, but you don't back up our act. Here we are; we're doing the best we can do—and nothing happens. You tell us to believe in healing and pray for healing, but you're not doing anything. Oh, God, it's not fair!" I was brokenhearted. After a few minutes I came to my senses and looked up only to see the other men lying there with me, calling out to God. We were all broken over the experience. I limped home and fell into bed, wondering what the future held.

## BREAKTHROUGH

The next morning I was awakened by the phone ringing; one of our newest members was on the line. He said, "I just got a brand new job, and I've got to go to work today. My wife is sick with a fever. I can't stay home and take care of the kids, and we can't find a babysitter. Can you come pray for her?"

"I'll be right there," I said.

I hung up the phone and stared at the ceiling. "God," I said, "look what you've got me into this time. This guy really believes this stuff. He's going to lose his job, or I'm going to have to take care of his kids today."

When I arrived at the house the husband led me into their bedroom. His wife looked terrible. Her face was red and swollen with fever. "Oh no," I groaned inwardly, "this looks like a hard one." I walked over and laid hands on her, mumbled a faithless prayer, and then I turned around and began explaining to her husband why some people do not get healed—a talk I had perfected during the previous ten months. I was well into my explanation when his eye caught something behind me. Then he started grinning. I turned around to see his wife out of bed, looking like a new person. "What's happened to you?" I asked.

"I'm well," she said. "You healed me. Would you like to stay for some coffee or breakfast?"

I could not believe it. She was well! I politely declined her offer of hospitality and left. Halfway back to my car, I fully realized what had happened. All the months of questioning and despair, excitement and disappointment, revelation and humiliation—the full force of these emotions and hopes washed over me. Then I became euphoric and giddy. And I yelled at the top of my lungs, "We got one!"

My despair from the previous night was instantly transformed into joy and exaltation. The period of gestation was over; the healing ministry was born in me, at the moment I least suspected it would be. I drove off knowing that I was embarking on a new journey of faith, not fully prepared for what was around the next bend in the road.

## SWEETER THAN HONEY

"It really works," I thought as I wended my way toward home, "and God used *me* as a vehicle of his healing mercy." Then I was jolted out of my jubilant mood by an incredible vision.

Suddenly in my mind's eye there appeared to be a cloud bank superimposed across the sky. But I had never seen a cloud bank like this one, so I pulled my car over to the side of the road to take a closer look. Then I realized it was not a cloud bank, it was a honeycomb with honey dripping out on to people below. The people were in a variety of postures. Some were reverent; they were weeping and holding their hands out to catch the honey and taste it, even inviting others to take some of their honey. Others acted irritated, wiping the honey off themselves, complaining about the mess. I was awestruck. Not knowing what to think, I prayed, "Lord, what is it?"

He said, "It's my mercy, John. For some people it's a blessing, but for others it's a hindrance. There's plenty for everyone. Don't ever beg me for healing again. The problem isn't on my end, John. It's down there." (For readers who have never had a vision or supernaturally "heard" God in this fashion, I did not *physically* hear God speak. I experienced more of an impression, a spiritual sense of God speaking to me. Time proved that what I thought I had heard was true.)

That was a moving and profound experience; certainly it revolutionized my life more than any other experience I had since becoming a Christian. I have never looked at healing the same way since that day.

What made this experience so powerful was that it confirmed my newfound conviction, rooted in Scripture, that God's abundant grace included divine healing, if only we would believe him for it. I learned this lesson from the story in Mark 9:14-32 of Christ's healing a man's son who was possessed by a spirit and as a consequence was mute. After the disciples had failed to heal the boy, the father approached Jesus asking if he could help. Jesus wasted no time in identifying the reason for the disciples' failure: unbelief.

After explaining to Jesus that his son had been possessed by a spirit since childhood, the man asked, "But if you can do anything, take pity on us and help us" (v. 22).

Jesus said, "'If you can'? Everything is possible for him who believes" (v. 23). The key to experiencing God's healing mercy was belief, belief in the God who heals.

"I do believe," the father said. "Help me overcome my unbelief!" (v. 24). With this confession—what Jesus called "faith as small as a mustard seed" in Matthew 17:20—he cast a deaf and mute spirit out of the boy, and the boy was instantly healed.

What God showed me through scriptures like Mark 9, my first healing, and the honeycomb vision was that he is much greater than I ever imagined him to be, and with only the smallest act of faith I could experience his compassion and mercy. I also realized that God's mercy is constantly falling on us, because everything that he does is related to what he is: "the Father of compassion [mercies, *oiktirmōn*] and the God of all comfort, who comforts us in all our troubles . . . " (2 Cor. 1:3; see also Exod. 34:6; Neh. 9:17). Psalm 145:9 says, "The Lord is good to all; he has compassion on all he has made." Titus 3:5 says the Lord saved us "because of his mercy."

But too often I did not see God in the fullness of his mercy and grace. I trusted him to lead me, but I did not trust him to provide for me; I had faith to receive forgiveness of sins and salvation, but I had no faith for divine healing. I never realized God's mercy was as readily and abundantly available to me as the honey was available to all under the honeycomb.

Through the honeycomb vision I also understood that my first healing was only the beginning of my experiencing God's mercy—if I would only choose to believe and to receive it. In the vision, some people rejoiced, freely received, and freely gave away. The more they gave away, the more they received. "There's plenty for everyone," the Lord said. "Don't ever beg me for healing again."

But others, full of unbelief and skepticism, could not receive the grace, blessings, and gifts of God. They could not see that God's mercy and healing are greater than their understanding of how he works. "The problem isn't on my end," the Lord said. "It's down there." It is we—not God—who place limitations and unbelief on God's compassion and mercy. We are invited to cooperate with his Spirit by entering into a divine partnership, a partnership in which he brings direction and provides for healing.

## WHAT I LEARNED

During the ten-month period of ineffectual prayer I underwent many changes. Before God spoke to me at John Amstutz's Wednesday night Bible study, I believed in divine healing, but I did not believe that I and most Christians were called to pray for the sick. After this time I and other members of my congregation began to pray in earnest, even though for months we saw no results.

This period of failure was a learning experience, a time in which I was purged of my pride and self-sufficiency. I was humiliated, and I was humbled. God had first to cleanse a vessel before it was fit to fill with his precious oil of healing. I believe God began healing the sick through me only after I came to a place of total dependence on his grace and mercy.

I also learned about obedience to God's word. In the past I had been able to get some good results without God's help. But praying for the sick was different. I realized that I could get no results without God's anointing. My job was to obey, pray, and rely on his sovereign mercy; his part was to heal.

My experience is not typical of what happens when most people begin praying for the sick. In fact, I have met and even trained many Christians who healed the sick the first time they prayed for them! They were successful because they received practical instruction about divine healing, something that I did not have during those difficult ten months. In fact, I have written the remainder of this book to inform you about how God heals and how you can pray for the sick. But as you read these chapters I remind you that none of the instruction will be of benefit if you neglect the fundamental principles of obedience to God's word and reliance on his compassion and mercy.

# PART II.

# What Does Jesus Heal?

# 4. Healing the Whole Person

Not only is God's mercy always available to all who will receive it, his mercy touches every area of our lives. The honey in the vision that I saw was freely available and covered the people entirely, just as God's grace his kindness, unmerited favor, and forgiving love—has been lavished on us (Eph. 2:4–9). Realizing the extent of this grace is especially important for divine healing, because too often healing is limited to only one kind, for example, only to the physical, emotional, demonic, or social. But the Bible teaches that healing is available for the whole person.

A key factor in determining the extent of divine healing is our understanding of the nature of humanity. The Old Testament asserts that our humanity is an essential unity, body and soul being different aspects of our makeup. In other words, the emphasis is on the unity of our nature (to be sure a complex unity), not on the separate parts. Men and women are integrated whole beings rather than collections of compartments. Genesis 1:26–27 and 2:7 say, "Then God said, 'Let us make man in our image, in our likeness.' . . . The Lord God formed man of dust from the ground and breathed into his nostrils the breath of life, and man became a living being." So we live in a paradox: we are separated from the physical creation because we bear the very image and majesty of God, yet at the same time we are the simple products of dust.

In saying men and women are image bearers of God I mean that we are godlike, we possess a moral nature having an ability to choose between good and evil (Matt. 7:18; 12:34). Before Adam's fall from grace in the Garden of Eden, our nature and the desires of our soul were good (Gen. 1:31); after the Fall, sin entered the race, inclining us toward evil.[1]

God created human beings, body and soul, to experience everlasting communion with him. That relationship with him was lost when sin entered the race. The image of God was sullied, dirtied, tarnished; we died spiritually. We lost kingdom of God rule.

This is not to say our humanity was obliterated, that every part of our being is absolutely sinful. We are still capable of altruistic works and thoughts; we still have spiritual capacities, though on our own we always fall short of union with God and fulfilling his will. It is more accurate to say that every part of our being has been affected by sin, though not obliterated by it. These areas include our physical, psychological, emotional, intellectual, sexual, social, and, of course, spiritual functions. We are only a shadow of what God originally intended, always falling short of full communion with him (Gen. 3:8, 10, 24; Rom. 3:23).

The New Testament also teaches that our humanity is a unified whole. In 1 Thessalonians 5:23–24 Paul writes, "May your whole spirit, soul and body be kept blameless at the coming of our Lord Jesus Christ. The one who calls you is faithful and he will do it."

This view of humanity is quite different from the Greek concept that emphasized the different parts of the human being as body and soul or as body, soul, and spirit.[2] The Greek understanding pivoted around the idea of an immortal soul, an idea that Plato popularized. The goal of the soul was said to be release from the body, an idea that Paul thought unnatural (2 Cor. 5:1–4). Theologian G. C. Berkouwer summarizes the Greek view of humans as follows:

The soul was regarded as, on the one hand, immaterial, and on the other hand, adapted to the body. Insofar as it appropriated the *nous* [mind] or *pneuma* [spirit], it was regarded as immortal, but in so far as it was related to the body, as carnal and mortal.[3]

In the early church Athanasius and Augustine, then during the Reformation Luther and Calvin affirmed our humanity as an integrated whole with different aspects and maintained that our every act is done by the total person. Our souls alone do not sin: men and women sin. Our bodies alone do not die: men and women die. Our spirits alone are not redeemed: men and women are redeemed.

While it is true that the soul and body are separated at death, Christ's bodily resurrection assures us that our salvation will someday be made complete, reuniting soul and body, redeeming our humanity.

## IMPLICATIONS FOR A HEALING MINISTRY

From this understanding of our humanity it follows that sickness may strike a variety of places in our lives with repercussions affecting the whole person. Healing comes in the corresponding areas.

1. *Healing of the spirit.* This refers to healing spiritual sickness caused by sin.
2. *Healing of the effects of past hurts.* This is frequently referred to as "inner healing," by which most writers mean the healing of hurtful memories and damaged emotions. Of course, the memories in themselves are not healed; people are healed and released from the *effects* of hurtful memories and bondage to their emotions, effects like guilt, shame, and depression. Inner healing is the application of God's grace and forgiveness in those areas of our inner lives that hold us back from experiencing the abundant life. With these obstacles removed, people are freed to live fully for God.
3. *Healing of the demonized and mental illnesses.* Demonization, the influence of demonic activity in a person's life, is frequently incorrectly diagnosed as mental illness in Western culture. (In Eastern cultures the opposite tends to be the case—*all* psychological disorders are thought to be the result of spirits.) Both the external influence of

evil spirits and internal emotional disturbance can cause illness and both need healing.

4. *Healing of the body.* This includes healing of illnesses in which the tissues of the body have been damaged (for example, as through accidents or infection). It also includes healing of disorders in which structures that appear to be normal are malfunctioning (such as in irritable colon or muscle contraction headache).

5. *Healing of the dying and the dead.* This involves both comforting and strengthening those who are dying, and—infrequently—raising the dead.

The following chapters explain each of these in detail. Illness may strike any part of our being, its effects spilling into other areas of our lives. For example, people who suffer from severe psychological disorders may have related physical problems such as ulcers, high blood pressure, and so on. In many cases physicians are not sure which is the primary cause of the sickness. That is, does the mental illness cause physical problems or vice versa? Regarding divine healing, this means that we cannot affect one part of a person without affecting the whole person.[4]

## A SURPRISING CONCLUSION

Jesus also used the healing of disease to illustrate on a physical plane what he wants to do for us spiritually. In John 9, where he healed a man who had been blind from birth, Jesus told his disciples that the man was born blind "so that the work of God might be displayed in his life" through healing (v. 3). The "work of God" was physical healing that attested to Christ's messiahship and confounded the Pharisees. The disciples had asked whether the source of blindness was the man's sin or the man's parents' sin; their assumption about an indissoluble line between sin and sickness was the same as that of the teachers of the law in Mark 2. Clearly in

Jesus' thinking the spiritual reality that the healing pointed to—forgiveness of sins and the progressive revelation of Christ's messiahship—was more important than the physical miracle itself.

Later in John 9 Jesus drives home his point when approached by unbelieving Pharisees, men who claim that he "is not from God, for he does not keep the Sabbath" (v. 16). After telling the healed blind man that he, Jesus, was the Son of Man (v. 35, thus indicating he was the Messiah), Jesus said: "For judgment I have come into this world, so that the blind will see and those who see will become blind" (v. 39). Commenting on this verse, Leon Morris writes:

His coming represents a judgment, for men divide according to the way they react to that coming (see John 3:18; 8:15). In this passage the thought is worked out in terms of sight and blindness. The result of Jesus' coming is that blind men see. This has obvious relevance to the happenings of this chapter, and it must be understood to include the recovery of spiritual sight as well as of physical sight.[5]

Jesus goes on to tell the Pharisees, "If you were blind, you would not be guilty of sin; but now that you claim you can see, your guilt remains" (v. 41). The implication of Christ's words—no doubt a surprise to the Pharisees, who likely expected him to say that they were blind—was that those who have spiritual knowledge (those who can "see") yet do not believe in him can never receive spiritual healing. Leon Morris comments further on this passage:

His meaning is that they have enough spiritual knowledge to be responsible. Had they acted on the best knowledge they had they would have welcomed the Son of God. But they did not act on this. They claimed to have sight, but acted like the blind. Therefore their sin is not taken away. It remains with them.[6]

The Pharisees knew the sacrificial system (a set of practices involving burnt offerings, cereal offerings, peace offerings, sin offerings, guilt offerings; see Lev. 1–7) and the forgiveness that it points to, yet they failed to see that Christ was the fulfillment of that system.

Many people believe the root cause of the "divine healing" of physical disorders is in fact psychological, not spiritual. There is some basis for this belief. Recent medical research, especially into the immune system and cancer, indicates "psychosomatic ailments are real and not faked."[7] I believe psychosomatic influence may have some effect on people's healing. But crediting the psychological "power of suggestion" as a primary or exclusive source of healing in prayer overstates the case and cannot be proved scientifically.[8] In fact, the healing of mental illness is in most instances more difficult and probably more complex than the healing of physical disease. Among all modern medical specialists, psychiatrists and psychologists have a success rate that is far from what they would like it to be.

This leads to a surprising conclusion: physical problems are the least complex illnesses to pray for. What complicates divine healing of physical illnesses are associated spiritual, psychological, and demonic problems. For example, Mercedes ("Mequi") Herrera, a member of the Agape Community in Costa Rica, writes that the key to her physical healing was inner healing:

It all started when I heard Lynn Marshall, a visiting sister from Ann Arbor [Michigan], testify at a special weekend retreat for our community about how the Lord had healed her of scoliosis. I suffered from this back problem too but had accepted it as something I had to live with. But Lynn's sharing made me think that perhaps the Lord did want to do something for me.

What worried me most was that I felt unworthy. I greatly wanted to see the Lord's action in my life but couldn't help thinking that this was for others only. These thoughts were in my mind during one of the weekend prayer sessions, when there was a word of knowledge concerning people with spinal problems. I went forward—only because some other sisters in the music group made me—with a mixture of anguish and expectation. I was terribly afraid of feeling let down if I wasn't healed.

Three sisters, including Lynn, began praying over me and at first it seemed that my fears were being realized. But at the point when my frustration had become almost overwhelming, the Lord brought to my mind some memories I wasn't expecting right then. I burst into tears and cried till I had no more tears to shed. Through that I became so filled with the Spirit and with a great peace that I simply opened my heart to the Lord and his healing power. That's when Lynn laid hands on my back. At that moment, I had a vision in which I saw my spine straightening up and taking its original shape. Then I heard the sisters shout for joy as the vision was realized before their eyes!

Now I am about an inch taller than before, and I take this physical healing as a sign of the even greater inner healing I experienced during those couple of hours when the Lord came to me and embraced me very tightly. With this permanent remembrance as proof, I can never forget how much he loves me![9]

Notice that for Mercedes Herrera the "greater" healing was her inner healing, the overcoming of a feeling of personal unworthiness and the rejection that literally bent her over.

## GOD'S LOVE

Practitioners of modern medicine tend to treat physical and mental illness on a material plane only, largely ignoring the complex psychological and spiritual dimensions of health care. As one Christian physician admitted, "People resent the fact that they are treated as though they were a loose conglomeration of organ systems rather than as a whole person."[10]

There are at least two extreme attitudes toward modern medicine that Christians should avoid. The first is practicing healing prayer only, refusing any help at all from modern medicine. In many instances this means missing out on significant healing that can be provided by modern medical treatment. For example, many types of mental illness may be controlled through drug therapy.

The second extreme to avoid is limiting the way God heals only to modern medicine. Because our nature is such that one area of our lives may affect another, and because modern medicine does not deal with some of the areas where the cause of a problem may lie, total treatment may be ineffectual. For example, frequently I pray for people with a physical ailment who, I discover, have serious sin in their lives. After they confess and repent of their sin, the physical condition disappears. My point is that physical illness may often be caused by spiritual, emotional, or even demonic influences.

This integrated understanding of human nature has another implication: *as we pray for a person's condition to be healed we should also pray for the person.* Jesus was always kind and considerate when he prayed for the sick, showing love and affection for the person. He never scolded anyone for his or her condition. When prayer for divine healing is lubricated with love, God's compassion constrains and controls how we pray. God's grace and compassion are given to people to heal certain conditions, but the focus is on the whole person. This means that God's mercy should always be communicated with love and gentleness, warmth and compassion; we should do for others as we would want done for ourselves.

## HEALING OF THE SPIRIT

The healing of our spirit, in which our relationship with God is renewed and restored, is the most fundamental area of healing. Without doubt the healing of our spirit is the linchpin around which all other areas of healing revolve.

The human spirit is the capacity in our inner being through which we relate to God and the spiritual world. Genesis 2:7 says that God first formed man from the earth and then "breathed into his nostrils the breath of life, and man became a living being." It is this "breath of life" that separates us from the rest of creation as God's image bearers (Gen. 1:27; Ps. 8:5–8). David C. Needham points out:

It is certainly true that God's original and ultimate intention for man is that he exist bodily. Our bodies, both our present unredeemed ones and our future glorified ones, are not to be thought of as sinful in themselves or of minimal importance. But time after time God takes pains to remind us that we are most essentially spirit beings.[11]

Paul told the Corinthian Christians, "Dear friends, let us purify ourselves from everything that contaminates body and spirit, perfecting holiness out of reverence to God" (2 Cor. 7:1; see also 1 Thess. 5:23). The writer of Hebrews declared that the word of God "penetrates even to dividing soul and spirit" (Heb. 4:12); that is, it penetrates and searches out our innermost being. In both these passages the authors are concerned about the health and purity of people's lives, including their spirits.

The origin of our sickness of spirit goes back to the familiar story, in Genesis 3:1–24, of the Garden of Eden, in which Adam and Eve were tempted by the serpent. The episode began with the spiritually healthy Adam and Eve walking through the garden, enjoying an open relationship with God and each other. Satan then appeared in the form of a serpent, tempting the woman to sin by eating fruit from the tree of the knowledge of good and evil, an act that the Lord had clearly forbidden the man and woman to do. Eve disobeyed, as later did Adam, and sin entered the human race. The results were catastrophic.

First, "the eyes of both of them were opened, and they realized they were naked" (v. 7). Sin awakened shame in them, and the corresponding response to shame was an attempt to cover up: "they sewed fig leaves together and made coverings for themselves." Adam later tried to lay the responsibility for his sin on Eve (v. 12), a further indication of their alienation from each other. Eventually the Lord "made garments of skin for Adam and his wife and clothed them" (v. 21), possibly an early indication of God's provision to cover the shame of our sin through the shedding of blood (in this case the blood of the animals from which the garments were made). So sin brought about social and relational disruption.

Second, "they hid from the Lord God among the trees of the garden" (v. 8). In other words, Adam and Eve's sin created guilt feelings, which caused them to run and hide from God. Later the Lord banished them from the Garden of Eden (v. 23–24). So sin brought about spiritual disruption, the cutting off of their relationship with God. They died spiritually when they sinned.

God had said that if they ate from the forbidden tree they would surely die. While they did not die physically at that moment, they did die spiritually. This is not to say that they ceased to have any capacity to relate to God or other spiritual beings. Rather, their capacity to know God fully and freely was altered and cut off; because he is holy and without sin, God could no longer have free fellowship with them.

But the nature of their spiritual death went deeper than God cutting himself off from them. Their humanity, their heart, the core of their being was changed by sin. They were incapable of either fully desiring a free and open relationship with God or freely knowing God.

Third, when found by the Lord the man said, "I heard you in the garden and I was afraid because I was naked; so I hid" (v. 10). Sin produced fear; Adam was no longer capable emotionally of carrying on an open and free relationship with God.

Fourth, their sin brought the frustration of physical work, toil (the land worked against them rather than for them), and death into the human race. We became mortals. The Lord told the woman: "I will greatly increase your pains in childbearing; with pain you will give birth to children" (v. 16). And to Adam he said, "By the sweat of your brow you will eat your food until you return to the ground, since from it you were taken; for dust you are and to dust you will return" (v. 19).

The ramifications of Adam and Eve's sickness of spirit were great indeed. Social, psychological, emotional, environmental, and spiritual aspects of life were set on edge. The human race has never been the same since. Martyn Lloyd-Jones, in his book *The Cross*, summarizes how spiritual sickness has affected us:

All the varied and complicated problems of the human race today, as they have always been throughout the running centuries, all emanate from just one thing, that man is in the wrong relationship to God. He is alienated from God. There is a state of warfare between man and God. That is the cause of all our troubles. Trouble came into this world as the direct and immediate result of man's rebellion against God, and it has continued ever since.[12]

## THE NEW TESTAMENT

The New Testament also has many illustrations of the relationship between spiritual sickness and other types of problems. Mark 2:1–12 describes how Jesus healed a paralytic. The paralytic had been brought to a crowded meeting by his friends (they had to lower him through a hole in the roof). Jesus, recognizing the friends' faith, said to the paralytic, "Son, your sins are forgiven" (v. 5).

There were teachers of the law in the room at the time who thought to themselves, "Who can forgive sins but God alone?" (v. 7). Jesus said, "Why are you thinking these things? Which is easier: to say to the paralytic, 'Your sins are forgiven,' or to say, 'Get up, take your mat and walk'?" (v. 8–9). Then, just as he had done with the paralytic's sins, Jesus declared his body healed: "I tell you, get up, take your mat and go home" (v. 11). The fact that Jesus forgave the man's sins first indicates that Jesus understood spiritual sickness, caused by sin, as the primary issue in the paralytic's life and that his paralytic condition was directly related to it.

John 5:1–15 describes one of Jesus' greatest miracles, the healing at the pool of Bethesda of a man who had been an invalid for thirty-eight years. He was an embittered, lonely man who seemed angry with life and people and was without hope (v. 7). Like many who suffer from chronic illness, he was full of unbelief, fueled by years of failed healing attempts ("he had been in this condition for a long time," v. 6).

Jesus asked the man if he wanted to get well, that is, if he wanted to turn away from his bitterness and anger as well as be healed of his physical problem. The invalid answered by trying to shift the blame for his unbelief: "I have no one to help me into the pool when the water is stirred. While I am trying to get in, someone else goes down ahead of me" (v. 7). That is, he thought that God could not heal him because of others' failure to help. This man illustrates our problem: that our faith and expectations are limited. Commenting on his response, John Calvin writes, "This sick man does what we nearly all do. He limits God's help to his own ideas and does not dare promise himself more than he conceives in his mind."[13]

Christ responded to the invalid's litany of self-pity and unbelief by healing him. What Jesus said when he healed him is very important. First, Jesus commanded that he "Get up!" (v. 8). Through these strongly spoken words the invalid's thoughts were jolted away from others' failures and on to taking responsibility for his own life. Then Jesus told him to "pick up [his] mat and walk" (v. 8). This call was to obedience and faith—obedience to Jesus' words, faith in Jesus' power. In commanding the invalid in this way, Jesus asked him to believe that God could still heal. As the invalid acted on Christ's words, he was healed.

What is often overlooked in this story is how Jesus later found the man at the Temple and instructed him, "See, you are well again. Stop sinning or something worse may happen to you" (v. 14). Apparently Jesus knew in this instance that the root of his problem was spiritual sickness brought on by sin. God's healing grace was abundantly given, but the invalid still had to believe and turn from the sin that had held him captive for thirty-eight years.

About five years ago a woman in her late forties asked me to pray for her healing. She suffered from chronic stomach disorders and arthritis. When I started to pray over her I received an insight that she was bitter. So I asked her if she was feeling hostility, anger, or bitterness toward someone; and I felt led to ask specifically if she felt that way toward her sister.

She stiffened up, then said, "No. I haven't seen my sister for sixteen years."

I inquired further. "Are you sure?"

Then she told me how her sister years ago had married a man she loved, then later divorced him. "I cannot forgive my sister for that," she admitted.

"If you don't forgive her," I told her, "your 'bones will waste away,' just as David complained his did when he kept silent about his sin of adultery with Bathsheba."

When she heard my words she relented. "What should I do?" she asked.

I told her to write her sister a letter forgiving her and asking to renew their relationship. She wrote the letter immediately, but she did not mail it for several weeks. During that time she became more ill, until she thought she was going to die. Then she remembered the letter. Somehow she summoned the strength to drive to the post office and mail it. The very *moment* she dropped the letter into the box, she experienced relief, and she was completely healed by the time she reached home.

## NEW MEN AND WOMEN

What we have seen in Adam and Eve and in New Testament illustrations is that spiritual sickness has other ramifications for our lives. It disrupts our emotions, our relationships, and even our physical bodies. Let us look now at the central and root act that God does to restore our spiritual life.

Our salvation is initiated in a one-time event in which we are born again (regenerated) by turning away from our sins and toward Christ. This "born-again" event produces many changes in our lives and is the basis for our spiritual healing. The clearest description of these changes is found in the first eight chapters of the book of Romans. In the first four chapters Paul teaches that we are justified through faith in Christ (that is, our sins are forgiven and we are declared righteous by the Father): "This righteousness from God comes through faith in Jesus Christ to all who believe. There is no difference, for all have sinned and fall short of the glory of God, and are justified freely by his grace through the redemption that came by Christ Jesus" (3:22–24).

"Justification by faith," as theologians call this cardinal truth of the Christian life, has two parts. First, God *forgives* the sins that we have committed, so we no longer have to live in bondage to guilt and fear; second, God *declares us righteous* with the same righteousness as that of his own Son.

The remarkable quality about our justification is that it is *free:* "But God demonstrates his own love for us in this: While we were still sinners, Christ died for us" (Rom. 5:8). This is difficult for many to accept, because there is something in us that wants to earn eternal life; we want to do it our own way, in our own strength. But God's gifts of grace and mercy cannot be earned; they can only be received.

God forgives us in Christ and declares us righteous. He adopts us as his sons and daughters. He changes us into his likeness.

So complete is our death in Christ that we are now a new creation: "For we know that our old self was crucified with him so that the body of sin might be done away with, that we should no longer be slaves to sin—because anyone who has died has been freed from sin" (Rom. 6:6–7). This is what being "born again" (what theologians call regeneration) means: we have new natures, new hearts, ones that now want to please and obey God.[14]

"If anyone is in Christ," Paul wrote in 2 Corinthians 5:17, "he is a new creation; the old has gone, the new has come!" *The key to our spiritual healing—and the one point that must be understood and experienced for the rest of what I write in this book to make any sense—is becoming new creations in Christ and living our lives as fully forgiven and reconstructed people.* In this regard our initial "healing of spirit" is more like a heart transplant operation, for God does not bring new life to an old heart so much as create a new heart in us with new desires and capacities to know him (Ps. 51:10). This is the fulfillment of God's promise found in Jeremiah 31:33: "I will put my law in their minds and write it on their hearts."

Paul makes the same point in Ephesians 1:4–6, where he writes, "In love he [the Father] predestined us to be adopted as his sons through Jesus Christ, in accordance with his pleasure and will—to the praise of his glorious grace, which he has freely given us in the One he loves."

Under Roman law an adopted son was recognized in the same way as a natural son. In fact, at the time of the adoption all records of the adopted son's previous life were destroyed, indicating he was a new person and that he had all the privileges of a natural son, including inheritance rights. That is what being a Christian is like: we no longer are tied to our old inheritance of sin and sinful desires; we are new creations (see also Col. 3:1–11; 1 John 3:6–7).

I used to tell people that "I was just a sinner saved by grace." But I no longer say that. True, I once was a sinner who repented and believed and as a result was saved by grace. But now I am a child of God, healed of my spiritual sickness, "set free from sin and [a slave] to righteousness" (Rom. 6:18). That is to say, my fundamental identity is that I am a child of God, a new creation.

David C. Neeham in his book *Birthright* comments on this new identity:

Contrary to much popular teaching, regeneration (being born again) is more than having something taken away (sins forgiven) or having something added to you (a new nature with the assistance of the Holy Spirit); it is becoming someone you had never been before. This new identity is not on the flesh level, but the spirit level—one's deepest self. This miracle is more than a "judicial" act of God. It is an act so real that it is right to say that a Christian's essential nature is righteous rather than sinful. All other lesser identities each of us has can only be understood and appreciated by our acceptance and response to this fact.[15]

## WHAT ABOUT SIN?

Saying that we are new creations and that our old natures are dead is not the same as saying Christians no longer struggle with sin. "If we claim to be without sin," 1 John 1:8 says, "we deceive ourselves and the truth is not in us." John was observing that in this age we will continue to struggle with sin. But he also teaches that we can live righteous lives: "No one who is born of God will continue to sin, because God's seed remains in him; he cannot go on sinning, because he has been born of God" (1 John 3:9).

Many Christians read this passage and get depressed. "I cannot overcome my sin," they think. "My old nature is still too strong." But how can something that has already died still have such a hold on us?

We continue to struggle, but there are no longer "two mes"—a good person and a bad person. I am a new creation in Christ; there is only one me.

In fact, many Christians do go on sinning and suffer from the consequences of sickness of their spirits by yielding to sin that still dwells in their bodies (Rom. 6:12). They give in to sin because they fail to understand and believe that they are new creations in Christ—forgiven, renewed, empowered for righteousness by the Holy Spirit (Rom. 8:9–12). So the effects of sickness of the spirit may take hold of Christians again and again through willful and unconfessed sin, bondage to certain sins, and the neglecting of their relationship with God and his people. The impact of their sin may bring great harm to their emotions and desires and to their psychological and physical health.

If the old self is dead, how does sin still live in our bodies? Our flesh, in which sin still dwells, is yet to be redeemed.

Our problem is that our converted new nature is tied to a body of flesh. The flesh (Greek *sarx*) is the "sin principle" at work in us and with which we are no longer identified as redeemed men and women. This "sin principle" tries to affect our whole being and needs to be progressively overcome. So there is a struggle to integrate our new nature with this reality.

I do not want to minimize the degree to which Christians experience a moral struggle, but we can and should expect the Holy Spirit to make a change in us to such an extent that the struggle is lessened. The change is in what we want—righteousness—and in what we do—obey God. So it is not that the Christian life becomes easy, but it does become easier to live a life of righteousness.

I am convinced that the most common reason for falling into sin is that people do not understand their true identity and purpose as Christians. Actions may be taken in which the effects of sickness of spirit will be healed. The following is a simple, five-step act of faith:

1. *Confronting sin.* Most people know their sins. When they agree with God, that he is right and they are wrong, they allow God's healing access to their spirits, minds, and bodies.

2. *Confessing sin.* Confession goes a step beyond acknowledging we have sin; it is the willingness, through prayer, to admit our sins to God and ask for his forgiveness.

3. *Performing appropriate actions of repentance.* Many sins require repentance to others whom we have wronged (for example, to family or church members), restitution (as when we have stolen something), or a change in life-style (for example, from an immoral relationship).

4. *Receiving God's forgiveness.* There are many people who agree with God about their sin, confess it, and even do acts of appropriate repentance. Yet they never fully receive healing, because they do not believe God has forgiven them. Receiving forgiveness requires humility,

acknowledging there is *nothing* we can do to earn God's grace. All we can do is believe, and to do that we must acknowledge our complete dependence on him.

5. *Forgiving others as God forgives*. Jesus said, "For if you forgive men when they sin against you, your heavenly Father will also forgive you. But if you do not forgive men their sins, your Father will not forgive your sins" (Matt. 6:14–15). God's grace has the marvelous characteristic of being inexhaustable; in fact, the more we give it away, the more it is multiplied in us. When we refuse to give away that which God has so freely given us (by holding people's sins against them), God's grace dries up and we develop sickness of the spirit. Our failure to forgive is bad for us.

Perhaps you are suffering from sickness of spirit as you read these pages. If so, the five steps I have just described are for you. As you take these steps, healing will come, your relationship with God will be restored (or established), and every part of your life will be affected.

# 5. Overcoming the Effects of Past Hurts

In September 1984, the Vineyard Christian Fellowship of Anaheim released over six hundred people to establish a Vineyard Fellowship in nearby Yorba Linda. At that time four thousand people attended the Anaheim Vineyard, so we gave up about fifteen percent of our church. But the figure for the number of people who left reveals only part of the loss to the Anaheim Vineyard and those of us who remained.

Bob Fulton, one of the original Anaheim Vineyard pastors and my brother-in-law, was called as the senior pastor of the new group. He and his wife, Penny (my wife's sister), had overseen the development of our small-group system (most people who attend our church are also involved in a weekly small group gathering of from fifteen to forty people). Further, many of the six hundred people who went to Yorba Linda were our earliest converts and closest friends. These included many of the key lay leaders in the church; until these mature Christians and trained leaders were replaced, the burdens of providing pastoral care would be increased. There were new relationships to be formed, young leaders to recruit, train, and deploy—and much hard work ahead of us.

Though it meant new challenges and more work at the Anaheim Vineyard, Carol enthusiastically agreed with starting the new Yorba Linda church. She knew that the new church was one way through which God would advance his gospel in Orange County. But Carol had not counted on the personal hurt that resulted from missed Sunday fellowship with her two natural sisters and most of her old friends. Soon after the new church began, she was struggling subconsciously with feelings of abandonment and loss.

"I was not able to articulate rationally what was happening inside of me," Carol now says. "If you would have asked me at the time how I felt, I would have told you, 'Great! Never been better.' But in my heart, my innermost part, I was hurting. I also began finding excuses for not seeing my sisters and friends during the week."

Throughout the summer and into the autumn of 1985 Carol's feelings of hurt and abandonment worsened. Then one Sunday in October she made an alarming discovery. "I had had a hectic week and was at a low point both physically and spiritually, when I discovered a large, lemon-sized lump in my breast. At first I didn't know what to do. What if it were malignant? What if I needed surgery?"

That night I prayed for Carol's physical healing, but with no effect. On Monday morning Carol made an appointment with her doctor for Tuesday. "That night I prayed, asking God what he wanted for me in all of this," Carol says. "As I did, he showed me that the lump in my breast was related directly to my feelings of loneliness and abandonment. Until that moment I had not realized how deeply hurt I was. During my childhood I had developed a fear of being abandoned, and I had allowed that fear to control my feelings toward the loss of regular fellowship with my sisters and my friends."

Carol came to me and told me that she suspected there was a relationship between her past hurt and her current sinful attitudes, and the lump. We did not understand the connection between the two, but we accepted God's revelation that they were related. So we prayed together, and she sincerely repented of her bitterness. Then from her heart she blessed her sisters and friends and their work in the new church. "The result was like a huge weight being lifted from my soul," she says. "God reassured me that he would never leave me, and I have been more confident in my relationships since then."

I then prayed again for the healing of the lump in her breast. When I asked the Holy Spirit to come on Carol, I felt a surge of power go through my hands and onto her. "I felt the power of God come on me," Carol says. "The lump felt warm and numb, then it immediately began to shrink. By Tuesday morning the lump had shrunk to the size of a grape, so I cancelled my doctor's appointment. On Tuesday evening Blaine and Becky Cook came by the house and prayed for me, and by Wednesday the lump was gone." Carol's healing went beyond the disappearance of the lump: relationships with family and friends were renewed. Today she enjoys open and free fellowship with them.

## INNER HEALING

For years an irrational fear that God and her friends would abandon her lurked under the surface of Carol's strong and gifted personality. The apparent loss of family and friends by their move to the other church was tailor-made to bring out anxieties and to affect her behavior. That fear, when left to run its course, led to loneliness, depression, avoidance of friends, and a lack of trust in God. The final symptom was the lump in her breast.

When Carol focused on God's promise that he would never leave her, and when she repented of her sinful attitudes and actions toward her sisters and friends, she received Christ's forgiveness and was healed of psychological and emotional damage that had its roots in childhood experiences. She no longer saw herself as a victim of past hurts; their significance receded as she began to see past experience from God's perspective.

A by-product of her healing was renewed relationships. Relating well to others in an open, free, caring, and trusting way reinforced the healing that she received when she repented and believed God's truth. Now Carol's friends tell her that neither they nor God will ever abandon her.

Emotional and psychological hurts linger in the form of bad memories (thoughts of hurtful experiences from the past) and form barriers to personal growth. They may even lead us into various forms of sin, emotional problems, and physical illnesses.

Emotional and psychological hurts, including bad memories, are caused both by our sin and by our being sinned against. The healing of these past hurts restores the inward (unseen and unseeable) part of men and women, as opposed to purely physical, visible, or outward healing. Therefore, the healing of past hurts is commonly called "inner healing."[1]

According to David Seamands inner healing is "ministering to and praying for damaged emotions and unhealed memories."[2] Michael Scanlan writes:

Inner healing is the healing of the inner man. By inner man we mean the intellectual, volitional and affective areas commonly referred to as mind, will and heart but including such other areas as related to emotions, psyche, soul and spirit. Inner healing is distinguished from outer healing commonly called physical healing.[3]

Dennis Bennett says more succinctly, "Inner healing is simply cooperating with the Lord to let him cure and remove from our psychological natures the things that are blocking the flow of the Holy Spirit."[4]

I define inner healing as *a process in which the Holy Spirit brings forgiveness of sins and emotional renewal to people suffering from damaged minds, wills, and emotions.* It is a way of bringing the power of the gospel to a specific area of need.

## INNER HURTS

Most hurtful and damaging experiences that lead to the need for inner healing fall into one of three categories. The first category is damage that comes as a result of being born into a sinful world. These experiences are not the result of the purposeful actions of other persons against us. They include many experiences that are not of our own choice and that are outside our control; inherited diseases, accidents, and poverty are three examples. These experiences beyond our control contribute to what psychologist Karen Horney calls basic anxieties, feeling isolated and helpless in a hostile world.[5]

A second category is wounds inflicted by others. Parents and family members, friends, acquaintances, even strangers may have sinned against us, intentionally or unintentionally. Children of alcoholic parents or children of parents who physically and psychologically abused them fall into this category. This category includes all kinds of unkind things done to us, too numerous for all to be recounted, though some abuses deserve special mention. Some of the most damaging and complex problems that I pray for involve failed relationships with unloving fathers. Also, I encounter many instances of sexual abuse like rape and incest in which the victim is enslaved by rage and anger toward the wrongdoer.[6]

The last category is damage that comes as a result of the personal sin we commit. Frequently these are behavioral sins like fornication, adultery, and homosexuality. In recent years I have prayed with many women and men for damage that has come from the sin of abortion. Sinful attitudes like greed, competitiveness, and jealousy also lead to emotional and psychological damage. These sinful actions and attitudes result in guilt and guilt feelings. I have prayed many times for people who know that God forgives them, yet still they suffer from guilt feelings. What they know intellectually has not penetrated their hearts.

Poor choices may also create emotional damage in us. Poor choices are not necessarily sinful, though they are unwise and result in failure. Poor choices frequently lead to problems with guilt feelings and anger. Sometimes wounds inflicted by others combine with our own sins, creating weakness in us.

For example, Michael Flynn, an Episcopal priest, received this letter from a woman after he had spoken about inner healing at a conference she attended:

[After the conference] I was hassling with the devil over a problem of a sexual nature and I cried out to God to show me where the "hook" was that Satan had over me. He took me back to a situation where I was working many years ago with a group of people who had very loose life-styles and were influencing me greatly. He then recited some words to me that I had actually said—an inner vow. And then he showed me how much it had hurt him. . . . So I broke the vow, confessed my sin, and asked him to forgive me. The power of God came and I felt a shock go through my body and I knew that bond was broken and I was free. I knew I truly was able to follow Jesus if I chose. Such sweet victory! I was shocked when Satan showed up at that very moment and tempted me again. I was still revelling in my newfound joy. How dare he? And then I realized the battle was still on. I turned to Jesus, and he said, "You don't have to do that anymore, because we took care of it." I saw him as my rock, my Savior, and my protector. And Satan left.

One does not have to be a victim of abuse or have committed a sexual sin to need inner healing. For example, there are those who suffer from an "older brother syndrome." Like the older brother in the parable of the prodigal son (see Luke 15:11–32), our pride leads to resentment and bitterness when expectations, based on an inflated view of ourselves, are unfulfilled.

There is also the problem of overscrupulosity, commonly found among those raised in evangelical and Roman Catholic families. I once prayed for a man who suffered greatly from guilt feelings that came from a minor childhood incident. When he was ten years old his mother had discovered in his trouser pocket a playing card with the picture of a nude woman. (He had found it on the way home from school.) She disciplined him for having the card, and he had suffered under the guilt of it for over thirty years! His suffering was as great as that of many people I have prayed for who committed far more serious sins.

## DIAGNOSIS

Hurtful and damaging experiences leave us with remembered and remaining emotional responses that limit our freedom to experience God's grace fully. Leading practitioners of inner healing have observed that certain behavioral and emotional patterns arise in people who have not adequately applied Christ's grace and forgiveness to the problems created by hurtful memories. The following characteristics, described by Theodore Dobson, Michael Scanlan, Francis MacNutt, and Rita Bennett are found frequently in people needing inner healing:

The burden of pain that all of us carry drains our energy from creative and productive activity and makes us feel unworthy, guilty, hopeless, broken, and unforgivable.

This burden would be destructive enough if its effects went no further, but such is not the case. These negative feelings, now converted over a period of time into attitudes, begin to develop within us negative patterns of behavior, and our past begins to destroy our present. That which is so negative begins to want to destroy itself, and so we develop habits of self-destruction or habits of sin.[7]

Some of the initial manifestations were a judgmental spirit that is harsh and demanding on self and others, a strong perfectionist attitude demanding the impossible from self and others, a strong pattern of fearing future events, a sense of aloneness and abandonment whenever there are times of decision, a preoccupation with one's own guilt and a compulsive reaction to compete for position and success. . . . Usually there is a constant expectation of growth or breakthrough to a new spiritual freedom, but it hasn't happened. It doesn't happen because the heart is hurting.[8]

Inner healing is indicated whenever we become aware that we are held down in any way by the hurts of the past. We all suffer from this kind of bondage to one degree or another, some severely, some minimally. Any unreasonable fear, anxiety, or compulsion caused by patterns built up in the past can be broken by prayer, provided the person is also doing his best to discipline his life in a Christian way. So many Christians are hindered in their lives by such things as a haunting sense of worthlessness, erratic fits of anger or expression, anxiety and unreasoning fears, compulsive sexual drives, and other problems which they would like to change, but find they cannot cope with on the basis of repentance and a decision to change.[9]

A Christian, even one who is a recognized leader, may still have great need for inner healing. What are the things he or she may need to cope with? Here are a few: poor self-identity; self-hatred; feeling God doesn't love him or her; hatred of others; unforgiveness of self or others; self-aggrandizement; self-centeredness; bad temper; a hyper-critical attitude; embarrassment from a physical, emotional or mental handicap; loneliness; rejection; depression; persecution; divorce; false guilt; various sexual problems.

There may be yet unhealed needs from the death of someone close and dear; from being in or causing an accident; from fears or memories of pregnancy and giving birth.[10]

When the emotional and psychological affects of hurtful memories are not dealt with, physical problems like migraine headaches, indigestion, nightmares, dizziness, and many other functional disturbances may develop.[11] This was the case for Carol when she developed a lump in her breast.

## HEALING WITH A PURPOSE

The purpose and goal of inner healing is emotionally healthy persons, people who are released from the emotional and psychological bondage that past experiences have produced. I use the term "emotions" in a broad sense that includes all the internal reactions we feel to situations around us or to things happening in ourselves. Emotions are inner reactions that we are conscious of and that influence our behavior.

I make a distinction between reactions and responses. An emotion is our reaction; what we do or say is our response. In some ways this distinction is not always clear to us, because it is not always easy to distinguish exactly which emotion we are having that is causing a certain response or why we are having it. But this distinction is helpful because it underlines something that is crucial about the healing of past hurts: our goal is to have emotional reactions that reinforce the love of God and neighbor, so that negative reactions that lead us astray are not out of control.

Emotionally healthy persons are:

1. *People whose emotional reactions help them live the Christian*

*life.* That is, their emotions tend to reinforce righteousness and love. These people have what psychologists call well-integrated personalities, which makes it possible for them to believe and receive all that God has for them. James 1:5–8 describes persons who are unsure of their identity in Christ, whose emotional and psychological life is at odds with what God says is true about their being new creations in Christ:

If any of you lacks wisdom, he should ask God, who gives generously to all without finding fault, and it will be given to him. But when he asks, he must believe and not doubt, because he who doubts is like a wave of the sea, blown and tossed by the wind. That man should not think he will receive anything from the Lord; he is a double-minded man, unstable in all he does.

The Greek word translated in this passage "double-minded" is *dipsuchos*, which means a man with two souls, or two minds, within him. William Barclay comments, "One believes, the other disbelieves; and the man is a walking civil war in which trust and distrust of God wage a continual battle against each other."[12] So emotionally healthy persons have one mind, the mind of Christ, which forms and informs their emotional and psychological lives.

2. *People whose emotional reactions instinctively work correctly.* When we think about emotions, it is easy to assume that we should reflect first, then respond to a given situation. But this is repression of our emotions and is usually based on the fear that we cannot handle them rather than an attempt to find the right place for them in our lives. The scriptural view is that in Christ we have a new nature—including emotions—which enables us to respond instinctively in the right way.

Michael Scanlan describes this situation as having the peace of Jesus. "The peace of Jesus Christ is a distinct gift from the Lord" that has many signs: rejoicing, unselfishness, prayer, watchfulness, and the fruit of the Spirit (Phil. 4:4).[13]

3. *People whose emotional reactions are subordinate to right responses.* Emotional reactions are not supposed to run our lives.

They are meant to support right responses, to be servants of righteousness and love. This means our emotions should be subordinated to the scriptural truth of our new nature in Christ. This stresses learning to trust what God says about us rather than how we may feel about ourselves. Steve Scott and Brooks Alexander write:

The biblical depiction of our nature is surely a truer and more trustworthy evaluation than that provided by our fears, angers, and memories, not to mention the accusations of the Adversary (Rom. 8:1–2). *Inner healing should help to re-educate us (via the word of God) as to who we are in Christ.* As we understand how God sees us, as well as the provision he has made for our growth, we will begin to develop a self-esteem that corresponds precisely to our reliance on Christ's righteousness rather than our own. (Rom. 12:3) [Emphasis mine][14]

## MEMORIES OF THE WAY WE WERE

It is impossible to correct dysfunctional attitudes and emotions that result from past hurts without in some way changing how we cope with the painful memories of those bad experiences. These attitudes and ways of thinking, so deeply embedded in our hearts, subconsciously hold us back from believing what God says is true about us.

Paul's Letter to the Ephesian Christians teaches us that we can experience a life of wholeness, blessing, and freedom to serve God on earth: "Praise be to the God and Father of our Lord Jesus Christ, who has blessed us in the heavenly realms with every spiritual blessing in Christ. For he chose us in him before the creation of the world to be holy and blameless in his sight" (1:3–4). Notice that his giving us "every spiritual blessing" is an accomplished act; all that remains is for us to trust him for the blessings!

God decided long ago—"before the creation of the world"—that we should inherit forgiveness of sins and the riches of his grace. Now we are sons and daughters of God, participants in his glory and freedom:

And you also were included in Christ when you heard the word of truth, the gospel of your salvation. Having believed, you were marked in him with a seal, the promised Holy Spirit, who is a deposit guaranteeing our inheritance until the redemption of those who are God's possession—to the praise of his glory. (Eph. 1:13–14)

But when we are held back by the guilt and pain coming from hurtful memories, we miss out on experiencing what is already ours. Michael Scanlan says that these painful memories often result in brokenheartedness, by which he means "the center of love within is shattered, never again to be the same source of giving and receiving love."[15] The broken heart is restored through release from the bondage to hurtful memories, a process that includes forgiveness and emotional reconstruction under the guidance of the Holy Spirit.

Many people cannot face their painful memories and suffer the inevitable emotional trauma. They need, Scanlan says, the power of the Holy Spirit and the gift of faith to be able to face the past, thus freeing themselves to live fully in the future. Understood in this way, the "healing of memories" is not the elimination of painful memories from our consciousness; it is God's Spirit taking away their sting and healing the resultant emotional damage. This was Carol's experience when she confessed her sin and believed God's assurance that he would never leave her. She was freed instantly from the grip of painful memories, though she can certainly still recall the experiences.

Another way of thinking about the healing of bad memories is that though God does not eliminate the memories, he does reframe memories so they are no longer significant factors in how we feel, think, and act. Their hurt recedes to the back ground as the knowledge and assurance of our identity in Christ comes forward. We may now think of ourselves as new creations in Christ, not as victims of past hurts—no matter how terrible or unjust those hurts may have been.

The way our brain stores memories is a complex subject, though discoveries in modern medicine have unlocked some interesting facts. In the early 1950s Dr. Wilder Penfield, a neurosurgeon at McGill University in Montreal, performed brain surgery on epileptic patients under a local anesthetic. During the course of surgery he performed several experiments. In one of the experiments he electrically stimulated the cerebral cortex of the brain with a small electrode. The patients reported dreamlike experiences that were in fact recorded memories from the past, many of which they had forgotten. As a result of these experiments, Dr. Penfield drew the following conclusions:

1. The brain records all of our experiences.
2. It also records our perception of the feelings associated with these experiences.
3. Through the function of remembering, we can be aware of the present while reliving a past experience.
4. Recordings of many of our experiences remain in the brain even though we are not consciously aware of them; some may be recalled at any time, while others are buried deep in the subconscious mind and are available through dreams or external stimuli (if at all).
5. These past experiences not only influence the present but also the future, shaping, guiding, and sometimes limiting our behavior. [16]

Penfield's research confirms that memories have a powerful influence on behavior and attitudes. When we remember the facts surrounding certain events we also experience the emotions associated with those events. If those emotions include terror, depression, anger, guilt feelings, and so on, we may develop crippling emotional problems.

Even when we do not consciously remember painful events, we still feel the effects of them. Theodore Dobson writes:

Accumulated hurts may come out as uncontrollable "fits" of anger, jealousy, or depression. Accumulated guilt may be expressed in physical or psychological illness. Phobias—irrational fears of harmless or only ordinarily dangerous things—may be the result of fearful forgotten episodes in a person's history. These kinds of pain are more harmful and destructive than the original pain that caused them, for they are more difficult to deal with and find remedies for.[17]

Michael Scanlan maintains that a distinction must be made between "surface" and "root" memories. By surface memories he means memories that "can be called forth into the consciousness of the person."[18] Examples of surface memories are an embarrassing incident, a time of fright, or an action filled with guilt feelings. Through the power and grace of the Holy Spirit these memories may be consciously recalled, faced, and prayed for; the person may then experience peace and release from their hold.

Root memories are more difficult to discover. They are embedded deeply in people's subconscious minds, below the level of their awareness. Scanlan writes:

Where a root memory is involved there are many disturbing memories built upon one root memory. Praying for individual surface memories yields little success. These memories are but parts of the iceberg above the water. There is a reality to be healed beneath the water. . . . Sometimes a recent memory of rejection is the object of healing; sometimes it is a hidden repressed memory of early life; sometimes it is a series of memories; sometimes it is a pattern of life that continues almost independently of any memories. . . . When the root is healed, new freedom is experienced in a whole series of other memories.[19]

The Holy Spirit is capable of probing deeply into the unconscious mind and rooting out effects of past hurts that hold us back.

## FORGIVENESS

The most essential ingredient in inner healing prayer, the kind of prayer that gets to the deeper memories and associated hurts that hold us back from true freedom in Christ, is the two-sided coin of repentance and forgiveness (both forgiving others and ourselves).

James's prescription for double-mindedness was hearty repentance: "Come near to God and he will come near to you. Wash your hands, you sinners, and purify your hearts, you double-minded. Grieve, mourn and wail. Change your laughter to mourning and your joy to gloom" (James 4:8–9). Repentance is not feeling bad about ourselves; it is feeling bad about our sins and turning from them. And repentance is the doorway to receiving forgiveness.

The parable of the unmerciful servant, found in Matthew 18:21–35, illustrates the importance of receiving and giving forgiveness. The occasion of the parable was Peter's question about how many times we should forgive someone who has sinned against us. "Up to seven times?" Peter asked. Jesus answered, "I tell you, not seven times, but seventy-seven times" (v. 21–22). Jesus introduced the parable by saying there is no sin committed against us that we cannot forgive; then through the parable he taught we can always forgive others because God has already forgiven us far more than we will ever need to forgive someone else.

In the parable a servant who owed ten thousand talents was brought before his king to settle accounts. The servant was unable to pay, so the king ordered that he, his wife, and children be sold into slavery. The servant then fell to his knees, asking for more time to repay the debt. Instead, the king "took pity on him, canceled the debt and let him go" (v. 27). Ten thousand talents is equal to billions of dollars (the total GNP of Palestine at that time was perhaps 1000 talents!), an impossible sum for any individual to raise.[20] The Lord forgives unforgivable sins. The point is that when we have wronged God or someone else, we must learn to receive forgiveness, no matter how great our sins.

But there is more to this parable. After the servant left the king, he went out and "found one of his fellow servants who owed him a hundred denarii" (v. 28). A hundred denarii is only a three months' salary, a paltry sum in comparison to the debt the king has forgiven. The first servant "grabbed him and began to choke him. 'Pay back what you owe me!' he demanded" (v. 28). Then, when the debtor asked for time to repay the debt—the same request the servant had made to the king—the servant had no mercy, refused to forgive him, and had him thrown into prison. When the king learned about his, he said, "You wicked servant, I canceled all that debt of yours because you begged me to. Shouldn't you have had mercy on your fellow servant just as I had on you?" The passage continues, "In anger his master turned him over to the jailers to be tortured, until he should pay back all he owed" (v. 32–34).

The king was angry because the servant would not forgive as he had been forgiven. Notice that the debtor who owed the hundred denarii had not asked for forgiveness; he had asked only for time to pay the debt. Jesus was teaching that we should extend forgiveness to those who do not even ask to be forgiven. Why? I believe it is because having no mercy is a crippling burden that leads to hostility (anger directed toward others), guilt (anger directed toward ourselves), and anxiety (fear without an appropriate object).

Finally, Jesus taught that unforgiveness will cause all types of personal torment on earth—spiritual, mental, emotional, physical, and social. All of this culminates in eternity in hell. "This is how my heavenly Father will treat each of you," he said, "unless you forgive your brother from your heart" (v. 35). The principle is simple: God has given us mercy so we may extend it to others, and if we forgive others we will continue to experience God's forgiveness.

There is one last principle regarding forgiveness that is important to maintaining emotional health: each Christian is responsible in every conflict to put things right by receiving or giving forgiveness. We have no right to withhold forgiveness or refuse to receive forgiveness, because God has extended his mercy to us.

In Matthew 5:23–24 Jesus says: "Therefore, if you are offering your gift at the altar and there remember that your brother has something against you, leave your gift there in front of the altar. First go and be reconciled to your brother; then come and offer your gift." If we have sinned against someone, we have the responsibility to apologize, ask for forgiveness, and, when necessary, make restitution.

Jesus also taught that if we have been sinned against, we have the responsibility to approach the offender and work it out: "If your brother sins against you, go and show him his fault, just between the two of you. If he listens to you, you have won your brother over" (Matt. 18:15). Extending forgiveness is a prerequisite for reconciliation in these situations.

## CONVERSION THERAPY

A second ingredient in healing prayer is seeing our past experience from God's perspective. People who come to see their past hurts through the lens of God's mercy undergo what I sometimes refer to as "conversion therapy." They learn to evaluate their emotions and past experiences on the basis of new criteria, the gospel's.

Peter's denial of Jesus and his eventual restoration is one of the greatest episodes of conversion therapy in the New Testament (see Luke 22:31–34, 54–62; John 21:15–22). After Jesus' arrest Peter followed him to the house of the high priest, where he sat down around a fire in the courtyard. During the night three retainers of the high priest who had never seen him before accused Peter of being Jesus' colleague. Peter vigorously denied their assertions and in so doing denied his relationship with the Lord.

At the third denial, "the Lord turned and looked straight at Peter. Then Peter remembered the word the Lord had spoken to him: 'Before the rooster crows today, you will disown me three times'" (Luke 22:61). Peter was overwhelmed by his own unfaithfulness and failure, and "he went outside and wept bitterly" (v. 62). From that moment on, whenever Peter thought of Jesus' face he must have remembered his own denial and the Lord's gaze.

Peter "wept bitterly." Tears of bitterness are not the same as tears of repentance. Tears of bitterness are born out of self-pity. He went out and wept, "Oh, woe is me. It all came true. I committed the worst sin possible, the very thing that I had promised the Lord I would not do." At the Last Supper he had said, "Lord, I am ready to go with you to prison and to death" (Luke 22:33). Soon after this at Gethsemane Peter wielded a sword in defense of Jesus. But when the Lord took the sword out of his hand, Peter did not know how to fight: he did not know how to fight the inward fight in the spiritual realm. Peter had been sure of his own strength and ideas, but knew little of God's strength and ways. And after he denied Christ all that remained was disillusionment with himself.

Satan tried to gain control of the disciples through the emotional and spiritual trauma of Jesus' crucifixion. Jesus knew this would happen, and at the Last Supper he prayed that Simon's "faith may not fail" during this time of sifting (Luke 22:31–32). Peter was sifted in the courtyard, and it remained for the Lord to restore him after the resurrection.

Peter returned to Galilee and to his profession of fishing. In his post-resurrection appearance, Jesus brought back to Peter the memory of his calling through the miracle of a large catch of fish, thus renewing in him hope (see John 21:2–7; Luke 5:4–11). Then, while sitting around the campfire, Jesus asked him three times, "Peter, do you love me?" (John 21:15–19). Three times Peter had denied the Lord, and now three times Jesus recommissioned him to "Feed my sheep," which renewed him spiritually, emotionally, and relationally.

In the third exchange between Jesus and Peter, Peter said, "Lord, you know all things; you know that I love you" (John 21:17). What Peter said was, in effect, "You know all about me, including what I am going to say to you now. I have denied you; I have been a fool and a turncoat. I have done it all. You know the depth of my heart." When Peter acknowledged that Jesus knew his limitations and weaknesses he was able to receive Jesus' commission to "Feed my sheep." In his simple commission Jesus in effect said, "You are Saint Peter now. I love and forgive you. I have great confidence in you. You are not thinking of yourself more highly than you ought."

Peter never again saw himself as a betrayer. From this point on, he believed that he was a new creation in Christ and lived on that basis. The book of Acts never mentions Peter's past failures. His Letters are full of faith in God and confidence in his grace and forgiveness. He became a fully healed and emotionally healthy person.

## RESTORATION NOW

Peter's restoration illustrates how quickly healing from crippling memories may happen when people open their hearts and minds to the work of the Holy Spirit and believe that what God's word says about them is true. After Carol was healed of her breast lump last year, she reevaluated how she had been praying for people's healing from the effects of hurtful memories. "I would spend weeks, months, sometimes even years working with people who were trying to recover from various kinds of childhood traumas," she said. "But after my healing, which happened in only a few minutes, I realized that much of what we were doing was aimed at healing the old person, not helping people to believe they are new creations in Christ. Further, I observed that in cases like Peter's, people are restored quickly."

Hurtful memories affected people's ability to believe passages of Scripture like 2 Corinthians 5:17, "Therefore, if anyone is in Christ, he is a new creation; the old has gone, the new has come!" So instead of focusing on past hurts, Carol thought, she should focus on the core of people's present beliefs; her assumption was that many people do not truly believe what God says is true about them.

To test her theory Carol, along with Gloria Thompson, began accepting appointments to pray for people every Monday. They decided that people should have significant improvement immediately and that they should not have to see them more than a few times. Their underlying assumption was that God's grace is sufficient for inner healing now.

Over the next few months they had remarkable results, helping people substantially after only one or two prayer sessions. "What we discovered," Carol says, "is that often people do not truly believe. When we questioned them about receiving Christ's forgiveness and believing that they were new creations in Christ, they became hesitant and usually admitted that they 'couldn't possibly be forgiven for the terrible things they did' or for the terrible things that were done to them.''

At one conference around this time Carol was asked to pray for a woman whose stiffened fingers curled toward her elbows and whose arms and shoulders contracted every time she entered a room of worshiping people. "She looked crablike and tormented," Carol said, "a phenomenon I have seen in others." After taking the woman to a private room, Carol interviewed her. Connie (not her real name) was twenty-five years old and had been a committed Christian for four years. After Carol discerned that her problem was not demonic in origin (in Part III I describe in detail how this is done), she continued the interview. Here is Connie's story:

When I was thirteen years old my parents divorced, and at that time I knew they did not love me or care for me. I was abandoned by them. So, to get back at my parents for their selfishness, I became promiscuous. Over the next seven years I had many men . . . and two abortions. I also had a problem with masturbation, something that I still struggle with.

When Connie committed her life to Christ at age twenty-one, it was a life-changing experience. Her life-style changed immediately; she turned away from promiscuity and immersed herself in a strong, healthy church. Though she inherited eternal life, a new life-style, and new friends, she never fully accepted forgiveness for her sins nor did she extend to her parents forgiveness for their sins against her. So when she

entered an environment in which the Holy Spirit was working—especially a worship service—she experienced crippling
*emotional trauma* associated with the hurt of her parents' divorce and her promiscuous life-style.

During the interview Carol began to suspect that Connie
was not conscious of how her past sins and the sins committed
against her were related to her present condition. These memories and associated emotional trauma were embedded deeply
in her subconscious mind. But when the Holy Spirit came on
her, shame, guilt, and fear flared into her consciousness, resulting in bizarre body language and the inability to pray and
worship freely.

Carol invited the Holy Spirit to come on Connie and gently
reveal his grace and mercy to her. Then Carol asked Connie to
repent and receive forgiveness for the sins of hatred of parents,
promiscuity, masturbation, and abortion. At first Connie could
not do this, because she was convinced her sins were too
great. "God could never forgive me," she said, "I'm so dirty."
So Carol read aloud from Ephesians 1 about God's grace and
forgiveness; the word of God ignited a flicker of hope and faith
in Connie. That flicker touched something in her heart: she
began to believe God's forgiveness for her sin, and by the end
of the session she was able to forgive her parents. As Connie
received and extended forgiveness, her body relaxed and the
crablike grip disappeared. She attended the rest of the conference, and for the first time in her Christian life was able to
worship God freely. She was completely healed.

# 6. Healing the Demonized

Judy was the twenty-eight-year-old wife of a missionary who had just returned home from Europe to California. Soon after arriving, she complained to her husband about seeing strange and twisted faces over her own face when she gazed into windows at night. She also told him of having terrifying dreams, something that started in France after she prayed for a man who had claimed to have demonic problems. She was confused and frightened by the strange faces and terrifying dreams. Judy (not her real name) also had other psychological problems that had been lifelong struggles for her. For example, as long as she could remember she had become infatuated with married men, fantasizing sexual intercourse but never actually becoming physically involved with them.

Judy's family background helps explain why she had these experiences. Both of her parents had been involved in the occult—they were married in a spiritist church. They divorced when Judy was a young girl and she had been raised by her mother. Judy was never personally involved in the occult, and she claimed to have been a Christian since the age of four. She had married a strong Christian. Still, as long as Judy could remember she struggled with impure thoughts, and now these strange and twisted visions and dreams were tormenting her.

Soon after returning to California, Judy attended a small-group meeting that was led by Blaine and Becky Cook. During the meeting Judy behaved in a bizarre manner. For no apparent reason, she cried out, fell to the floor, and began thrashing around. She had never behaved this way before. When Becky Cook approached Judy to help her, something in Judy said, "I hate you." The words that Judy uttered seemed hardly her own; they were not her normal speech at all. Judy later said she felt like a spectator during the experience, as though she had no control over what was happening. Blaine then picked Judy up and took her to another room for prayer by a team. On the way Judy hit Blaine in the mouth. By now Blaine suspected that Judy was under the influence of a demon, so he commanded the spirit to stop its violent attacks.

During the prayer time Blaine and the team identified demons that brought out feelings of defiance, anger, and fear, and the desire to commit adultery in Judy. Blaine put his hand on her and said, "You demons who are producing defiance, the temptation to commit adultery, anger, and fear, be gone from this child of God." As Blaine prayed, Judy fell to the ground, then she experienced immediate and dramatic relief from her oppression. Since then she has had no problems with habitual sexual fantasies, demonic dreams, or seeing evil spirits on her face. For a short period of time she continued to have a problem with anger, but the problem gradually went away as she continued to meet with Blaine for counseling and prayer and with a small group of other Christians for encouragement and instruction. She also experienced a significant improvement in her ability to relate well to others. Today Judy is back in Europe serving the Lord as a missionary.

## DO DEMONS ACTUALLY EXIST?

The phenomena that Judy experienced—both her behavior and post-experience testimony—strongly suggest that she was affected by evil spirits. But many modern, secularized people ask: "Do demons actually exist? Or do they belong only to the world of myth and folklore, delusions of demented or superstitious people who are unenlightened by modern science?" Some people think that much of what is thought to be supernatural activity is better explained in psychological or physiological terms, and that belief in the devil is neither progressive nor up to date.

This way of thinking is not confined only to secularists. Many Western Christians struggle with the same kinds of questions. At one time people attributed everything to the direct intervention of the devil; today modern men and women attribute nothing to the devil. Now it is a worldview problem: we are forced to choose either the devil or science, but not both! For example, recently an evangelical psychologist, Christian Hageseth, only half jokingly asserted, "The rate at which people diagnose [demon] possession is inversely proportional to their education in the behavioral sciences."[1] Yet I believe that the understanding of Jesus and the apostles about the significance of Satan and evil spirits is so much a part of the New Testament that we cannot ignore their existence and influence.[2]

C. S. Lewis, in his classic description of demonic strategy, *The Screwtape Letters*, predicted the rise of a strange mixture of science and religion. The book is written in the form of a series of letters from a senior demon (Screwtape) to a junior temptor (Wormwood). In the seventh letter Screwtape describes what he sees as a promising trend in modern society:

Our policy, for the moment, is to conceal ourselves. Of course this has not always been so. We are really faced with a cruel dilemma. When the humans disbelieve in our existence we lose all the pleasing results of direct terrorism, and we make no magicians. On the other hand, when they believe in us, we cannot make them materialists and skeptics. At least, not yet. I have great hopes that we shall learn in due time how to emotionalize and mythologize their science to such an extent that what is, in effect, a belief in us (though not under that name) will creep in while the human mind remains closed to belief in the Enemy. The "Life Force," the worship of sex, and some aspects of Psychoanalysis may here prove useful. If once we can produce our perfect work—the Materialistic Magician, the man, not using, but veritably worshiping, what he vaguely calls "Forces" while denying the existence of "spirits"—then the end of the war will be in sight. But in the meantime we must obey our orders. I do not think you will have much difficulty in keeping the patient in the dark. The fact that "devils" are predominantly *comic* figures in the modern imagination will help you. If any faint suspicion of your existence begins to arise in his mind, suggest to him a picture of something in red tights, and persuade him that since he cannot believe in that (it is an old textbook method of confusing them) he therefore cannot believe in you.[3]

Ultimately the answer to the question of Satan's and demons' existence is found in Scripture. The New Testament clearly teaches the existence of both Satan and demons (Luke 10:17, 20; Rev. 12:7–10). Jesus' life and ministry were marked by continual confrontations with demons (Luke 4:31–37, 41; 6:18; 7:21; 8:2, 26–39; 9:37–43; 11:14–26), and he gave authority to his followers to cast out demons (Luke 9:1, 49–50; 10:17–20; Mark 16:17). The New Testament contains teaching from the early church on Christians' authority over demons (1 Cor. 2:6–8; 10:20–21; Eph. 6:10–18; Col. 1:13–16; 2:20), and numerous incidences in which exorcisms took place (Acts 5:16; 8:6–8; 16:16–18; 19:11–12).

There is undeniable evidence for belief in demons throughout the history of the early church. All of the church fathers and all of the reformers believed the devil exists and that his works are painfully manifest among us.[4] Human experience itself testifies to the devil's existence, as Judy's story demonstrates.[5] Do the devil and demons actually exist? Scripture, church tradition, and human experience all answer an emphatic yes.

## SPIRITUAL WARFARE

Once the existence of Satan and demons is accepted, it is necessary to understand their relevance. The Father sent Jesus to destroy the kingdom of Satan and its evil works (John 12:31; 1 John 3:8) and to establish the kingdom of God. In fact, one cannot understand the significance of Christ's mission on earth without understanding the significance of the kingdom of God. There are four key points in Jesus' instruction on the kingdom of God:

1. God's reign came into the world in the person of Jesus (Matt. 12:28).
2. By repenting of personal sin and believing in Jesus Christ,

men and women are redeemed from the world, the flesh, and the devil, and they come under the reign of God's kingdom (John 3:1–21).

3. The kingdom of God is destroying the kingdom of Satan (1 John 3:8).
4. At the return of Christ, when he ushers in the fullness of the kingdom of God, Satan will be eternally destroyed (Matt. 13:36–43).

Jesus' public ministry had two elements: *proclamation* of the good news of the kingdom of God and *demonstration* of its power through casting out demons, healing the sick, and raising the dead. During his first sermon in the synagogue at Capernaum Jesus encountered a demon in a man who asked, "What do you want with us, Jesus of Nazareth? Have you come to destroy us?" (Mark 1:24). Jesus came as a divine invader to destroy demons and release men and women to eternal life, which explains why the Lord's presence caused demons to tremble and fear. Jesus' ministry was marked by continual conflict with Satan and demons for the purpose of establishing God's reign on earth.

Jesus commissioned the Twelve and the Seventy-two to preach the kingdom of heaven, heal the sick, and drive out demons (Matt. 10:5–15; Luke 10:1–20). We too have been commissioned to preach the kingdom of God and have been given authority to cast out demons. The nature of our authority over demons reflects the dilemma of living in the time before the return of Christ and the new age, the fullness of his kingdom. Jesus defeated Satan at the cross, and through his victory we have authority over Satan. But we have yet to exercise that authority fully until Christ's return. So though the kingdom of Satan was decisively defeated through Jesus' death and resurrection, we do not yet enjoy the fullness of the kingdom of God. In other words, until Christ's return we are still in a battle with the world, the flesh, and the devil and his demons (John 16:33).

In coming into a relationship with Christ we receive eternal life, forgiveness of sins, and a new nature. We are also released from bondage to the kingdom of Satan, and we are given life in the kingdom of God. As we walk with God we gain access to protection from Satan's harm (1 John 5:18) and overcome Satan (1 John 2:13–14; 4:4). But Satan is still alive, and "the whole world is under the control of the evil one" (1 John 5:19). Those who have not turned to Christ are Satan's prey, but he continues to war on the saints (Rev. 12:17). So though we have all that we need now for eternal life, nevertheless we live in a hostile environment, one ruled by Satan. This means that Satan may attack us in many areas of our lives.

Michael Scanlan and Randall Cirner point out:

The fact is that many Christians do not live in the full freedom of the sons and daughters of God because many areas of their lives are in bondage to Satan. Sins, unwanted habits, physical illness, emotional wounds, psychological problems, "bad luck," disunity in relationships, problems in relating to God, fears, and compulsions are just some of the ways Satan wages war against the children of God.[6]

This is not to imply that these problems are always or even frequently caused by demons, only that their cause may be from the influence of demons. And their cause may be complex, a combination involving psyhological, physical, and demonic factors.

The fact of Satan's open warfare on the saints, combined with Christ's command that we "make disciples of all nations" (Matt. 28:19–20), means we are locked in spiritual warfare until Christ's return. We are called to liberate territory for Jesus Christ, to take back ground from deceiving spirits who speak through hypocritical liars (1 Tim. 4:1–2). As we succeed in this warfare, the victims of Satan's power are released and the time for the ending of Satan's dominion and for the establishment of God's rule on earth comes near.

We must face the enemy; we must fight. Like Jesus himself, we have a job to do: *proclaim* the kingdom of God and *demonstrate* it through healing the sick and casting out demons (John

20:21). This task also includes teaching, discipling, caring for others, living the corporate life, and so on. Scripture is clear about the seriousness and centrality of spiritual warfare for the believer:

Be self-controlled and alert. Your enemy the devil prowls around like a roaring lion looking for someone to devour. Resist him, standing firm in the faith, because you know that your brothers throughout the world are undergoing the same kind of suffering. (1 Pet. 5:8–9)

Finally, be strong in the Lord and in his mighty power. Put on the full armor of God so that you can take your stand against the devil's schemes. For our struggle is not against flesh and blood, but against the rulers, against the authorities, against the powers of this dark world and against the spiritual forces of evil in the heavenly realms. (Eph. 6:10–12)

What every Christian needs to know about spiritual warfare is that while Satan is strong, Christ is stronger. We have nothing to fear from Satan or demons, as long as we live faithfully and righteously, never backing down when challenged by evil.[7]

## WHAT ARE DEMONS?

Scripture and church tradition offer insights into the nature and origin of Satan and demons. But first a comment is in order about who and what Satan is *not*. Satan is not an uncreated, eternal being like God, only opposite in nature. As C. S. Lewis points out, "Satan, the leader or dictator of devils, is the opposite, not of God, but of Michael."[8] We flatter Satan and misunderstand God's eternal goodness when we raise Satan to the level of being a god. No, Satan is no god, and we need not fear him as being one.

In the beginning God created Lucifer ("Lightbearer") to serve and love him, but he rebelled and became Satan ("Adversary"). Some believe Isaiah 14:12–15, which refers directly to the king of Babylon, is also a description of the fall of Satan. In this passage one called the "morning star" in the New

International Version (which is translated "Lucifer" in the Latin Vulgate) is cast down to earth after attempting to overthrow God. He wanted the supreme authority of God! In the Isaiah 14 passage, he says, "I will ascend to heaven; I will raise my throne above the stars of God; I will sit enthroned on the mount of assembly, on the utmost heights of the sacred mountain. I will ascend above the tops of the clouds; I will make myself like the Most High." He rebelled in pride and, eventually, came to covet what did not belong to him. He is called the "ruler of the air" (Eph. 2:2), indicating the earth is his abode for now. The time will come when he will be cast permanently into hell (Rom. 20:10).

In the third century Origen (ca. 185–254), a theologian from Alexandria, wrote:

In regard to the devil and his angels and opposing powers, the ecclesiastical teaching maintains that these beings do indeed exist; but what they are or how they exist is not explained with sufficient clarity. This opinion, however, is held by most: that the devil was an angel; and having apostasized, he persuaded as many angels as possible to fall away with himself; and these, even to the present time, are called his angels.[9]

The few glimpses we receive from Scripture confirm Origen's opinion.

As is usually true for all sin today, Satan's rebellion affected others—in this instance other angels. The New Testament indicates demons are angels who sinned and were cast into hell or down to earth. "They do not differ in nature from good angels," C. S. Lewis writes, "but their nature is depraved."[10]

Three passages in the New Testament describe demons' origin and current condition:

God did not spare angels when they sinned, but sent them to hell, putting them into gloomy dungeons to be held for judgment. (2 Pet. 2:4)

And the angels who did not keep their positions of authority but abandoned their own home—these he has kept in darkness, bound with everlasting chains for judgment on the great Day. (Jude 6)

And there was war in heaven. Michael and his angels fought against the dragon, and the dragon and his angels fought back. But he was not strong enough, and they lost their place in heaven. The great dragon was hurled down—that ancient serpent called the devil or Satan, who leads the whole world astray. He was hurled to the earth, and his angels with him.

Then I heard a loud voice in heaven say:
"Now have come the salvation and
   the power and the kingdom of our God,
and the authority of his Christ.
For the accuser of our brothers,
   who accuses them before our God
      day and night,
   has been hurled down.
They overcame him
   by the blood of the Lamb
   and by the word of their testimony;
they did not love their lives so much
   as to shrink from death.
Therefore rejoice, you heavens
   and you who dwell in them!
But woe to the earth and the sea,
   because the devil has gone down to you!
He is filled with fury,
because he knows that his time is short." (Rev.
   12:7–12)

We learn from these passages that there are two groups of demons. The first group is those who have been confined to "gloomy dungeons" and "bound in everlasting chains" (see also Col. 2.15, 1 Pet. 3:18–22). I suspect that these are too harmful to be allowed to move about freely on earth. The second group is those who are free to roam about the earth and in some way serve under Satan (see also Matt. 12:24–26; Rev. 9:1–11; 20:1). They are numerous and well organized, another indication that Satan can be quite effective in warring on humanity (Eph. 6:11–12).

Other passages in the New Testament reveal the following characteristics about demons:

- They have intelligence (Acts 16:16–18; 19:15–16);
- They are spirits (Matt. 8:16; 12:43–45; Luke 10:17–20; 24:39; Rev. 16:14);
- They manifest themselves in different forms (2 Kings 6:17; Rev. 9:1–12; 16:13–14);
- They are malevolent (Matt. 12:43–45; Mark 1:27; 3:11; Luke 4:36; Acts 8:7; Rev. 16:13);
- They know their own end (Matt. 8:29; 25:41; James 2:19);
- They have supernatural strength (Matt. 12:29; Mark 5:4; Luke 8:29; Acts 19:13–16); and
- They must bow to Jesus' name (Matt. 8:28–34; Mark 5:7; Luke 8:26–33).

## HOW DO EVIL SPIRITS AFFECT US?

Christians have been born into a conflict with Satan and demons because we are identified with Christ, who is Satan's prime target (1 Pet. 4:12–13). This is serious warfare; the kingdom of Satan is powerful, well organized, and it can affect men and women in many ways (Eph. 6:12; 1 Pet. 5:8). Many people experience chronic problems—spiritual, psychological, physical—from which they never find true healing through medicine, psychology, psychiatry, or prayer. I believe that often demons are the cause of these problems.

Satan attacks us in three ways:

1. *Temptation.* Scripture sometimes talks about the struggle between the spirit and the flesh (Gal. 5:17, where the NIV translates *sarx*, the Greek word for "flesh," as "the sinful nature") and in other instances speaks of Satan tempting men and women (1 Thess. 3:5). The two influences often work together: the flesh opens us to satanic influence, and Satan is the author of temptation.

I believe that most temptations are the result of our own choices and the influence of the world (Jer. 17:9; Mark 7:20–23; James 1:14–15). But Scripture also describes a second category of temptation that involves more direct demonic influence. For example, in the wilderness Satan directly tempted Christ (Matt. 4:1–11); he tempted Ananias to lie about his personal finances (Acts 5:3); and he incited David to sin by taking a census in Israel (1 Chron. 21:1).

The world, the flesh, and the devil work in concert to tempt us. They have a diabolical interrelationship that seeks to trap men and women in sin and death. When we yield to the temptations of the flesh and the world, we become more vulnerable to further demonic temptation.

Satan is the mastermind, the manipulator, of the flesh and the world. For example, Satan capitalized on David's sin of pride through the influence of the world, which weakened his ability to resist the temptation to take a census (1 Chron. 21:2–8). Judas's love of money made him susceptible to Satan's temptation to betray Jesus (John 12:4–6; 13:2, 27). So the more we sin, the more susceptible we are to demonic temptation (John 8:34, 2 Pet. 2:19).

The biblical word for temptation also implies testing, for God allows temptation to test and strengthen Christians' faith. In this regard a person who is tempted and does no wrong does not incur guilt. Satan's temptations are only effective if we yield to them (James 1:14–15).

2. *Opposition.* Michael Scanlan and Randall Cirner write:

Satan and his evil spirits also attack mankind in general and Christians in particular by trying to prevent the preaching of the gospel and the spreading of the kingdom of God. In the lives of individuals, they will attempt to block a person's coming to the Lord or growing in a deeper relationship with the Lord.[11]

These are not temptations to wrongdoing. I am talking about accidents, counterfeit supernatural gifts, and other diversions.

Opposition usually comes in the form of attacks like making someone sick, causing an accident, making a scene, and so on.

Examples of demonic opposition include "the prince of the Persian kingdoms" (apparently a demon exercising influence over the Persian realm in the interests of Satan) resistance to the heavenly messenger who had come to Daniel's aid (Dan. 10:1–15), the magician Elymas opposing Paul and Barnabas on the island of Paphos (Acts 13:6–10), and the slave girl who had a spirit of divination and created a sideshow when Paul tried to preach (Acts 16:16–18).

3. *Demonization.* Satan and demons may also attack men and women by getting a grip on people's personalities or physical lives. Scripture describes three areas of our lives that may be affected by demonization: the physical, mental, and spiritual. Physical afflictions were numerous, including dumbness and blindness (Matt. 9:32; 12:22), epilepsy (Mark 9:14–29), high fever (Luke 4:38–39), and crippling (Luke 13:10–17).

Some forms of demonic bondage were the cause of habitual patterns of temptation or moral weakness not changed by repentance, for example, having difficulty pronouncing the words of a name, praying, or acknowledging God. In many cases these were accompanied by emotional problems like fear, anxiety, and lust. In the Old Testament Saul's insanity is perhaps the best illustration of this (1 Sam. 16:14–23). Many were deceived into believing and telling lies. For example, the serpent deceived Eve in the Garden (Gen. 3:1–5), he filled Ananias's heart to lie (Acts 5:3), and James describes an instance in which bitter envy and selfish ambition are inspired by demons (James 3:15). Paul warns Timothy "that in later times some will abandon the faith and follow deceiving spirits and things taught by demons" (1 Tim. 4:1).

Sometimes these habitual patterns of temptation or moral weakness were accompanied by violent action (Luke 8:26–29). Two points are worth making in this regard.

First, Scripture makes a distinction between natural and demonic causes of physical and mental illness. In some instances the sick were described as being "demonized," and in others they were simply called "sick." In seventeen instances in the Gospels and Acts this distinction is made (Matt. 4:24; 8:16; 10:1; 10:8; Mark 1:32–34; 3:10–11; 6:13; 16:17–18; Luke 4:40–41; 6:18–19; 7:21; 8:2; 9:1; 13:32; Acts 5:16; 8:6–7; 19:11–12).

Second, in these examples Christ and the disciples prayed differently for the sick, depending on the cause of their illness. Those whose physical or mental illness was caused by demons had demons cast out. Those whose sickness had a physical cause were not delivered of evil spirits (see Matt. 8:1–4, 5–13; 9:1–8, 18–26; 20:29–34; Luke 17:11–19; John 5:1–15; 9:1–12; Acts 3:1–10; 14:8–10).

The Bible frequently describes people who "have demons." The Greek terms used to describe people having demons are imprecise. In fact, many English translations are misleading when they describe people who "have a demon" as "demon possessed." The original Greek terms may not be translated this precisely. This translation is unfortunate, because the word "possession" conjures up images of demons owning and being in absolute control of people at all times. But I do not believe that demons may own people absolutely while they still live on earth; even when demons gain a high degree of control, people are able to exercise a degree of free will that may lead to deliverance and salvation. The Greek word used for having a demon (*daimonizomenoi*) is more literally translated "demon-ized" (see Matt. 4:24; Mark 1:32; Luke 8:36; John 10:21), which means to be influenced, afflicted, or tormented in some way by demonic power.

The demonized suffer under varying degrees of bondage. A demonized person may be tormented by troubling thoughts or may be fairly well controlled by a demon (what is commonly inferred from the English term "possession"); yet the New Testament would only say that both are "demonized." So referring to all demonized people as being possessed is not biblical; it is inaccurate and tends only to confuse and emotionally upset people. I prefer not to use the term "possession." Instead, I will speak of severely demonized people.

The term "demonized" refers to people who are in varying

degrees or levels of demonic bondage. In all instances of bondage people are subject to periodic attacks by one or more demons that may affect them physically, mentally, and spiritually. In literature on demonization, terms used to describe more mild forms of demonization include influence, oppression, obsession, and subjection. More severe forms of demonization are described as demonic attack, assault, and possession.

In mild demonization, the influence of evil spirits varies from harassment to more extreme forms of bondage. Demonic oppression results in blindness and hardness of heart toward the gospel (2 Cor. 4:4), apostasy and doctrinal corruption (1 Tim. 4:1; 1 John 4:1–3), and indulging in sinful, defiling behavior (2 Pet. 2:1–12).

Demonic influence can create many of the same spiritual, emotional, and physical problems as severe demonization, but they are not the same. The difference is a matter of degree: the severely demonized person goes through long and frequent periods of demonic manifestation. Merrill Unger writes:

In demon possession, one or more evil spirits dwell in a person's body as their house and take complete possession of it *at times*. In this condition the personality and consciousness of the victim are completely "blacked out," and the personality of the demon takes full control. He thinks, speaks, and acts through the body of the possessed. . . . [12]

Instances of severe demonization are rare, whereas demonic influence is more common.

## SEVERE DEMONIZATION

Jesus' healing of the demented man in the region of the Gerasenes (the name of the region varies in the Gospels and the textual traditions) provides a classic illustration of severe demonization (Matt. 8:28–34; Mark 5:1–20; Luke 8:26–39—I refer to the Lucan account below). This is the story in which demons, when they were cast out of the man, went into a herd of pigs. The result was the complete healing of the man. A close examination of this account reveals characteristics that distinguish severe demonization from mild demonization and from mental illness:[13]

1. The severely demonized person still has *some* control over his or her own life. The demonized man from the region of the Gerasenes met Jesus when he came across from Galilee; his coming forward to meet Jesus was perhaps an indication that he wanted healing.

2. Inhabiting demons exercise influence episodically, often precipitating epileptic-like seizures with convulsions and other symptoms like rigidity, screaming, and foaming at the mouth. For example, when the demonized Gerasene saw Jesus, "he cried out and fell at his feet, shouting at the top of his voice" (v. 28). Sometimes the attacks are self-destructive, and they may last for only a few minutes or go on for several days.

3. Evil spirits may actually reside in a severely demonized person. Scripture says that "many demons had gone into him" (v. 30). They take over almost complete control of the person at will, even blotting out the person's consciousness. Sometimes the person may be unable to speak or hear (Mark 9:25; Luke 11:14). He or she becomes a slave to the demons, their tool.

4. Frequently a severely demonized person has unusual physical strength. "Many times it [the evil spirit] has seized him, and though he was chained hand and foot and kept under guard, he had broken his chains and had been driven by the demon into solitary places" (v. 29; see also Acts 19:16).

5. The severely demonized person frequently projects a new personality. The demon speaks directly to others through the person it inhabits. The demon refers to itself in the first person, bystanders in the second person, and the person it is inhabiting in the third person. The

man approached Jesus when he first came ashore, then the demon in him threw him down and begged Jesus not to torture it (v. 27–28).

6. A severely demonized person has a strong resistance and opposition to Jesus. "What do you want with me, Jesus, Son of the Most High God? I beg you, don't torture me!" is what the demon said when Jesus came near (v. 28).

7. A severely demonized person often has the ability to convey knowledge that the inhabited person did not have access to in his or her normal state. The man knew immediately who Jesus was, even though the man had never met him before. He also recognized Jesus' authority to cast the demon out (v. 29, 31; see also Acts 16:16–18).

8. Severely demonized people often speak with voices and languages other than their own. The man was described as "shouting at the top of his voice," an unnatural way to speak (v. 28). Many times I have witnessed people who spoke with strange voices—for example, women who spoke like men. Later, after a demon is cast out of them, they do not speak with that voice again.

9. Severely demonized persons are marked by moral depravity, depending on the personality of the demon who inhabits them. Frequently they go about naked. This man had "for a long time . . . not worn clothes or lived in a house, but had lived in the tombs" (v. 27). Every severely demonized person for whom I have prayed has struggled with some form of serious sexual sin. Many struggle with alcohol and drug abuse.

10. Immediate deliverance from the evil spirit is possible for the demonized. For those whose mental illness is caused purely by demons, the cure is immediate. Those whose mental illness is other in origin must go through a long and costly process of psychological healing. The severely demonized man was immediately and completely healed:

"When they came to Jesus, they found the man from whom the demons had gone out, sitting at Jesus' feet, dressed and in his right mind; and they were afraid. Those who had seen it told the people how the demon-possessed man had been cured" (v. 35–36).

11. Last, when demons leave a person they seek out other bodies to inhabit. "The demons begged Jesus to let them go into them [a herd of pigs], and he gave them permission. When the demons came out of the man, they went into the pigs, and the herd rushed down the steep bank into the lake and was drowned" (v. 32–33).

In 1975 William P. Wilson, a medical doctor at Duke Medical Center in Durham, North Carolina, described an incidence of what he believed to be severe demonization in one of his patients. The following was reported in a paper presented before a symposium sponsored by the Christian Medical Association in January of 1975 at the University of Notre Dame:

This thirty-two-year-old, twice-married female was brought in because of falling spells which had been treated with all kinds of anticonvulsant medication. She was examined on the neurosurgical service and after all examinations including EEG, brain scan, and a pseumoencephalogram were negative, she was transferred to the psychiatric service. Her mental status examination was unremarkable and all of the staff commented that she seemed normal until she had her first "spell."

While standing at the door of the day room she was violently thrown to the floor, bruising her arm severely. She was picked up and carried to her room all the while resisting violently. When the author [Dr. Wilson] arrived, eight persons were restraining her as she thrashed about on the bed. *Her facial expression was one of anger and hate.* Sedation resulted in sleep. During the ensuing weeks, the patient was treated psychotherapeutically and it was learned that there was considerable turmoil in her childhood home, but because she was "pretty" she was spoiled. She married the type of individual described by Jackson Smith as the first husband of a hysterical female. She was a "high liver" and after her separation and divorce, she was threatened with rejection by her parents. She remarried and her second husband was a "nice" but unexciting man. She continued to associate with her "high living" friends. When her husband demanded that she give up her friends and her parties, she started having the "spells."

The usual psychotherapeutic treatment for hysteria including interviews under sodium amytol only aggravated her spells. Seclusion in the closed section brought her assaultive and combative behavior to an end but she would have spells in which she became mute, especially when religious matters were discussed. More dramatically, when the names Jesus or Christ were mentioned she would immediately go into a trance. On one occasion while in a coma, in desperation, a demon was exorcised and her spells ceased. She subsequently accepted Christ as her Savior and has been well since.[14]

I am frequently asked if a Christian can be demon possessed. If the question means, "Can a demon own and have the absolute control of a Christian?" the answer is no. But, as I have already noted, the concept of possession is not biblical.

A more biblical and significant question is: "Can a believer be demonized?" I believe that believers and nonbelievers alike can be demonized.

Two years ago I met a twenty-nine-year-old former pastor with serious emotional and spiritual problems that, it turned out, were the result of serious demonic influences. Bill (not his real name) was an only child who had been raised by Christian parents in the Midwest. His childhood was by all appearances normal, middle-class, and uneventful. He was raised in an evangelical church, and at age ten he was converted to faith in Christ at a Christian camp. As a teenager Bill felt God calling him to become a pastor, and soon afterward he attended Bible college. He was graduated near the top of his class, and then served in several interim pastoral assignments.

But at age twenty-seven Bill left the ministry. When I met him he was under psychological care. In fact, it was his psychologist who arranged for me to meet with Bill and her. She had attended a course I taught at a nearby seminary and thought I might be able to help Bill. Bill told me that he had a lifelong problem with the desire to look at pornographic pictures and make obscene phone calls. During two of his pastorates his sinful behavior was discovered by members of the congregations and he was forced to resign. In each instance his problem was not dealt with. He currently was employed by a major parachurch organization. His psychologist was trying to change his antisocial behavior by dealing with his problem of self-hatred, though she was making no headway. She was trying to deal with the outcome of all these problems—guilt—rather than their root—demons.

At our first meeting a demon manifested itself through Bill, which was the first time something like this had happened to him. Bill's voice and personality changed, his face became contorted, and the spirit challenged my authority to be there. Until this time Bill had ruled out the possibility that he might be under the influence of demons, because he had been taught and believed that demons could not influence Christians today. I said, "Identify yourselves." They said they made Bill use pornography and practice masturbation; they caused his rage and self-hatred. I said, "In the name of Jesus, leave Bill right now" (see Luke 10:17). At first the demons resisted my commands, so I prayed further and again told them to leave. After about thirty minutes of prayer, they were gone. Bill told me that for the first time in years he felt free from compulsions to sin sexually.

A week later we again met with Bill, because though he no longer struggled with the desire to view pornography and make obscene phone calls, he still felt a great deal of anxiety. During this second session we cast out spirits that created fear, self-abuse, and a false religiosity.

Recently I met with Bill, and after almost two years he is still no longer involved with pornography or obscene phone calls. He is still meeting with his psychologist, but his problems are no longer demonic.

Stories like Bill's raise another question regarding Christians and demons: "What protection does a Christian have from demonization?" The answer is that we are promised absolute protection from demonization (though not attack) if we walk in faith and live righteously. Colossians 1:13–14 says, "For he [the Father] has rescued us from the dominion of darkness and brought us into the kingdom of the Son he loves, in whom we have redemption, the forgiveness of sins." In 1 John 4:4 it says, "You, dear children, are from God and have overcome them [evil spirits], because the one who is in you is greater than the one who is in the world." Further, we now have new natures through the indwelling of the Holy Spirit (John 14:16; 2 Cor. 5:17). We are vessels of God's glory, not Satan's tools (1 Cor. 6:19).

But Christians can be affected and even controlled by evil spirits if they live in unconfessed and serious sin. Our situation with demons is analogous to our situation with the flesh and the world. We are forgiven and born again in Christ, but if we choose to believe the lies of the world and yield to our flesh, we will live in sin. Demonization works the same way: we have been delivered from the power of demons yet we can still be affected by them. Satan has yet to be "thrown into the lake of burning sulfur" and "tormented day and night for ever and ever" (Rev. 20:10).

Scripture has several illustrations of believers who were demonized. In the Old Testament, Saul was a believer who had been anointed by the Holy Spirit and prophesied (1 Sam. 10:1, 9–13). After sinning (his sin was likened to witchcraft by Samuel in 1 Sam. 15:23), Saul was tormented by an evil spirit (1 Sam. 16:14). His symptoms—fits of anger, murder, fear, witchcraft, and suicide—are all symptoms of a demonized person.

The New Testament also has examples of demonized believers. In Luke 13 Jesus healed a crippled woman whom he described as "a daughter of Abraham, whom Satan has kept bound for eighteen long years" (v. 16). In another place Jesus indicated that a "son of Abraham" was one who had received salvation (Luke 19:9), and Paul in Galatians 3:7 writes, "Those who believe are children of Abraham." Judas was one of the Twelve, yet he ended his life as a severely demonized man (Luke 22:3). Jesus indicated that Satan was going to sift Peter as wheat (Luke 22:31–32). The purpose of sifting was to determine the good wheat from the bad wheat; Satan wanted to sift Peter to discover his weakest point, the demonic pathway into his life. For Peter, the access point may have been his pride (Luke 22:33), and his denial of Jesus may have been the result of demonization (22:54–62). Later Peter warned believers that "Your enemy the devil prowls around like a roaring lion looking for someone to devour" (1 Pet. 5:8).

The New Testament teaches that when Christians live in sin, they risk being turned over to Satan. Satan was the cause of Ananias's and Sapphira's deaths in that he tempted them and they fell and suffered the consequences of God's wrath (Acts 5:1–11). Peter said, "Ananias, how is it that Satan has so filled your heart that you have lied to the Holy Spirit. . . ?" (Acts 5:3). At the time they were numbered among the believers mentioned in Acts 4:32–45.

Christians can also be demonized if inherited demons (demons that are passed from parents to children) or demons that they pick up through other means are not cast out of their lives. This was the outlook of the early church, which performed the rite of Christian exorcism on all new converts and believers, infant and adult. Hippolytus (ca. 170–236), who was perhaps the most important third-century theologian of the Roman church, wrote a treatise entitled the *Apostolic Tradition*. In it he encouraged candidates for church membership to be exorcized (prayed over for deliverance from evil spirits) by their godparents at the end of each weekly instruction by their teacher and immediately before baptism by their bishop. (The Roman Catholic rite of baptism still includes exorcism.) The early church also used exorcism on things (water and food), places (especially church sites), and persons other than candidates for church membership (including believers).[13]

## ENTRY POINTS

Demons gain a foothold in people's lives through a variety of ways. The first, as mentioned above, is through sin. Unrighteous anger, self-hatred and hatred of others, revenge, unforgiveness, lust, pornography, sexual wrongdoing, various sexual perversions (like transvestism, homosexuality, beastiality, sodomy), and drug and alcohol abuse commonly open the door to demonic influence.

Scripture makes special mention of the danger of involvement in the occult (Exod. 20:3–5; Lev. 19:31; 20:6–8). So when I pray for people who I suspect are afflicted by evil spirits I always ask if they or a close relative have been involved in the occult or false religions, particularly Eastern religions. If a person has been involved with the occult, it almost inevitably means he or she has a demonic problem.

I received the following letter in 1985 from a pastor in Oregon. The first part of his letter recounted how he and his wife had recently prayed for the ill baby of a new couple in their church. He then continued to tell their story:

The next event that occurred was when we were away visiting [another couple] in Vancouver, British Columbia. [At our church's small group meeting] the mother of the baby that my wife and I had prayed for showed up distraught. She began behaving in a strange manner, saying that she was being told by voices to murder her husband. The small group leader and assistant began to pray for her. At that point classic manifestations of demon activity began (altered voices, eyes and facial expressions that weren't normal, stiffening up of the body, shrieking, etc.). They began praying against the sources of these manifestations. After a while she calmed down and the person that we knew seemed to be in control again. They took her home at her request to pray for her and the house that she lived in. Once there they found that she was engaged and had engaged heavily in the occult. As they began to pray the [demonic] manifestations began again. Apparently her house was full of objects that had been used for occult purposes. To make a long story short, they were there until

3 A.M. Their prayer was assisted by another minister that was called in by a friend of the woman being prayed for. He had many years experience in these matters and was able to expel several demons from her. My wife and I visited this individual the next day to follow up. (I was really upset when I had heard about all this, as this area was to my mind the least developed area for us theologically and experientially. Apparently God was not interested in my concerns.) As we interviewed her and then prayed over her I became convinced that this was indeed a genuine deliverance. We prayed for the infilling of the Holy Spirit. . . . She completely renounced any involvement in the occult and had all objects removed and destroyed. At this point I better understand why her baby had been afflicted so suddenly a few days before. There are so many things we don't understand concerning this ministry. For instance, the next day when we talked to her, she didn't remember anything that happened the night before. . . .

Demons may also gain access to men and women through sins done against them. "I, the Lord your God," the Ten Commandments say, "am a jealous God, punishing the children for the sin of the fathers to the third and fourth generation of those who hate me" (Exod. 20:5). While this does not mean that demons are always passed from one generation to another, in some cases they may be. For example, people who have been sinned against sexually usually have serious demonic problems. Seventy percent of all children of alcoholics become alcoholics themselves; I believe in many instances demonic influence contributes to their problem.

Many times I have discerned the cause of people's physical and emotional illnesses are spirits that have come to them from their parents. Curses spoken by relatives, teachers, and friends may also be avenues for demonic influence, as can all sorts of witchcraft practiced by others against unsuspecting people. Trauma such as rape, abandonment by parents, and serious accidents also create fear and terror that are avenues for demons.

Again, my point is that until Christ's return we live in enemy territory, a sinful world that is in bondage to Satan's terror. So we should not be surprised about the extent of his evil deeds and influence.


## OUR WEAPONS

So far I have painted a grim picture of Christians' circumstances. Our powerful and crafty enemy is everywhere, always seeking to destroy us through his many means. That is bad news. But the good news is that Christ has equipped us adequately for the battle.

Our weapons are described in Ephesians 6:10–18:

Finally, be strong in the Lord and in his mighty power. Put on the full armor of God so that you can take your stand against the devil's schemes. For our struggle is not against flesh and blood, but against the rulers, against the authorities, against the powers of this dark world and against the spiritual powers of evil in heavenly realms. Therefore put on the full armor of God, so that when the day of evil comes, you may be able to stand your ground, and after you have done everything, to stand. Stand firm then, with the belt of truth buckled around your waist, with the breastplate of righteousness in place, and with your feet fitted with the readiness that comes from the gospel. In addition to all this, take up the shield of faith, with which you can extinguish all the flaming arrows of the evil one. Take the helmet of salvation and the sword of the Spirit, which is the word of God. And pray in the Spirit on all occasions with all kinds of prayers and requests. With this in mind, be alert and always keep on praying for all the saints.

The Greek word translated "finally" at the beginning of this passage could just as easily be translated "henceforth" or "for the remaining time." Paul may be warning the Ephesians that until Christ's return there are no cessations of hostilities with Satan, not even a cease-fire or temporary truce. The entire universe is a battleground involving tactically shrewd and ingeniously deceptive rulers, authorities, powers, and spiritual forces of evil—all names for different classes of evil spirits.

Paul was a prisoner when he wrote the Letter to the Ephesians (3:1; 4:1). In this chapter he calls himself "an ambassador in chains." The custom of that day was to chain prisoners by the wrist to a Roman soldier (6:20). I can imagine Paul praying about how he could help equip the Ephesians for spiritual warfare, then looking up and see the soldier's armor as a perfect analogy. First he tells them to "be strong in the Lord," that is, to rely on God's strength and not their own. Then he tells them to "put on the full armor of God, so that when the day of evil comes, you may be able to stand your ground" (6:13); that is, he tells them they must cooperate with God in fighting the forces of evil. Divine enablement and human cooperative are the keys to overcoming the forces of evil. Paul uses six pieces of equipment as analogies for spiritual weapons (plus one other that has no counterpart in Roman armor):

1. *The belt of truth.* The belt was used by the Roman soldier to tuck up his tunic, and it was the first piece of armor he put on. It ensured him that he could fight unimpeded by a flowing garment. Another use for the belt was to hold his weapons, both his large and small swords. Paul says that the Christian's belt is truth; with it we can move freely and quickly. Putting on God's truth means living out his word—being honest and sincere in our faith, and not full of religious hypocrisy. So the "belt of truth" refers to Christian character and integrity, a life-style that conforms to Scripture. Character, not brute force, is the first step in winning battles against Satan.

2. *The breastplate of righteousness.* The breastplate covered both the front and back of the soldier. It was a major piece of equipment that protected the soldier's heart. In Proverbs 4:23 it says, "Above all else, guard your heart, for it is the wellspring of life."

In 4:24 and 5:9 Paul uses righteousness to refer to upright character and conduct. Righteousness is first of all a condition of the heart, and the heart is what determines the course of our lives. Good character, not words, is the best defense against accusations.

3. *Feet fitted with readiness.* Roman soldiers wore protective and supportive footgear. Tied to their ankles and shins with ornamental straps, their boots equipped them for long marches and gave them a solid stance. Paul is making two points. First, we are to be prepared to share the gospel of peace at any time. This means knowing how to tell others about Christ and being open to the Holy Spirit's leading in specific situations. Second, Christians can stand firmly on the gospel of peace, that is, we are always to be spiritually prepared to share the gospel because we are at peace with God.

4. *The shield of faith.* The shield referred to here is the larger of the two shields that the Roman soldier carried. It normally measured four and a half feet high by two and a half feet wide and was oval-shaped. It consisted of two layers of wood glued together and covered with leather. The soldier would plant the shield and squat behind it.

The incendiary missiles ("flaming arrows") were dangerous weapons in those days. They were dipped in pitch, lit, and fired at the enemy. Frequently before battles the soldiers would dip their shields in water so they would extinguish the flaming arrows.

When we take the great commission seriously and go on the offensive in challenging Satan, he fights back with flaming arrows. He attacks us and everything associated with us: our church, spouse, children, business—everything. Our shield against these attacks is faith, a belief in God's ability to protect us and a confidence in his word.

5. *The helmet of salvation.* This piece of equipment was usually made of a tough bronze or iron alloy. It often had a hinged visor that added protection. Nothing short of an axe could penetrate it. Of course, it protected the head. The head is the seat of our thought life. Many Christians are incapacitated because they do not know how to protect their thought lives. Satan will bombard us with fear, hatred, suspicion, depression, mistrust, and a host of other mental distractions.

The Christian's helmet, our protection, is salvation, which is deliverance from evil. Our salvation provides both forgiveness of past sins and strength to conquer future sin. As we trust and thank him for our salvation, both for our forgiveness and confidence for his future blessing, our thought lives are protected.

6. *The sword of the Spirit.* This piece of armor is the only one that can be used for attack as well as defense. The type of sword Paul refers to was a small, twelve- to fourteen-inch knife like instrument whose tip was pinpoint sharp and whose blade could cut in any direction. It was used in close, personal fighting. The Roman soldier would look for chinks in his opponents's armor and then attack them with his little sword.

The word of God is the Christian's sword. It is both our weapon of defense against sin and of offense against demonic invasion. Two Greek words are usually translated "word," *logos* and *rhema.* Paul uses *rhema,* which means a word that is spoken, in this verse. Here Paul is referring to words spoken by the power of the Spirit to assist us in defending ourselves against the enemy. This is exactly what Jesus did when he encountered Satan and demons: he rebuked them and drove them away.

7. *Pray in the Spirit.* Though mentioned last and not likened to any piece of Roman armor, this is perhaps the Christian's greatest weapon. Paul calls us to constant, intense, and unselfish prayer that is controlled by the Spirit.

In summary, living as free as possible from sin (especially avoiding involvement with the occult) and living as consistently as possible in the power of the Holy Spirit are the greatest deterrents to demonic influence. We have been given total authority over demons. But this does not mean that we should be surprised when we encounter them. God has equipped us for battle, and he expects us to use all the armor to advance the kingdom of God.

## DEFEATING THE ENEMY

Most people who are demonized are not aware of it, but there are many symptoms present in demonized people that help us to identify demons. A caveat is in order here: *the presence of one or more of these symptoms indicates the possibility though not necessity that the person is demonized.* Not all symptoms that look demonic are demonic. From my experience, I have observed that most people who claim they are demonized are not. Keep that thought in mind as you read the following incomplete list of symptoms:

1. Contorted physical reactions, especially when the power of the Holy Spirit is present, as in a worship service or prayer meeting;
2. Addiction to drugs or alcohol;
3. A problem with compulsions such as eating disorders, lust, fornication, pornography, masturbation, homosexuality, stealing, murder, lying, or suicide;
4. Bondage to emotions such as fear, depression, anxiety, and rage;
5. Bondage to sinful attitudes like self-hatred, unforgiveness, bitterness, resentment, and contempt;
6. Chronic physical sickness, especially sicknesses that have been in the family for several generations;
7. A history of occult involvement;
8. A disturbed family history involving, for example, incest, alcoholism, and various forms of child abuse.

Perhaps as you read this chapter you began to suspect that you have a demonic problem. If so, there is something you can do about it right now. Release from the bondage of demons is called deliverance. Michael Scanlan and Randall Cirner describe four types of deliverance. The first is personal or self-deliverance, "where bondage is broken by the individual apart from a special ministry session."[16] If you suspect a personal problem with demons, I encourage you to follow these steps right now:

1. In faith turn to Christ, committing every area of your life to his lordship.

2. Confess and renounce the area of sin and temptation with which you are having difficulty.
3. Take on the authority and power that is rightfully yours in Christ and command any spirits that you sense present to leave. This may be done with a simple prayer like: "In the name of Jesus, I command you, spirit of [fear, homosexuality, etc.] to leave and stay out of my life."
4. Destroy all objects associated with the area of sin you are struggling with, especially occult objects and books.

Some people are too severely demonized for self-deliverance to be effective. They need other types of deliverance. Fraternal deliverance is when Christian brothers and sisters help cast out demons. Pastoral deliverance, ministry from pastors, is helpful in more extreme cases of demonization. In these instances there is usually need for ongoing pastoral care after the person has been delivered. The last type of deliverance comes from people who God has given "special gifts of discernment, revelation, and authority to overcome Satan and evil spirits at their most profound levels of activity."[17] I have more to say about these last three types of deliverance in Part III, where I describe how to help others in need of deliverance.

# 7. Healing the Body

Of the different types of human healing, divine healing of physical conditions is the most difficult for most people in Western civilization to believe in; it appears far easier to pray effectively for spiritual or psychological hurts than for physical hurts caused by sickness or accidents. Surely the influences of modern materialism and rationalism contribute to why most people are skeptical about physical healings.

This does not mean that physical healing is in fact more difficult than healing of the spirit. There is no greater miracle than forgiveness of sins. The problem for most people is *verification* of a healing. Anyone can say, "Your sins are forgiven" and not have to worry about any demonstration of the words' effect; how does one measure forgiveness? But demonstrability is not a problem when they say, "Be healed of your paralysis." Such a claim may be proved or disproved on the basis of the prayer's result: if the person walks, there is a likelihood he or she was healed.

Of course, the skeptic could also say that even the ability of the paralytic to walk after healing prayer only proved an *apparent* paralysis was "healed," or that a real paralysis was healed for reasons other than supernatural intervention. George Bernard Shaw once made this point. While touring the Shrine of Lourdes in France, Shaw was shown a pile of discarded crutches left behind by those who no longer needed them to walk. He commented that a few wooden legs would have been more convincing.

This was precisely Jesus' situation in Mark 2, when he pronounced a paralytic's sins forgiven and was immediately challenged by teachers of the law who asked, "Who can forgive sins but God alone?" Jesus responded by taking up their challenge:

Which is easier: to say to the paralytic, "Your sins are forgiven," or to say, "Get up, take your mat and walk"? But that you may know that the Son of Man has authority on earth to forgive sins. . . . He said to the paralytic, "I tell you, get up, take your mat and go home." (v. 9–11)

According to the Jews' faith, only God could forgive sin. For a man to forgive sin was blasphemy that deserved punishment by death, preferably by stoning (see Lev. 24:16). Their problem was they did not recognize Jesus was God and, as God, he had every right to forgive sins.

But Jesus challenged the teachers' reasoning and blindness when he healed the paralytic. This meant that they were forced to admit that the greater miracle of forgiveness of sins had also occurred and that Jesus' claim to deity was true. Still, spiritual blindness is powerful, filling people with unbelief and hatred; the teachers refused to accept the revelation of Jesus' deity or, secondarily, his miracles of forgiveness and healing.

The Pharisees and teachers of the law held a well-developed theology of forgiveness of sins based on the Old Testament sacrificial system. When Jesus pronounced the paralytic forgiven, he challenged their religious practices and prejudices. They were threatened and reacted defensively, failing to recognize that Jesus was in fact the fulfillment of their system. At the same time the teachers' theology, practice, and experience did *not* exclude divine healing. Their concern was rarely to question the possibility of miracles; they questioned the source and meaning of Christ's miracles, and how the miracles supported or undermined their theological system. So they tried to trap Jesus by getting him to perform a miracle on the Sabbath (see Luke 14:1–14); he thereby violated their interpretation of the Sabbath so they could invalidate his work.

Western Christians are incredulous about the Jewish teachers' understanding of forgiveness, but I suspect the teachers would be no less incredulous about many Western Christians' attitude toward divine healing. The irony is that the Jewish teachers' attitude toward divine healing demonstrated far greater faith in God's ability to work supernaturally than many Western Christians have today. Western Christians often deny even the *possibility* of miracles; they have no theology, model, practice, or experience with divine healing, so—as the Pharisees did with Christ's forgiveness—they reject it.

My point is that most Western people, even Christians, do not think rationally about physical healing. Instead they react with suspicion to any new model or practice that suggests change in their current understanding. With divine healing most Western Christians have few models in the church and very little positive experience.

## CATEGORIES OF HEALING

The Bible contains both good news and bad news about our physical conditions. The bad news is that one of the results of the Fall was that death entered the human race. Physical suffering from disease, accidents, genetic disorders, and, ultimately, physical death affects all men and women. So deeply felt yet contrary to God's original intentions for us are the effects of the Fall that Paul writes, "We know that the whole creation has been groaning as in the pains of childbirth right up to the present time . . . [and] we ourselves, who have the firstfruits of the Spirit, groan inwardly as we wait eagerly for our adoption as sons, the redemption of our bodies" (Rom. 8:22–23).

The good news is that through Christ's bodily resurrection we are assured of immortality. "Listen," Paul told the Corinthian Christians, "I tell you a mystery: We will not all sleep, but we will all be changed—in a flash, in the twinkling of an eye, at the last trumpet. For the trumpet will sound, the dead will be raised imperishable, and we will be changed" (1 Cor. 15:51–52).

There is also good news while we still live on the earth. The Bible contains examples of the healing of many different kinds of diseases, though the words used to describe these diseases are not the same as those commonly used in modern medicine. The Old Testament contains illustrations of divine healing of the body, as I have commented on in Chapter 2 (see also Appendix C). In the New Testament, the Gospels contain twenty-six accounts of the physical healing of individuals. The book of Acts contains five. But physical healing is mentioned only incidentally in the Letters (in two of the four listings of the gifts, 1 Cor. 12:8–11, 28–30). James 5:13–16 is the only passage in which we find specific instructions on how to pray for the sick.

There are several reasons for the decline in emphasis on divine healing in the Letters. First, and most pointedly, information about healing does not have to be repeated for us to understand it. There is nothing in the Letters that leads us to modify the Gospel's teaching about healing. Why is it required that the Letters say anything on the topic of healing? Are not the Gospels and Acts adequate? If healing is taught in one place, it does not have to be taught in another place. The Letters do not alter what is already a part of revelation in the Gospels. Praying for the sick was taken for granted by the time the Letters were written. In James 5 and 1 Corinthians 12 there is no hint that divine healing was controversial or divisive in the early church.

At the Anaheim Vineyard Christian Fellowship on Sunday mornings I have preached on divine healing only three times in the past three years. Why? Because prayer for divine healing is a normal part of our church life, something available every day of the week from many members of the church. (Of course, new members need to learn about divine healing, and for them we offer a course at our weekly training center.)

Further, there are many examples of one section of Scripture assuming in-depth knowledge on the part of readers about a topic taken from another section. For example, Hebrews 6:1–2 refers to the "elementary teachings about Christ" and the "instruction about baptisms"; the writer assumes knowledge about baptism that is found in the Gospels. Healing is not the only important topic that tapers off in the Letters. There is very little teaching about evangelism and church initiations. The Letters, unlike the Gospels, have much to say about church life, Christian morality, the work of the cross, and speech patterns. Why? Because a primary focus of the Gospels is begetting new Christians, while a primary focus of the Letters is raising believers to Christian maturity. In my earlier book, *Power Evangelism,* I argued that the spiritual gifts, especially healing, were important for effective evangelism. No wonder divine healing is described mostly in the Gospels.[1]

Looking into the Gospels and Acts we discover three categories of healings in the New Testament; two of these are physical and a third (mental illness) often has physical causes or related symptoms:[2]

1. *Organic disorders* are those in which damage to body tissue or structures can be observed or detected by a physician. Organic disorders include congenital defects (defects from birth such as Down's syndrome or congenital heart disease), infections, traumatic injuries (such as fractures), toxic disorders (those caused by contact with agents such as drugs, chemicals, pollutants, and so on), endocrine disorders (for example, thyroid and adrenal gland problems), neoplastic disorders (benign and malignant tumors), degenerative disorders (the breakdown of systems from age—for example, osteoarthritis), and cardiovascular disease (for example, strokes and heart disease). Organic disorders may result from life-style problems, for example, smoking, which in many instances leads to chronic obstructive lung disease, cardiac disease, and cancer.

Examples from Scripture of organic disorders include fevers (Matt. 8:14; Mark 1:30; Luke 4:38; John 4:52); an incised wound (Luke 22:50); nervous system diseases such as paralysis (Matt. 9:2; Mark 2:3; Acts 8:7, 9:32–35) and blindness (Matt. 9:27, 20:30; Mark 8:22; John 9:1; Acts 9:8–9, 17–19); deafness and defective speech (Mark 7:32); and a fatal head injury (Acts 20:9). Most of Jesus' healings rectified conditions in this category.

The following is a typical report of the healing of an organic disorder:

July 6, 1986

Dear Pastor Wimber:

Let me share one story of God's amazing grace and love with you, as a result of your last visit here in March, 1984. On Friday night when you were teaching, there was a young mother with her four-and-a-half-year-old baby right down in the front row. This youngster was born terribly brain damaged and is a microcephalic, which means she does not have all of her brain. She was totally dysfunctioned, could not feed herself, had never even sucked her thumb, was unable to speak, and her body would go through a constant array of terribly contorted disfiguring, purposeless movements except for a few hours of rest each night. Her arms and legs were rigidly spastic, her eyes were usually back in her head and she could not hold her head up even for a moment. That night God clearly spoke to me and four other people in that audience that he wanted to heal her.

The child's name is Tina. The following Wednesday we gathered with Tina's family to see what the Father was about. The five of us clearly could witness to the fact that God had unmistakenly spoken to us that he was going to heal Tina, and so we just laid claim to that in Jesus' name and to the glory of the Father. That began a whole series of miraculous events. First of all we began to notice immediate change in Tina. The purposeless movements ceased within three weeks. The rigidity of her arms and legs began to diminish on a very visible plane and within four or five weeks she no longer drooled and her eye movement was nearly normal and she was very attentive to those around her. She now sucks her thumb, something she never did from the time of her birth. . . . She now is starting to use her arms and legs in a synchronous way and is beginning to crawl ever so slightly but clearly and definitely. She can now propel herself across the living room, an estimated distance of approximately fourteen to fifteen feet. She is making repeated overt attempts to sit. She had a nasty habit of constantly biting everyone, and that has disappeared. She goes to a special school for handicapped, brain damaged children and the teachers' notes are an accurate chronology of this miracle.

The miracle of miracles, though, is happening in the family. Three weeks after we began [prayer], Debbie [Tina's mother] accepted Christ as her personal Savior. This is absolutely amazing considering the type of traumatized background that Debbie came from. Abused as a child, abused and degraded as a young woman, terribly traumatic marriage to an alcoholic, the birth of this devastatingly damaged baby then the awesome responsibilities of trying to raise her as a single parent, providing for herself and the child's needs, being more and more rejected by the world. Anyway, she was miraculously transformed and two weeks ago we had the privilege of baptizing her along with two other members of her family. . . .

Your brother in Christ,
James R. Friend, M.D.
Bakersfield, California

Dr. Friend describes in great detail the organic disorders of Tina, but the spiritual and emotional healing in her mother was greater. Here God used a physical healing to evangelize a family.

2. *Functional disorders* are those in which there is definitely a disturbance in the way the body is functioning but the offending organ or organs appear to be structurally normal. An automobile engine offers a good analogy for understanding the difference between organic and functional disorders. A faulty spark plug that affects engine performance is like an organic disorder; an engine that idles too fast, even though all the parts are in good condition, is like a functional disorder.

Functional disorders are often difficult for doctors to diagnose and frustrating to treat. "Doctors do have considerable difficulty with functional complaints," a Christian physician comments, "that is, the complaints for which there is no identifiable pathology. A patient will come in complaining, for example, about a lot of aches and pains, or stomach cramps, or headaches."[3]

Examples of functional disorders include some forms of headaches, backaches, stomach disorders, and high or low blood pressure. One of the more common functional disorders is irritable bowl syndrome, in which over a period of years a patient may suffer episodically from abdominal cramps.

Scripture does not record the healing of stomach disorders or headaches, although it is possible that many functional disorders were healed when Jesus ministered to big crowds (Matt. 4:24; 8:16; Mark 1:32, 39; 3:10–12; 6:13; Luke 4:41; 6:18; 7:21).

In April 1986 I received this report from D. M., a Vietnam veteran who recently had attended a healing seminar that was led by Bob and Penny Fulton in the Atascadero (California) Vineyard Christian Fellowship:

Saturday
No Headache!

[During the ministry time] I went up and hung out until Bob [Fulton] asked what my problem was.

Bob got someone from their team and some of my friends, including my wife, to pray for me. I explained about my headaches and how sometimes they last as much as six days at a wack, and how I would love to be rid of them.

They began to pray and it didn't seem to me that much was happening. They asked me what I felt and I said [that I felt] nothing, so they prayed some more. They were binding things like the spirit of fear and the spirit of oppression and asking the Holy Spirit to come and take over and to bring to mind anything or anyone that might be related to why I was having headaches.

Again they asked what I felt or saw. This time I saw a grass hut like those in Vietnam and I also saw myself dripping with blood, other peoples' blood. I knew I was responsible for that blood. I saw words floating around and shooting back and forth like lightning.

By this time I was losing control, wailing and starting to fall over (we were all standing in a circle). So they sat me down and someone went to get help. . . . They kept asking me things like what do you feel, what do you see, what are you doing right now, and most of the time things were happening so fast that I couldn't keep up. For example, I was coming into a L.Z. (landing zone) in a helicopter, or I was setting fire to a village, or I was shooting across rice paddies, I was shooting, shooting, shooting.

The words I saw going back and forth, up and down fast, slow, every way you can think of were words like murder, hate, kill. And no matter what I saw and heard I could always see my self with blood dripping off me. It seemed like it would come off of everything but my hands.

All this seemed to go on for ever and in the background I could hear the ministry team praying . . . in power. They would ask something and I would tell them something in return, and they would address that particular thing and then help me to deal with it using the Word of God and a lot of love and patience. This was done over and over again, always having me ask God for forgiveness and then forgiving myself and asking forgiveness of those I hurt even though they weren't there.

Each thing was taken to the cross and either nailed to it or was laid at the foot of it. At one point God gave me a vision of his kingdom bathed in golden light. He took my hands that were dripping with blood and seared his cross in both of them. He took the names that I gave to myself—words like murder and hate—and gave me a new name which is "Life Giver." And he blessed me again and again and again.

. . . My desire for me and my family is to be made useable for God and then to be used by God.[4]

Some people propose that almost all Christian healing today falls in this category (or the area of mental illness, which they do not associate in any way with demons). The implications are that because functional diseases cannot be diagnosed as having an organic cause, their healing may be attributed merely to psychological influences. But what if many functional disorders are in fact psychological in origin? Cannot the Holy Spirit bring psychological healing that results in physical healing? And are not the physical disorders nevertheless real? D. M.'s physical healing appears to be related to psychological and spiritual damage from his Vietnam experience, but it took the work of the Holy Spirit to uncover its cause and bring God's forgiveness, truth, and healing power to him. As a result of psychological and spiritual healing, his headaches were also healed at that time.

Even when the origin of a functional disorder is psychological in origin, the Holy Spirit may still be the agent of healing. The Holy Spirit has the ability to untangle disorder in every area of our lives, including complex psychosomatic disorders.

3. *Mental illness.* In mental illness personality and emotional disturbances result from brain disease, emotional factors, or demonization. Jesus regularly healed illnesses in this category. They include:

—Schizophrenic disorders which include problems with language communication, delusions (such as people believing that thoughts not their own have been placed in their heads), hallucinations (in particular hearing voices that come from outside), blunted emotions, and loss of contact with the world and with others;

—Paranoid disorders, which include delusions of being persecuted and extreme and unjustified jealousy;

—Affective disorders, which include disturbances of mood as characterized by major depressions or mania;

—Anxiety disorders, which include phobias (such as intense, unwarranted fears of objects or persons), generalized anxiety disorders, and obsessive-compulsive disorders;

—Somatoform disorders, which are disorders that have no known physiological cause and include multiple physical complaints for which people have taken medicine or consulted doctors, loss of motor or sensory function such as a paralysis or blindness, severe and prolonged pain, and the misinterpretation of minor physical sensations as serious illnesses (an example of a somatoform disorder [a physician provided this illustration] would be the sudden paralysis of the legs of a young woman whenever she comes under stressful conditions); and

—Dissociative disorders, which include amnesia, fugue (in which a person suddenly and unexpectedly travels to a new locale, starts a new life, and is amnesic for his or her previous identity), and multiple personality.[5]

John Wilkinson has pointed out that in Scripture in many

instances serious physical conditions are associated with demonic and emotional problems: epilepsy (Mark 1:26; Luke 4:35); acute mania (Matt. 8:28; Mark 5:2–7; Luke 8:29); mutism (Matt. 9:32–33); and mutism accompanied by blindness (Matt. 12:22).[6]

The causes of illnesses in all three of these categories—organic, functional, and mental—are quite complex. The origin of physical illness may be demonic, emotional, spiritual (from sin), psychological, or chemical.

## GOD HEALS

Scriptural examples of healing teach us many things about how physical healing works. In 2 Kings 5:1–15 we read that Naaman, commander of the army of the king of Aram (probably a reference to Ben-Hadad II, 853 B.C.), was healed of leprosy, an organic disorder. From a Jewish slave he had heard that through Elisha the prophet people were healed. Naaman received permission—and a large gift—from his king to travel to Samaria and seek healing.

When he finally found Elisha, Naaman made two mistakes in seeking healing. First, he thought he could buy his healing by offering Elisha money (v. 2, 6, 15). Elisha refused to accept anything from Naaman, even after he was healed.

When God anoints people to heal, it is common for those healed to offer gifts. I have made it a matter of policy never to accept gifts for healing. Greed and materialism are perhaps the most common cause of the undoing of many men and women with a healing ministry.

Just as tragic is the harm done by faith healers who become caught up in opulent life-styles, rationalizing their material wealth as a sign of "God's blessing." When I pray over people for God to give them a healing ministry, I always instruct them *never* to accept money for healing.

Naaman's second mistake was assuming Elisha should pray for him in a certain way: "I thought that he [Elisha] would surely come out to me and stand and call on the name of the

Lord his God, wave his hand over the spot and cure me of my leprosy" (v. 11). Elisha had told him to go wash himself seven times in the Jordan. Naaman was offended; his pride almost cost him his healing. "Are not Abana and Pharpar, the rivers of Damascus, better than any of the waters of Israel?" he said, "Couldn't I wash in them and be cleansed?" Of course the answer was no, because the source of healing was not the water of a specific river, but the God who commanded him to obey. Elisha instructed him to wash seven times in the Jordan as an act of faith.

Fortunately for Naaman, his servants reasoned with him, and he had a change of heart. He humbled himself, went into the Jordan seven times, and immediately "his flesh was restored and became clean like that of a young boy" (v. 14). Finally, his physical healing created in him a heart for God. Naaman told Elisha, "Now I know that there is no God in all the world except in Israel" (v. 15).

Stories like Naaman's are not confined to biblical times. Several years ago a young man from the Anaheim Vineyard Christian Fellowship was in a cafe, sitting near an elderly gentleman who suffered from severe palsy of his hands. The older man was shaking so much that he kept dropping his food as he tried to eat. The young man, full of compassion, walked over and grabbed the man's hands, then said, "Jesus will heal that." The shaking stopped immediately. Everyone in the cafe looked on in stunned silence. Then the young man said, "Now Jesus will heal your heart just as he healed your hands." Within a few minutes the older gentleman was praying a prayer of repentance and faith in Christ.

## WHAT ABOUT MEDICAL TREATMENT?

In 2 Kings 20:1–11 we read about the healing of Hezekiah, who was king of Judah from 729 to 687 B.C. In 701 B.C., after Jerusalem was miraculously spared from the Assyrian army, Hezekiah "became ill and was at the point of death" due to a boil. Through revelation God told the prophet Isaiah that Hezekiah was to die. Because of this Isaiah did not pray for Hezekiah's healing. Instead he told him: "Put your house in order, because you are going to die; you will not recover" (v. 1).

Hezekiah recited his good deeds and wept bitterly before God, pleading for mercy and healing (v. 3, see also Isaiah 38:10–18). Hezekiah responded in a despondent way. But he had the courage and faith to talk to God about his problems, and God heard him. God answered Hezekiah's prayer, telling Isaiah to "Go back and tell Hezekiah . . . 'I have heard your prayer and seen your tears; I will heal you. . . . I will add fifteen years to your life'" (v. 5–6). So God gave Hezekiah a promise of healing.

Isaiah then administered natural medicine (a poultice of figs) to the boil, and Hezekiah recovered. The story of Hezekiah's healing demonstrates that God sometimes uses medical treatment to produce healing. Some Christians quote 2 Chronicles 16:12–13 as proof that they should never consult physicians: "In the thirty-ninth year of his reign Asa was afflicted with a disease in his feet. Though his disease was severe, even in his illness he did not seek help from the Lord, but only from the physicians. Then in the forty-first year of his reign Asa died. . . . " But in those days "physicians" used occult practices to heal disease. Asa's sin was not seeking the Lord for healing, which is not antithetical to seeking legitimate medical care.

Paul encouraged Timothy to use a little wine for his stomach ailments, because the wine had medicinal benefits (1 Tim. 5:23). Oil and spittal were regarded as having healing qualities and were used by Jesus and his disciples in their healings (Mark 6:13; 7:33; 8:23; John 9:6). Whether or not these treatments possessed scientific healing qualities is not the issue. Jesus associated with medical treatments; in fact, he seemed to sanction them. Therefore, as Isaiah demonstrated with Hezekiah's illness, divine healing does not preclude medical treatment. God is the source of healing, and he heals through a variety of means.

I encourage most of the people whom I pray for to seek medical help, especially if they have a life-threatening disease. This letter is a good illustration of the positive interplay between modern medical treatment and divine healing:

December 17, 1984

Dear Pastor Wimber,

I spoke to you at the November 5–7, 1984, seminar in Anaheim about the healing my mother received when she visited the Vineyard in late September. Here it is in writing.

. . . At the end of the service you had a word of knowledge for a lady with the left leg broken in three places from a bad accident several years earlier. I asked the Lord if it was Mom and he said, "Yes!" We all went to the prayer room and . . . two [prayer team members] prayed for healing of Mom's leg and also for her lung cancer. While we were praying for the cancer Suzy said she could feel the tumor disappear.

Mom went in for her scheduled checkup after she got back to Portland, Oregon. There was no sign of the tumor on the X-ray, where previous X-rays taken from the same angle had shown a mass larger than a golf ball. The blood tests confirmed the cancer was gone.

Last summer after finding the lung cancer Mom underwent seven weeks of radiation to destroy as much of the tumor as possible. During the whole time she has been prayed for weekly at her church. S. [her friend] prayed for her daily before her treatments.

From the medical viewpoint the tumor was not expected to go away completely. Instead she sailed through with only minor discomfort (sensitivity of skin and a slight cough) and she put on weight.

As for her leg, the day after prayer she walked up and down the Queen Mary ship and the Spruce Goose aeroplane, which she could not have done before. Her knee cap, which was hard to find and rigid before (so hard to find that her current doctor at first thought it had been removed), is now easily visible and it moves as it should.

Sincerely,
J. P.
Pasadena, California

Perhaps the best advice about the use of prayer and medicine is found in the apocryphal book of Ecclesiasticus (or, as it is also called, the Wisdom of Jesus the Son of Sirach), written by a Jewish scribe probably around 180 B.C.:

Honor the physician with the honor due him . . . for the Lord created him; for healing comes from the Most High. . . . The Lord created medicines from the earth, and a sensible man will not despise them. . . . My son, when you are sick do not be negligent, but pray to the Lord, and he will heal you. . . . And give the physician his place, for the Lord created him; let him not leave you, for there is need of him. There is a time when success lies in the hands of physicians, for they too will pray to the Lord that he should grant them success in diagnosis and in healing, for the sake of preserving life. (38:1, 2, 4, 9, 12–14, RSV)

## FAITH

In Matthew 8:5–13 we read of the healing of the centurion's slave, who was paralyzed and suffering terribly. A centurion was a Roman military officer in charge of a hundred soldiers. For a man of his stature to approach Jesus (Luke in his Gospel says he actually sent intermediaries, Jewish elders and friends) and ask for prayer for his servant took great humility. Jesus immediately responded to the request: "I will go and heal him" (v. 7).

Without exception, in every recorded instance where he was asked to pray for the sick, Jesus complied (though in one instance Jesus delayed prayer; see John 11, the story of the death of Lazarus). I wrote earlier that when I pray over people for the healing ministry, I always instruct them never to accept money; I also instruct them never to deny prayer for healing to anyone who asks for it.

Jesus healed the slave because of the centurion's faith. The centurion was so humble that he said, "Lord, I do not deserve to have you come under my roof. But just say the word, and my servant will be healed" (v. 8). Undoubtedly the centurion knew that a Jew ceremonially defiled himself when he entered the home of a Gentile, and his statement revealed his deep sense of humility before Jesus.

The centurion's faith was marked by three characteristics: first, a humble sense of unworthiness; second, a realization of and belief in Jesus' authority and power over the created order; and third, a belief in the power of Jesus' word. He knew that God could not be bound by time or geography, and he had faith that if Jesus spoke the command, his servant would be healed.

After marveling over the centurion's faith, Jesus healed his servant through a spoken command. "Go!" Jesus said to the centurion. "It will be done just as you believed it would" (v. 13). Here was a man, Jesus said, whose faith was so mature that Jesus did not need to heal the servant in person. That very hour the servant was healed.

Faith is the medium through which God releases his healing power. Most divine healing comes as a result of someone's faith in God. After healing someone Jesus frequently said, "Your faith has healed you" (Luke 18:42; see also Luke 8:48; 17:19). Paul, in Lystra, recognized healing faith in a man who was crippled: "Paul looked directly at him, saw that he had faith to be healed and called out, 'Stand upon your feet!' At that, the man jumped up and began to walk" (Acts 14:9–10). After a similar incident Peter told onlookers that it was "by faith in the name of Jesus [that] this man whom you see and know was made strong. It is Jesus' name and the faith that comes through him that has given this complete healing . . . " (Acts 3:16).

But it would be a mistake to assume that faith exercised by the person being prayed for is always required for healing. In fact, Scripture is full of examples of people *other than* the person being prayed for as sources of healing faith, as was the case of the centurion whose servant was healed. In the passage describing the paralytic's healing that I discussed at the beginning of this chapter, Jesus forgave the paralytic's sins and eventually healed him when he saw the faith of the men who had lowered him through a hole in the roof (Mark 2:5).

Relatives are also frequently sources of healing faith. After the synagogue ruler Jairus received the news that his little daughter had died, Jesus told him, "Don't be afraid; just believe" (Mark 5:36). Soon after, she became the first person raised from the dead in Jesus' ministry.

A third group of people whose faith is an avenue for healing is those who pray for the sick. Jesus healed the man born blind and *later* asked him, "Do you believe in the Son of Man?" (John 9:35). Jesus' question—and the man's response ("Who is he, sir?")—indicates that the man was a passive recipient of God's grace. Jesus exercised faith for healing before the blind man had any knowledge that he was the Son of God. Only after the healing did the man say, "Lord, I believe" (v. 38).

In the New Testament only those who pray for others' healing are berated for any lack of faith; the sick person is never chastised for lack of faith. Jesus spoke some of his harshest words to the disciples when they failed to heal the boy with an evil spirit in Mark 9. "O unbelieving generation," he said, "how long shall I stay with you? How long shall I put up with you?" (v. 19). After Jesus delivered the boy of the evil spirit, the disciples asked Jesus why they had failed. "This kind," he said, "can come out only by prayer" (v. 29). They had ceased to believe completely in God's power to heal.

In John 14:12 Jesus said, "I tell you the truth, anyone who has faith in me will do what I have been doing. He will do even greater things than these, because I am going to the Father." Whose faith is most important for divine healing? The sick person's? Friends'? Relatives'? That of the people who pray? The answer is *"anyone* who has faith" in Jesus for miracles.

This has practical applications when praying for the sick. Whenever I pray for the sick I always look among those present for the people who have faith—other members of the healing team, the person being prayed for, relatives (even children, who usually have great faith for healing), friends, and, of course, myself. When I recognize them, I instruct them to place their hands on or near the part of the body that needs healing, then I ask God to release his healing power.

## THE POWER OF GOD

In Mark 5:25–34 we read of the healing of a woman who had been bleeding for twelve years. The precise nature of her problem is not known, but "she had suffered a great deal under the care of many doctors and had spent all she had, yet instead of getting better she grew worse" (v. 26). According to Jewish law, anyone who touched her was ceremonially unclean (Lev. 15:25–30), a fact that must have produced serious social and emotional problems for her.

Jesus was passing through a crowd on the way to Jairus's home to heal his daughter when he "realized that power had gone out from him" (v. 30). Because of her faith, when she touched Jesus' cloak, immediately "her bleeding stopped and she felt in her body that she was freed from her suffering" (v. 29). "Trembling with fear," she told Jesus what she had done, and he said to her, "Daughter, your faith has healed you. Go in peace and be freed from your suffering" (v. 34). For twelve years she had been seeking healing; in disappointment after disappointment she persisted. She had lost everything—friends, finances, peace of mind—but she had not lost faith in God. Now instead of trusting in doctors she was trusting in Jesus. "If I just touch his clothes," she thought, "I will be healed" (v. 28). She could see herself doing it; she did it; and she was healed.

Jesus healed her through her touch. There was a flow of healing power out from him. They both felt it, and she was immediately healed—physically and emotionally (v. 34). The power that we are told of here is difficult to understand or describe. Over the years I have felt something like it several hundred times when praying for people's healing.[7]

## HEALING PRAYER

In Mark 7:31–37 we read about the healing of a deaf and mute man at the Sea of Galilee. Other people, perhaps his friends or family members, brought the man to Jesus, "and they begged him to place his hand on the man" (v. 32). Almost all of Jesus' healings were performed in public, because the healings were usually a catalyst for faith in the witnesses as well as in the person healed. But in this instance Jesus took the man aside, away from the crowds.

I have been in many situations where an emotional atmosphere created by friends and family members present has quenched faith for healing. They are so desperate and full of fear and anxiety that it is difficult for me or the person I am praying for to have much faith for healing. I usually ask them to leave, allowing only those who know how to pray and are not caught up emotionally in the situation to remain. I suspect Jesus took aside the deaf and mute man for the same reasons.

Jesus then did something unusual: he put his fingers in the man's ears, then spit and touched the man's tongue. Secular literature in the first century indicates that saliva was thought to have medicinal properties, but I believe Jesus did these things for other reasons. By placing his fingers in the man's ears and pulling them out, Jesus indicated to him that his ears would be opened; by touching his tongue with saliva, Jesus indicated to him that his tongue would be healed. Still, it was an unusual way to heal the man.

Sometimes the Father performs healing through unusual means. One time I was praying for a man with a severe gum problem that produced great pain. As I prayed I sensed the Lord wanted me to slap him. I could not bring myself to do it; instead I tapped him on the shoulder lightly. Nothing happened, because tapping was not what God wanted me to do. So I struck him on the forehead with the palm of my hand (not enough to hurt him), and the pain in his gums left instantly. What was the correlation between my striking him and his healing? I do not know! (Later his dentist said his gums had returned to normal.)

I have seen many other strange things done by those praying for healing. For example, several years ago I was in Cape

Town, South Africa, at a meeting in which a man who was crying said, "Is there a blind person in here?" Another pastor heard him ask, and it so happened that a man who was blind in his right eye was nearby. The weeping man then said, "The Lord said that if I take the tears from my eyes and put them in his, he will be made well." So the pastor took some tears and placed them on the blind man's eye. He was instantly healed. I was flabbergasted. Later the pastor told me that all he did was perform a function and there was very little faith on his own part. My point is that sometimes God heals through strange means.

Jesus prayed with compassion and authority. After touching the deaf and mute man, he simply commanded his ears to be opened, and immediately the man could hear and speak properly. Most of the healings in the New Testament were immediate, though not all. For example, in Mark 8:22–26 Jesus had to pray twice for a blind man to be healed. After spitting in his eyes and laying hands on him, Jesus asked if he saw anything. "I see people," the man said. "They look like trees walking around" (v. 24). So Jesus once more put his hands on the man's eyes, "and he saw everything clearly" (v. 25). Clearly there was a process of healing taking place here, which teaches us that we should not be impatient when praying for others. Francis MacNutt writes:

One of the great discoveries in my life has been that when a short prayer doesn't seem to help, a "soaking" prayer often brings the healing we are looking for. Over and over I have checked the effect of prayer by asking groups how many were *totally healed* when we prayed a short prayer and how many were *improved*. The number of people who experience some real improvement usually outnumbers those who are totally healed by five to one. This led me to realize that a short prayer usually has some physical effect (and always a spiritual effect) upon a person, but that most of us need more time when we pray for the sick.[8]

Most physical healing is a process, because sometimes there are other factors—emotional, psychological, demonic—that must first be dealt with. Sometimes, though, no matter how much we pray, the sick do not get better. Why this happens is the topic of the next chapter.

# 8. Not Everyone Is Healed

In January of 1983 I, along with two of my friends, went to England to pray for a close friend, David Watson. David had just been informed by his doctors that he had cancer of the liver. They gave him about one year to live. Earlier on the phone I had told him that I was praying for his healing. In fact, my congregation, the Vineyard Christian Fellowship of Anaheim, California, was praying for him. I prayed for his healing with a combination of desperation (for he was my dear friend) and confidence (because in the past I had seen some people healed of the same condition).

When I and my associates arrived in London our first concern was to express love and care toward David. Because we had flown all night, we decided to go directly to the hospital, greet David, and tell him that we would pray for his healing the following day when we were better rested. But that morning, a Wednesday, did not go as planned.

After arriving at the hospital, we chatted about the events that had led up to his hospitalization and I began explaining our plan to return the next day. I noticed that David was quite anxious about his condition, so in my heart I asked God to make us vehicles of his love and peace. As we spoke we sensed the presence of God in the room; I felt the sensations that I have come to associate with the Holy Spirit's presence, a beautiful calmness that dispels fear and unbelief. I suggested that we should go ahead and pray. We prayed quietly, thanking God for his compassion and mercy.

Through prayer and worship our attitudes were transformed from fear and anxiety to trust and peace. Then we prayed for David's healing, and we all received insights into David's spiritual condition of which we had no prior knowledge. Scripture calls insights like these "words of knowledge." The Holy Spirit revealed these insights to us, and they helped us greatly in knowing how to pray for David. In fact, after the prayer time and throughout the rest of the day we continued to receive insights about David's condition; this indicated to us that God had truly led us there to pray. That morning we prayed for over half an hour, fully aware of God's presence and peace. When we finished I said, "I sense that the work we came over to do is done." Although I said that we would come back again to pray, I believed that this had been the key prayer time.

David experienced the sensations and presence of the Holy Spirit that on similar occasions I have observed occur in the bodies of those who were eventually healed of cancer. He felt heat and tingling, what he described as "energy" coming into his body. (Many people use terms like "energy" or "electricity" to describe sensations they feel during healing prayer. God's healing power is not literal energy or electricity. When I pray for the sick I am not looking for energy or electricity; I am looking for God's presence.) We all had a sense of peace about what happened. I told David that these healing signs might indicate that, in the future, the cancer would die. What we had come to do—pray—was accomplished; now it was up to God. I said neither that I thought he was healed nor that his future healing was assured.

In a letter written to C. Peter Wagner dated March 15, 1986, Anne Watson commented on how I approached healing prayer with David. She graciously granted me permission to reproduce part of it here:

John Wimber never promised David a guarantee of healing or ever proclaimed him healed in my hearing. In fact the very opposite was true. On more than one occasion he impressed on us the fact that he did not claim or promise healing and asked us if we understood and accepted that before he agreed to pray. I was not at the hospital when John and his other pastors prayed for David initially but David himself told me what he experienced. I asked him about the healing issue and he told me what I have written above.

Though I was cautious about promising healing, I was not reluctant about praying again and again for David's healing. In December of 1983 Teddy and Margaret Saunders brought David Watson to my home in Yorba Linda for an eight-day visit. During this period healing teams from the Anaheim Vineyard Christian Fellowship prayed for David almost round the clock. We prayed over him for hours at a time. But fluids continued to collect in his body; I knew he was dying. I could hardly look at him, I loved him so much.

One day toward the end of his visit I had a long, frank conversation with him. Up to that time he had still been making plans for the coming year as though he were not ill. "David," I said, "you're a dying man, and you're denying it."

"I know," he said.

"Unless God sovereignly intervenes, you will die," I said. "Go home and get your affairs in good order. Your faith in Christ has been a constant source of encouragement to me. But you have to acknowledge that you are dying."

David said that, whether his health improved or not, his trust in God would not be shaken. Then I walked over and put my arms around him, and, for the first time since he knew he was ill, he wept. "John," he then said, "if I die, promise me that you will not stop preaching the gospel of the kingdom of God and praying for the sick." I assured him that I would continue.

David was not healed. He died in February 1984. Perhaps no one, with the exception of David's wife and children, is any more disappointed than I that David was not healed. I do not know why he was not healed—I lost one of my dearest friends— but I have continued to pray for the sick and always will.[1]

## FOUR WHO WERE NOT HEALED

I wish I could have written that David Watson is alive today and completely healed of cancer; I also wish I could tell that I

have been healed of the heart problems described in the intro-
duction to this book. But if I did it would not be the truth.
David Watson's death and my physical problems raise a larger
question about divine healing: what about those who are not
healed?

The Letters contain four specific instances where the
sick were not healed immediately and in at least two cases
possibly were never healed. The first case involves Epaphroditus, a leader in the church at Philippi who had
traveled to Rome to visit Paul in prison and contracted a serious
illness (we do not know the specific nature of the illness).
Paul wrote back to the Philippians: "Indeed he [Epaphroditus]
was ill, and almost died. But God had mercy on him, and not
on him only but also on me, to spare me sorrow upon sorrow"
(Phil. 2:27). Paul's concerns reveal a love for his friend and a
desire for his healing. Based on this, it seems likely that Epa-
proditus received healing prayer that had no immediate effect.
It may be that the disease ran its course or that later healing
prayer was effective. In either case, Epaphroditus came close
to death.

The second case involves Timothy. In 1 Timothy 5:23 Paul
advises Timothy to "stop drinking only water, and use a little
wine because of your stomach and your frequent illnesses."
Paul had more to say about faith than any other person (except
Jesus) in the New Testament, and Timothy, Paul's most beloved
disciple, had many titles—evangelist, pastor, teacher, apostle.
Yet Paul told him to use a little wine for his stomach's sake,
which was at that time considered sound advice for healthy
eating habits.[2] Why did Paul give this advice? Most likely
because to that date healing prayer had not been effective for
Timothy's illnesses.

The third case involves the Gentile Christian from Ephesus,
Trophimus, who was Paul's traveling companion on his third
missionary journey (Acts 20:4) and, unwittingly, who was the
cause of Paul's later arrest in Jerusalem (Acts 21:27–29). In 2
Timothy 4:20 Paul writes, "I left Trophimus sick in Miletus."

There is the possibility, based on the Greek word translated in this verse "sick," that Trophimus had overworked and weakened his body.[3]

Indeed, the illnesses of Epaphroditus, Timothy, and, as we shall see next, Paul all could have been the result of the physical and spiritual strain associated with their ministries. In other words, they may have been guilty of what many pastors—myself included—do today: abuse their bodies by disobeying the natural laws of health, which include good exercise, enough sleep, proper eating, recreation, and so on. Yet, granting this theory about Trophimus's specific illness, we are still faced with the fact that Paul's prayers were not enough to heal him when he wrote 2 Timothy. If healing ever came to Trophimus, it was delayed.

The fourth case involves Paul himself. In Galatians 4:13–14 he writes, "As you know, it was because of an illness that I first preached the gospel to you. Even though my illness was a trial to you, you did not treat me with contempt or scorn." Some commentators have suggested Paul's illness was an eye affliction, while others have suggested malaria or epilepsy.[4] Regardless of what the specific illness was, Paul was not healed at that time.[5] Galatians was one of Paul's earliest Letters, written between A.D. 48 and 49 or A.D. 53 and 57, depending on which theory of dating is accepted. Because he never again mentions his illness, eventually Paul was either healed or recovered over time.

What makes these four instances of God not healing even more remarkable is that they involved men who were highly esteemed, gifted, and mature Christian leaders. Explanations such as personal sin, defective faith, or ignorance in those who were sick or those who prayed over them for healing are not plausible for these men.[6] Paul continued to have success in praying for the sick, even though in these four instances there was no immediate healing (Acts 28:8 9).

Another important insight into divine healing may be that God is selective about who he heals. For instance, on one hand

Jesus healed all who were brought to him (Matt. 4:24; 8:16; Mark 1:32; Luke 6:18–19), while on the other hand at the pool of Bethesda (the first-century equivalent of a hospital, full of people seeking physical healing) Scripture mentions Jesus healed only the man who had been an invalid for thirty-eight years (John 5:1–9). It could be that Jesus was selective in healing only one person.

The only conclusion that may be drawn from these examples in the Letters and from indications in the Gospels is that not all were healed when prayed for by the disciples.

There are many reasons that people are not healed when prayed for. Most of the reasons involve some form of sin and unbelief:

- Some people do not have faith in God for healing (James 5:15).
- Personal, unconfessed sin creates a barrier to God's grace (James 5:16).
- Persistent and widespread disunity, sin, and unbelief in bodies of believers and families inhibit healing in individual members of the body (1 Cor. 11:30).
- Because of incomplete or incorrect diagnoses of what is causing their problems, people do not know how to pray correctly.
- Some people assume that God always heals instantly, and when he does not heal immediately they stop praying.

## HEALING AND THE ATONEMENT

But what about those who persevere in healing prayer and believe God for healing, yet still are not healed? The answer to this question is discovered in the relationship between divine healing and Christ's death on the cross.

Theologians refer to Christ's death, the events surrounding it, and its results as the atonement. The Anglo-Saxon term "atonement" means "a making at one," indicating a process of bringing those who are estranged from God into unity with him. Sin is universal and cuts all men and women off from God (1 Kings 8:46; Rom. 3:23); it is serious (Hab. 1:13; Col. 1:21); and it is not something any of us can deal with by ourselves (Num. 32:23; Rom. 3:20). The atonement is central to Christianity because through it our sins are forgiven and we are brought into right relationship with God.

Christ's death on the cross is the foundation of Christianity, securing forgiveness and healing for our souls in this age. Everything in the Old Testament—especially the sacrificial system—points to the cross, and everything since then looks back to it. Through the mystery of Christ's death, God revealed his love for us by delivering his Son "over to death for our sins" (Rom. 4:25).

Not only did Christ die for our sins, he died *for us:* "For Christ's love compels us, because we are convinced that one died for all, and therefore all died" (2 Cor. 5:14). So deep was his identification with us that he took our places in judgment. The 2 Corinthians 5 passage goes on to say, "God made him who had no sin to be sin for us, so that in him we might become the righteousness of God" (v. 21). In fact, Peter teaches that this identification even touches the effects of sin in our physical bodies:

He himself bore our sins in his body on the tree, so that we might die to sins and live for righteousness; by his wounds you have been healed. (1 Pet. 2:24)

Everything the devil introduced to men and women was undone by Jesus at the cross, which of course includes sickness. Jesus, the new Adam, came to restore us, to reproduce his new nature in us—which touches every part of our beings. Matthew 8:16–17 says:

When evening came, many who were demon-possessed were brought to him, and he drove out the spirits with a word and healed all the sick. This was to fulfill what was spoken through the prophet Isaiah:

"He took up our infirmities and carried our diseases." (Isa. 53:4)

R. A. Torrey, commenting on this passage, writes:

It is often said that this verse teaches that the atoning death of Jesus Christ avails for our sicknesses as well as for our sins; or, in other words, that "physical healing is in the atonement." I think that is a fair inference from these verses when looked at in their context.[7]

The key phrase in Torrey's statement is "physical healing is in the atonement." This is an odd phrase, but what he means is that based on what Jesus experienced on the cross we as a consequence may experience one hundred percent healing here on earth.

There is much debate over whether or not healing is in the atonement,[8] and over what it means for healing to be in the atonement. At the least, we may infer on the basis of Matthew's statement that Christ's death "was to *fulfill* what was spoken through the prophet Isaiah," that the atonement is the basis for physical healing. Matthew is saying that Christ came to redeem the whole man from sin *and sin's effects*, which include sickness.

J. Sidlow Baxter asserts that "healing for our mortal bodies is *not* in the atonement":

This conclusion is supported at once by the fact that forgiveness of sins and cleansing from guilt are offered through the cross freely and certainly and at the present moment to all who sincerely believe, whereas healing for all our infirmities and sicknesses is *not* offered freely and certainly at present to all who believe. Not one of those who have believed for forgiveness and cleansing has ever been denied, but thousands and thousands who have believed for physical healing *have* been denied.[9]

Colin Brown also argues that healing is not in the atonement.[10] Like Baxter, Brown also objects to equating the availability of physical healing with spiritual healing and to asserting that "God overcomes disease in this age" is the same as "he overcomes sin." Forgiveness of sins is based on covenant grace: God intends that *everyone* who trusts in him will experience forgiveness of sins. But, Brown says, physical healing is different: many are healed, and many are not:

We need to recognize that there are distinctions between what God has covenanted to do and what he has not covenanted to do, between what God may do and what he has promised to do. God is the healer (Exod. 15:26) and the one who is behind all healing. But in the Old Testament health and healing were not automatically guaranteed by membership in the covenant. . . .

The new covenant does not promise healing for all now. It promises forgiveness of sins (Matt. 26:28). There is no specific, unqualified promise of health and healing in the New Testament to those who have faith. But there are promises of forgiveness and grace to those who repent and believe (e.g., Matt. 11:28; John 1:12; 3:16–18; Acts 2:38–39; 16:31; 17:30) The church is given authority to pronounce the forgiveness of sins in the name of Christ and the authority of the Spirit (John 20:23; cf. Matt. 18:15–20). But it has no parallel authority to heal. If God heals, it is an uncovenanted mercy. But when he forgives, it is a covenanted mercy.[11]

Though Baxter and Brown reject the notion that physical healing is in the atonement, they both believe divine healing is for today. In fact, Baxter writes that the atonement is the *basis* for physical healing: "It is still true, however, that divine healing for sickness comes to us *through* the atonement, just as all the other blessings of salvation do."[12]

Baxter is not splitting hairs when he differentiates between healing *in* the atonement as opposed to healing *through* the atonement. Because our sins are forgiven at the cross and our future bodily resurrections are assured through Christ's resurrection, the Holy Spirit can and does break into this age with signs and assurances of the fullness of the kingdom of God yet to come.

By asserting physical healing is an outcome of the atonement rather than in the atonement, Baxter and Brown avoid drawing erroneous conclusions. For example, some who believe healing is in the atonement conclude that all should expect and experience physical healing in this age, and if they are not healed it is always because of their flawed faith.

## THE WHOLE OF SCRIPTURE

Not all of those who believe physical healing is in the atonement conclude healing is automatic and immediate. Donald Gee, a British Pentecostal who does believe healing is in the atonement, nevertheless balks at concluding that this means we should expect full deliverance from physical illness in this age. To do so, he says, violates the whole of Scripture, which teaches that the fullness of the kingdom and resurrection life is yet to come (Rom. 8:16–25; 2 Cor. 5:1–5). Gee writes:

To assert that healing for our bodies rests upon an identical authority with healing for our souls in the atoning work of Christ our Savior can involve serious problems of personal faith and confidence for those weak in the faith if, and when, they see manifest cases where divine healing, though "claimed," has not been received.[13]

Gee continues: "In the final analysis . . . we make our own problems of divine healing because of our inveterate tendency to push any truth revealed to us to extremes."[14]

He outlines these two extremes:

1. *Presuming on God's sovereignty.* "We have erred by refusing any place in our doctrine, or at least a very insufficient place, for the sovereign will of God. To ask for divine healing without any accompanying 'nevertheless not my will but thine be done' seems to pose an attitude out of keeping with every other right attitude we take in prayer. . . . We make our own problems because the Almighty does not always do what we, in our haste or our imperfect ideas, think he ought to do."[15]

2. *Assuming all divine healing happens supernaturally.* "We seem to have unreasonably refused any place for physical healing to be ministered to us in the will of God except by entirely supernatural and miraculous means."[16]

## THE ALREADY AND THE NOT YET

Baxter, Brown, and Gee agree that divine healing is for today. They also agree that while forgiveness of all sins is given without delay to all men and women who repent sincerely of their sins, divine healing is not given in the same way. Another way of saying this is that our souls are saved completely in this age, but we long for the time when "we will be changed" and " . . . the perishable [will] clothe itself with the imperishable, and the mortal with immortality" (1 Cor. 15:52–53; also see 2 Cor. 5:4). So the body is not redeemed now as it will be after Christ's second coming, in the fullness of the kingdom of God.

This could explain why not everyone is healed when prayed for. We still live in a time that awaits the fullness of the kingdom of God, what Scripture calls the age to come or "the renewal of all things" (Matt. 19:28). In this age we "know in part," but we are assured of a time when we "shall know fully" (1 Cor. 13:12).

The fact that we are living between the first and second comings of Christ, what George Ladd calls living between the "already and the not yet," provides the interpretative key for understanding why the physical healing that Christ secured for us in or through the atonement is not always experienced today. His sovereignty, lordship, and kingdom are what bring healing. Our part is to pray "Thy kingdom come" and trust him for whatever healing comes from his gracious hand. And if in this age it does not come, then we still have assurance from the atonement that it will come in the age to come.[17]

The examples of Epaphroditus, Timothy, Trophimus, and Paul—and David Watson—are humbling reminders that the fullness of our salvation is yet to be revealed at Christ's return, that though the atonement provides for divine healing we have no right to presume that unless God heals in every instance there is something wrong with our faith or his faithfulness.

## OUR PROBLEM

There is another reason—I believe the most fundamental reason—why more people are not healed when prayed for today. We do not seek God as wholeheartedly as we should. In other words, God is able to do greater miracles than we have yet seen, if only we would persist in seeking him.

When Jesus and his disciples returned to Nazareth, his hometown, Scripture says that he could not do any miracles, and he healed only a few sick people (Mark 6:1–6). The explanation for these meager results was the people's lack of faith.

In Luke 11:1–13 one of the disciples asked Jesus how to pray. Jesus told a parable to teach the disciples the importance of boldness and persistence in prayer and to assure them that God answers prayer. In the story a man went to his neighbor late at night to borrow three loaves of bread, "because a friend of mine on a journey has come to me, and I have nothing to set before him" (v. 6). The neighbor, probably quite irritated, at first declined: "Don't bother me," he said. "The door is already locked, and my children are with me in bed. I can't get up and give you anything" (v. 7). But the first man kept knocking until he received the bread. "I tell you," Jesus said in conclusion, "though he will not get up and give him the bread because he is his friend, yet because of the man's boldness he will get up and give him as much as he needs" (v. 8).

The full meaning of this story is difficult to understand without insight into first-century Middle Eastern culture. At that time when a guest arrived at a village his care was a matter of honor and responsibility for the entire village. So the persistent man whom Jesus spoke about had the right to awaken his neighbor; the village's honor was at stake.

Jesus' application of this lesson to prayer was obvious: even as the village had the responsibility to provide for the guest, so God for the sake of his Son's honor has the responsibility to provide for his children. "So I say to you," Jesus said, "Ask and it will be given to you; seek and you will find; knock and

the door will be opened to you. For everyone who asks receives; he who seeks finds; and to him who knocks, the door
will be opened" (v. 9–10). In other words, as we seek God
with boldness and persistence, he will answer prayer. He is
bound by his honor to do so.

Our standard of faith and prayer for healing is not our
present experience. Our standard is God's heart, which is full
of grace and compassion. We should be grateful for today's
grace, but today's grace is not sufficient for tomorrow. He
wants us to ask for more. Jesus further applies the story of the
bold neighbor to our situation:

Which of you fathers, if your son asks for a fish, will give him a
snake instead? Or if he asks for an egg, will give him a scorpion? If
you then, though you are evil, know how to give good gifts to your
children, how much more will your Father in heaven give the Holy
Spirit to those who ask him! (v. 11–13)

There will be more grace, more mercy, more power, and more
divine healing . . . if only we persist in seeking him.


## WHAT ABOUT THE CHRONICALLY ILL?

Most Christians have friends or family members who have
suffered from an infirmity, multiple infirmities, or a series of
infirmities for many years. In some instances they have been
prayed over for divine healing literally hundreds of times without seeing any results. Frequently they give up hope for healing, resigning themselves to accept their condition or refusing
further healing prayer. Who can blame them?

This is not to imply that Jesus never healed the chronically
ill. For example, in Chapter 4 I wrote about Jesus healing a
man blind from birth (John 9) and about his healing a woman
who had been bleeding for twelve years (Mark 5). In fact, of
the forty one recorded instances of Jesus healing people, thirty-
three appear to have been chronic cases. So, for those who
have suffered for many years the possibility that God could

bring them healing in this age is not excluded. There *is* good news for those who are chronically ill. They should never give up receiving prayer for divine healing. But if in this age healing does not come, they are assured of their full restoration in the age to come.

One common denominator in many of Christ's healings of the chronically ill was evangelism. In preparation for a seminar that Michael Flynn, an Episcopal priest, led at a conference in February 1986 at the Anaheim Vineyard Christian Fellowship, he studied twenty-six cases in Scripture of healing the chronically ill. Here are the results of his survey (each case may be mentioned in more than one category):

- In seventeen instances, healings took place in evangelistic settings (Matt. 4:24; 8:16; 9:2–8; 9:32–33; Mark 1:23–28; 9:14–27; 10:46–52; Luke 8:42–48; 13:10–13, 16; 14:1–4; 17:11–19; John 4:28–30; 5:1–9, 14; 9:1–7; Acts 3:1–10; 8:5–8; 14:8–10).
- In sixteen instances, the healings had an evangelistic result (Matt. 9:2–8; 9:32–33; 12:9–13; Mark 1:23–28; 5:1–13, 18–20; 7:32–37; 9:14–27; Luke 5:12–14; 13:10–13, 16; 17:11–19; John 4:28–30; 9:1–7; Acts 3:1–8; 8:5–8; 9:32–35; 14:8–10).
- In twenty-one out of the twenty-six healings there was either an evangelistic setting or result.
- God seems to delight in healing difficult cases in evangelistic settings. These healings vindicate the preaching of the gospel and are demonstrations of God's power.

Based on these observations, Michael Flynn recommended that the chronically ill be brought to evangelical settings to receive prayer for healing, or if they are healed when prayed for in private that they then be brought to evangelical settings to testify about God's healing power.[18]

Yet evangelistic purposes provide an incomplete explanation for healing the chronically ill. James 5:14–15 instructs Christians:

Is any one of you sick? He should call the elders of the church to pray over him and anoint him with oil in the name of the Lord. And the prayer offered in faith will make the sick person well; the Lord will raise him up. If he has sinned, he will be forgiven.

This passage assumes that healing is a gift of God given freely to his people, not simply a means for winning new converts. So pastoral healing, God's mercy and blessing poured out on his children, is the most fundamental reason chronically ill Christians may have confidence that God will heal them.

Jesus first brought healing to the nation of Israel, but he did not withhold healing from anyone. In Matthew 15:21–28 we read about the Syrophoenician woman—a Gentile—who begged Jesus to heal her demon-possessed daughter. Jesus responded: "It is not right to take the children's bread and toss it to their dogs" (v. 26). This is one of the few places in Scripture where Jesus refused to heal someone immediately (see also Matt. 12:38–45; Luke 23:8–12). The Syrophoenician woman understood Jesus' words, and she said, "Yes, Lord, but even the dogs eat the crumbs that fall from their master's table" (v. 27). She believed that crumbs from Jesus' table were sufficient to heal her daughter. His response to her words is similar to his response to the Gentile centurion in Matthew 8:5 13: "Woman, you have great faith! Your request is granted" (Matt. 15:28). At that moment her daughter was healed.

I believe that Jesus was not putting off the Syrophoenician woman so much as clarifying the nature of his ministry: he came to give bread first to his children, then others. The significant point for the chronically ill is that Jesus, the bread of life, provides bread for his children. Today the church, those who are circumcised of heart, is the Israel of God (Rom 2:28–29; Gal. 6:16). So we may pray with confidence and faith for chronically ill Christians, because God wants to give his children the bread of healing.

## ON DEATH AND DYING

I frequently receive telephone calls from people asking if I will come pray for a close friend or family member who is dying. After I hear the details of the person's situation, I ask God, "Is this their appointed time to die?" If it is a person's time to die, we should release him or her to God. I pray this way because we are still waiting for the time for the full redemption of our bodies.

God does set the times of death for people. Scripture teaches that there is "a time to die" (Eccles. 3:2). These times vary greatly; in some cases God takes a baby or young child; in others, an elderly person. We are quick to question the death of a baby, but questions about a baby's death are subpoints under the larger question concerning death itself. Sin brought death into the creation, and Christ came to conquer death. That is what the atonement accomplished for us, the defeat of the power of death in our lives. "The last enemy to be destroyed," Paul writes, "is death" (1 Cor. 15:26; also see Rom. 5:12; Heb. 2:14). For God's people, physical death leads to healing: "We are confident, I say, and would prefer to be away from the body and at home with the Lord" (2 Cor. 5:8).

Several years ago I received a call from a distraught father. He was sobbing and could hardly talk. "My baby is here in the hospital," he said, "and they have tubes from machines attached all over her body. The doctors say she will not survive the night. Would you come?" I told him I would come to the hospital. After hanging up the phone I prayed, "Lord, are you calling this baby to you at this time?" I sensed the Lord saying no. I walked into the hospital with the knowledge that I was a representative of Christ, a messenger who had a gift for that baby girl.

When I entered the baby's room, I sensed death, so I quietly said, "Death, get out of here." It left, and the whole atmosphere in the room changed, as though a weight were lifted. Then I went over and began praying for the girl. After only a few minutes I knew she was going to be healed, and so did her father. Hope came into his eyes. "She is going to be okay," he said. "I know it." Within twenty minutes she improved greatly; several days later she was released, completely healed.

I am under no illusion about my own physical health. Even

if I am fully healed of my heart ailment, someday I will die of something else (unless Jesus returns first). My body is wearing out; it is subject to the effects of the Fall. But while I know that I cannot control the time when God will take me, I am also aware that I do not have to die from the effects of my personal sin before my appointed time.

In 1 Corinthians 11:17–34 Paul is writing to the Corinthian church about judgment that they had brought on themselves through abuse of the Lord's Supper. They were guilty of willful, unrepentant sin when they approached God at Communion. The result? "That is why many among you are weak and sick, and a number of you have fallen asleep" (v. 30). Because they were unwilling to obey God's word, they became sick and many died. The story of Ananias and Sapphira, found in Acts 5:1–10, is another illustration of how death could have been avoided through obedience and faith.

The way to avoid the fates of the Corinthian Christians and Ananias and Sapphira is to appropriate Christ's victory through faith and the Father's protection in turning away from sin: "We know that anyone born of God does not continue to sin; *the one who was born of God [Jesus] keeps him safe, and the evil one cannot harm him*" (1 John 5:18).

## MINISTERING TO THE TERMINALLY ILL

There are instances in which the Lord says, "The appointed time to die has come." For these people, offering a false hope for healing brings unnecessary pain and deflects their attention from trusting in God for eternal life. After all, good health and wisdom, though greatly to be desired, are pointless unless we are rightly related to God. Telling the truth in the face of death is one of the most helpful things we can do for a terminally ill person. That way he or she can talk about it and work through his or her relationship with God.

Dying has significance because of the atonement. Through the atonement men and women gain acceptance by God despite their sins and limitations. Notice that I said that we are accepted by God despite our sins *and limitations*. Limitations are not sinful: none of us is God. Many people think that if they live as they should, there should be no limitations to their lives. But when their time to die comes, and with it the reminder of their weaknesses, they have no way of coping with their limitations.

Many Christians find it difficult to accept their limitations, because all their lives they have served others, but have not themselves been served by others. These people have difficulty accepting help from others because they have never fully understood or accepted that "it is by grace [that we] have been saved, through faith—and this not from [ourselves], it is a gift of God—not by works, so that no one can boast" (Eph. 2:8–10). That is, they have neither understood nor believed fully that the atonement provides eternal life through God's faithfulness; they have worked hard at trying to maintain God's favor. Their faith is severely tested by their terminal illness, and they are greatly helped when they realize that they are justified on the basis of God's faithfulness and not their works.

Non-Christians in our society also find it difficult to accept their mortality. They have been raised in this modern, technological society in which death rarely is mentioned, and frequently they have not acknowledged that they will die. The only way they can learn to cope with their limitations and the guilt of their sins is through the healing of their spirit, which comes through repentance and faith in Christ.

We can offer the terminally ill a great gift of comfort and courage. One key to offering comfort and courage is our own freedom from anxiety about death, which begins with being rightly related to God. Facing a terminally ill person is difficult, for it reminds us of *our* limitations. Only when we can face death are we able to help others face death.

Samuel Southard, a professor of pastoral theology at Fuller Theological Seminary, has taught courses on ministering to the dying. He says that prayer—both for the counselor and the terminally ill person—is "one of the greatest spiritual resources which God has granted his children; it is a powerful medicine of the soul."[19] Prayer begins *before* we visit the terminally ill person. "Prayer should not be the last act in visitation; it should be an act of worship before we visit." If we have not prayed before we come, we will carry along tensions, anxiety, and hostility that we may have picked up from other activities. In this regard, our prayer is protection for the patient. Prayer also reminds us that God's Spirit goes before us, that he is the Comforter and not we ourselves.

Effective prayer for the terminally ill person begins with being a good listener (Prov. 20:5). Southard points out how important it is to listen to a sick person: "The attitude of prayer which is most meaningful to a sick person might be called responsive listening, sympathetic understanding, or communion of the spirit." Only when we understand the deeper meaning of the terminally ill person's words can be know how to pray effectively.

Finally, the Holy Spirit will speak to us, revealing to us the person's heart and the wisdom to know how to pray specifically. "When we have a listening ear, we may hear what God's Spirit has said to this sick person and what his Spirit would say to this person through us. The prayer that we pray at the sick person's request will then not be empty; it will speak to the true needs of his or her heart."[20]

Ministry to the terminally ill always leads to ministry to bereaved friends and relatives. They too need healing from the hurt of the loss of a loved one. Grieving without guilt is an important part of adjusting to the loss of a loved one. Sometimes the bereaved suffer from guilt over wrongdoing or neglect in their relationship with the deceased, and we can offer them Christ's forgiveness of their sins. Frequently they find it difficult to accept the loss or face the future. Each person is different. Perhaps the best advice is that we be compassionate, good listeners.

## RAISING THE DEAD

There are a few instances in Scripture in which the dead were raised. Jesus raised Jairus's daughter (Luke 8:40–56), the widow's son at Nain (Luke 7:11–15), and Lazarus (John 11:1–44); and Peter raised Tabitha (Acts 9:40–41), and Paul raised Eutychus (Acts 20:7–12). In these instances the kingdom of God breaks into the present age, revealing a glimpse of what will come at Christ's return (1 Cor. 15:24–26).

I find most interesting the incident at the time of Christ's death, recorded only in Matthew 27:52–53, of the tombs opening up and releasing "the holy people"—perhaps Old Testament saints—who "went into the holy city and appeared to many people." Life radiated from the cross, so that even the dead were raised! Surely this event was symbolic of Christ's conquering death through the atonement.

In sum, raising of the dead was a dramatic and infrequent event in the New Testament, but something that I believe is possible still today.

In this section of the book we have seen that Christ's healing power is available to every part of our lives. If we open our hearts to him we have no need to fear that he cannot heal. But believing in the possibility of Christ's healing is not the same as actually experiencing it. How to pray for the sick and experience Christ's healing power is the topic of the last section.

# PART III.

# How Does Jesus Heal Through Us?

# 9. An Integrated Model of Healing: Principles, Values, and Practices

The most effective way to train and equip people for any skill is by providing effective models and opportunities to practice the skill itself. This method is behind most evangelism training programs. So, shortly after I saw my first healing, I asked myself, "Is it possible to develop a model for healing from which large numbers of Christians may be trained to heal the sick?" I thought the answer was yes and became committed to developing that model.

Jesus used a show, tell, deploy, and supervise method of training. After calling the disciples he took them along with him, teaching and healing the sick as he went. Then, after he thought the disciples had seen and learned enough to try for themselves, he commissioned, empowered, instructed, and sent them out to do the same things (Matt. 10:1, 5–8).

The results of Jesus' training of the disciples are seen clearly in the book of Acts. The Twelve preached with great power and effectiveness, and they healed the lame and blind and cast out demons from the demonized. The Eleven also trained a second generation of disciples, people like Philip and Stephen, to preach and demonstrate the kingdom of God.

## A HEALING MODEL

I had to learn myself before training others. I did this in three steps. First, I began praying for the sick even though I knew little about divine healing. Second, I studied the theologies and practices of leaders from different schools of divine healing.[1] Third, I applied what I learned from these models to our situation in the Vineyard Christian Fellowship, asking specifically how it would help Christians learn to pray for the sick.

Throughout this process I developed teaching to explain the theology and methodology of divine healing. What emerged was what I call an "integrated model of healing," a model from which any Christian may learn to pray for the sick. I call this an "integrated model of healing," because it describes how God heals the whole person: body, soul, and spirit. After testing and adapting this model for several years in my congregation and at a course I helped teach at a local seminary, I developed a healing seminar in which people are trained to pray for the sick. Over the past few years thousands of Christians from Protestant, Catholic, and Orthodox traditions have been trained through these seminars, which are now conducted by me and about twenty of my associates.

## GUIDING PRINCIPLES

A good analogy for the different elements of a learning model are the parts of a building—foundation, supporting walls, plumbing, electricity, and heating and air-conditioning systems. The first task a builder performs is to excavate and lay a foundation. The length and width of the excavation determine the length and width of the building. The deeper and surer the foundation, the higher one can build. Principles are to a healing model as the foundation is to a building. I have mentioned most of these principles in other parts of this book, but they are worth summarizing together once more.

The first guiding principle is that *God wants to heal the sick today*. It is God's nature to heal people, and he has called us to reflect his nature. "He called his twelve disciples to him," Matthew writes about Jesus, "and gave them authority to drive out evil spirits and to heal every disease and sickness" (Matt. 10:1). Many Christians have never heard that God wants to heal today! I have observed that once people's skepticism about divine healing is removed, they are quite open to learning how to pray for the sick.

Another principle is *the importance of corporate ministry* (see 1 Cor. 14:26; Gal. 6:2; James 5:16; 1 Pet. 2:9; 4:10). Most people attend my healing seminars to learn how to pray for the sick, not for their own healing. When I do call forward the sick for prayer, it is to demonstrate healing and by example to teach others about divine healing. I rarely personally pray over the sick at my seminars. Instead, trained individuals pray while I describe to the seminar participants what they are doing and why they are doing it. So I do not hold healing services so much as equipping seminars, where everyone learns how to exercise the power God makes available to us.

Third, *our trust in God is demonstrated by action.* Jackie Pullinger in her book *Chasing the Dragon*[2] writes about her ministry to Chinese prostitutes. As a young girl she answered God's call to take the gospel to the most decadent in Hong Kong's ghettos. Jackie has told me that many times Christians ask her, "How can you do it?" She responds, "How can you not do it?" How can we not pray for the sick? I am not implying that everyone we pray over will be healed— surely they are not! But I am asserting that Scripture never qualifies who will be healed. Our task is to pray; God is the one who heals. We cannot do or teach less than what is in the Bible.

The reason all Christians can effectively pray for the sick is because *we are empowered by the Holy Spirit*, which is the fourth principle for the healing ministry. "You will receive power when the Holy Spirit comes on you," Jesus told the disciples shortly before Pentecost (Acts 1:8). And Paul writes that we are given "gifts of healing by [the] . . . Spirit" (1 Cor. 12:9). God's power, not human power, is the source of all divine healing. Our responsibility is to open our lives to the Spirit, to trust and honor him, and receive his power in our midst.

The fifth principle for divine healing is *the importance of loving relationships with our brothers and sisters.* Paul writes, "Love must be sincere. . . . Be devoted to one another in brotherly love. Honor one another above yourselves" (Rom. 12:9–10; see also 13:8). Healthy, supportive relationships with brothers and sisters in Christ are both a goal of healing and an effective environment for healing. The preparation, ministry, and follow-up necessary for divine healing can take place most often where there is sufficient commitment, responsibility, authority, and accountability among Christians. In other words, one of the primary benefits of our union with Christ is a life together with brothers and sisters.

The last principle is that *God wants to heal the whole person, not just specific conditions.* In John 7:23 Jesus asked the Jews who had just accused him of being demonized, "Why are you angry with me *for healing the whole man* on the Sabbath?" The Greek word translated "healing" *(hugiēs)* reflects a much more comprehensive understanding of health than that of modern popular thought. Commenting on this and other Greek words used in the New Testament for health, John Wilkinson writes:

Health is thought of in terms of wholeness, well-being, life, strength and salvation. . . . What modern man confines to the body, the Bible extends to the whole of man's being and relationships. It is only when man's being is whole and his relationships right that he can be truly described as healthy.[3]

I once heard someone say that it's more important to know what kind of person has the bug than what kind of bug has the person. By that he meant it is more important that we have information about a person's relationship with God and other people than that we have technical details about his or her illness. Keeping in mind that we pray for *persons* and not simply *conditions* ensures the protection of people's dignity. When I pray for a person's healing my goal is to leave him or her feeling more loved by God than before we prayed. One of the ways I express God's love is by showing interest in every aspect of a person's life. Often this means that praying for the sick takes a great deal of time, both in initial and follow-up sessions.

## VALUES

Values are to principles as supporting walls are to a foundation; they are visible extensions of our basic principles. Supporting walls hold the building together. Values determine the direction and flow of our limited resources of time, energy, and money. In other words, values determine what one does. The following four values flow from the guiding principles I described above and contribute to a vibrant healing ministry:

1. *A healing environment.* When the Holy Spirit is present and when people are full of faith in God for healing, healing often happens.

Jesus understood the importance of a healing environment. Mark 5:35–42 describes him raising Jairus's daughter from the dead. Jesus was on his way to pray for the girl when he was informed that she had died. Those who told him the girl was dead discouraged Jesus from going to the house. They had no faith that he could heal the little girl. But instead of giving up, Jesus insisted on going to Jairus's house, though he did not allow anyone other than Peter, James, and John to go with him. By excluding those who were full of unbelief, he created a healing environment.

He arrived at a home full of "commotion, with people crying and wailing loudly" (v. 38). When he told them to stop their wailing because the girl was asleep, they laughed at him. So "he put them all out, he took the child's father and mother and the disciples who were with him, and went in where the child was" (v. 40). For a second time he excluded those with little or no faith, and then he went into the room and, through a word of command ("Little girl, I say to you, get up!" v. 41), raised the girl from the dead.

Whenever I pray for the sick I look for a healing environment, an atmosphere full of faith and hope. I consciously look for faith in three places: first, in myself and others who are praying for the sick; second, in the person being prayed for; and third, in witnesses.

Usually I ask the person for whom I am praying, "Do you believe Jesus can heal?" If he or she answers positively, I then ask, "Do you believe Jesus will do it now?" If the answer is yes or if a witness or I have a strong sense that God wants to heal, I go forward with healing prayer. The point is that I always look for faith and gather people with faith for healing. If no one has that sense, I ask God for the faith. (I never blame the sick person for lack of faith if healing does not occur.) "Now faith," writes the writer of Hebrews, "is being sure [of the substance] of what we hope for and certain of what we do not see" (Heb. 11:1). I am rarely successful when that substance, that confidence of faith, is absent.

I have been in many healing situations where, like Jesus, I have asked those who are struggling with unbelief, fear, or anxiety to leave, while I ask others who I know have faith for healing to join us. I have also observed that frequently one healing is a springboard to many others. When a group sees someone healed, their faith increases greatly, resulting in a healing environment.

During the time of prayer for healing I encourage people to "dial down," that is, to relax and resist becoming worked up emotionally. Stirred up emotions rarely aid the healing process, and usually impede learning about how to pray for the sick. So I try to create an atmosphere that is clinical and rational (at my seminars the time of prayer is called a "clinic"), while at the same time it is powerful and spiritually sensitive. Of course, emotional expression is a natural by-product of divine healing and not a bad response. My point is that artificially creating an emotionally charged atmosphere militates against divine healing and especially undermines training others to pray for the sick.

One of the most significant ways to increase faith for healing is worship. As we draw close to God his Spirit works in us.

Because church gatherings include open, corporate worship, they can be powerful environments for healing. Most church meetings are for worship, the sacraments, and the proclamation of God's word—all three of which, incidentally, may lead to healing and other works of God. Here are some elements of how we approach worship:

- At the Vineyard Christian Fellowship we begin most church gatherings with at least thirty minutes of worship, and as we worship God our hearts open to God and faith for healing increases. We do not worship God so he will heal; we worship God because he is God and we are his people. We give God's love back to him in worship, and he sheds his light on us through the word and sacrament.

- We invite the Holy Spirit to come and minister to us. The Holy Spirit makes us more spiritually sensitive and we sense his powerful presence.

- If we believe in healing, then we must allow a place for it to occur when we gather together. I leave a place in the schedule of most church gatherings for divine healing, especially Sunday worship and small-group meetings. Most people know when they participate in Vineyard Christian Fellowship activities that there will be opportunity to receive prayer for healing or to pray for others.

When we are out in the marketplace we cannot worship aloud; nevertheless, God hears praise and thanksgiving in our hearts and sends his Spirit. Back in 1982 a friend of mine from Arizona wrote me a note in which he described his experience of the relationship between worship and effective healing prayer. Only a few weeks earlier he had written to ask why he was experiencing no success when he prayed for the sick. Since that time he had discovered his mistake:

It's happening, John! Six out of the seven things I've prayed for in the past five days for my family in the way of healing have occurred within two minutes! The only thing that hasn't been answered yet is

B's crossed eyes. I'm building up faith to see that healed, though. *I now realize what my mistake was: by just jumping in and praying for healing without worshiping God first, I was actually taking him for granted.* God showed me this while listening to one of your healing seminar tapes. After I repented in tears, I went upstairs and healed my daughter of a rash that covered eighty percent of her body. Jesus is so wonderful.

2. *Ministry time.* Learning to pray for the sick is like learning to ride a bicycle. At first the parent runs alongside the wobbly child to prevent serious injury. But in time the child is ready to go out on his own; inevitably he returns from his early solo rides with skinned knees and elbows. Most parents do not become overly concerned about these accidents. Instead, they encourage their child to get back on his bicycle and try again, because soon he will ride smoothly and safely. Learning to pray for the sick is a similar process: the first solo experiences are usually messy, but in time they become quite enjoyable. I am more interested in ministry than neatness, so I provide a place in which people know they are accepted and helped even when they fail. I do this by allowing time and space at my healing seminars and in other church gatherings for people to pray for the sick.

Each session at my healing seminar is divided into three parts: worship, instruction, and a clinic. In the clinic participants observe trained members of a healing team pray for the sick while I describe what is happening and why certain things are done. Then all the participants divide into ministry teams and do "hands-on" prayer themselves. (There are always people present who need healing.) Using this method, the majority of people pray for the sick even during the *first* session. I always make sure that trained people are on hand to help the novices, encouraging dialogue among group members for the purpose of understanding why we pray as we do.

I encourage people to pray for the sick in teams for several reasons:

- Spiritual power is multiplied when more people are praying (Matt. 18:19).
- Greater insights usually come by working with others, especially when an impasse is met.
- Teams provide a good healing and learning environment.
- Teams discourage individuals who experience success from thinking too highly of themselves.
- With team ministry, the person being prayed for is more likely to become dependent on Jesus than on the person who is praying for him or her.
- In teams there is always a witness to what takes place, which is a protection for the person praying (Matt. 18:16).
- In cases involving the casting out of demons, it is always best to have several people present (Lev. 26:8; Deut. 32:30).

Another excellent place for people to learn how to pray for the sick is in small home groups that are overseen by trained leaders. At the Vineyard Christian Fellowship we have many of these groups. We call them kinship groups. Of course, they are much more than healing meetings—they encompass worship, fellowship, Scripture study, and other activities that support successful Christian living—but they are a place where prayer for healing regularly occurs. This environment also provides excellent follow-up and support for those who are healed, thus decreasing the possibility of their condition returning.

In the seminars, healing teams, and small groups I encourage a climate of acceptance for those who pray, one in which they may succeed or fail as they learn this new skill. I tell them, "We are all learning about God's healing power together. Don't worry about failing—I fail every day! But the more I try, the more successful I am."

3. *Training.* I believe that training Christians to do God's works is one of the most important and least fulfilled jobs of leaders in the body of Christ. If leaders are properly trained, they will in turn train others. In Ephesians 4:11–13, Paul says,

"It was he [Jesus] who gave some to be apostles, some to be prophets, some to be evangelists, and some to be pastors and teachers, to prepare God's people for works of service, so that the body of Christ may be built up." The Greek word translated "to prepare" in the New International Version, *katartismon*, comes from the verb *katartizein*. The word was used in medicine for setting a broken bone or putting a joint back in place. In politics it was used to bring together opposing groups so a government could function normally. In Mark 1:19 it refers to mending nets and in Galatians 6:1 to disciplining a rebellious member of the body until he or she returns to unity and peace in the church. In other words, Paul is talking about equipping Christians fully, so that the body of Christ can be all that it ought to be. Leaders are not to do all the work for the people but are to train the people to do the work themselves. As the leaders equip the people, the body is built up in unity. I believe that I would be negligent if I were not training others to heal the sick.

Several obstacles prevent leaders from equipping others to heal the sick. One obstacle is a sense of personal unworthiness, a feeling that they are not mature enough, not successful enough. It is important for leaders to attempt to live free of sin, but I have discovered most healers are themselves wounded in some way. If leaders wait until they are perfect, they will have very little to offer this side of the return of Christ.

Some leaders have a fear that if they train others they will lose their ministry. (In many instances these leaders have healing ministries that attract large crowds, either in local churches or at healing conferences.) These leaders need to be reminded of a basic kingdom principle that always works in equipping: the more one gives away—whether gifts, skills, material possessions, or time—the more one receives from God. Jesus taught, "Give, and it will be given to you. A good measure, pressed down, shaken together and running over, will be poured into your lap. For with the measure you use, it will be measured to you" (Luke 6:38). The more people I train to heal the sick, the more people God gives us to heal.

4. A *life-style of healing.* Through a life-style of healing we give God's healing to the world. Healing is a way of life for me. When I am at home, in meetings, walking down the streets, in the markets or my workplace—under any and all circumstances—I am open to God using me to pray for the sick. While I am open to being used for divine healing any place and at any time, I do not automatically assume that healing is all God wants me to do. Divine healing is not the only action we take to advance the kingdom of God.

I have confidence about taking divine healing into the world. Because God is trustworthy, I assume that he leads and designs circumstances in our lives. When I feel led to do actions that contradict Christ's nature, I assume these feelings are not from God. (Of course, there are always situations that do not fall neatly under one of these two categories, but these are more the exceptions.) I am always asking myself the question, "Is this characteristic of how God works?"

For example, occasionally I sense that I should talk to someone, perhaps a stranger, about Christ. When I receive these inklings, I neither shrug them off as indigestion nor spend a great deal of time asking myself, "Is it really the will of God that I talk to these persons?" I always talk with them. Usually they respond positively to my words (many place their faith in Christ); sometimes they respond negatively. But I never question if I should have talked with them. Why? Because I know that God wants the gospel preached to every person in the world (Matt. 28:18–20).

The same thinking applies to helping the poor or meeting a need of a brother or sister in Christ. I think, "This is what Christ died for, that he may raise up a people to do his works on earth. His works include helping the poor and needy. Of course I will help."

I respond the same way when asked to pray for someone's healing or if I sense God telling me to pray for someone unsolicited. Frequently they are healed; occasionally they are not. But I never question if I should have prayed for them, because I am confident that my job is to obey and God's job is to heal. If, when I pray, God does not heal, I believe that it is still God's will that I prayed. I do not respond to the instances when there is no healing by thinking I am a failure or that I am not spiritual. How can *I* be a failure when God is the one who heals? Or, how can *I* take credit if someone is healed when God is the one who heals? So, because Christ is the healer, I have a life-style of healing.

The effects of a life-style of healing are physically and spiritually healthy churches, with many people won into the kingdom of God.[4]

## PRACTICES

Practices are like the plumbing, heating and air-conditioning systems, and electrical wiring in a building. We enjoy their benefits—running water, climate control, and electricity—though we rarely think about the complex support systems built throughout the structure that make them possible. Healing practices are the skills, attitudes, and activities that keep divine healing a growing and vital ministry in the church. They are what we do when praying for the sick.

The following are practices that must be mastered for an effective healing ministry. They flow out of the principles and values that I have listed above. I compare these practices to the physical senses of hearing, seeing, speaking, and touching:

1. *Hearing.* The most fundamental skill required for healing is openness to the Holy Spirit, emptying oneself and receiving his leading and power. Frequently I encounter people who want a method for healing, a formula they can follow that guarantees them automatic healings. But divine healing is neither automatic nor dependent on our right actions; it is rooted in a relationship with God and the power of his Spirit.

Divine healing is a gift from God, an act of his mercy and grace. Our part is to listen to him and carry out his word. "He has made us competent as ministers of a new covenant," Paul writes, "not of the letter but of the Spirit; for the letter kills, but the Spirit gives life" (2 Cor. 3:6). There are many ways in which we practice being open to God's presence and grow in hearing his word—Scripture study, worship, prayer, and meditation being foremost.

When I speak of listening to God's voice, I mean developing a practice of communion with the Father in which we are constantly asking, "Lord, what do you want to do now? How do you want to use me? How should I pray? Whom do you want me to evangelize? Is there someone that you want to heal?" Sometimes he gives me specific insights about people for whom I am praying. These come as impressions: specific words, pictures in my mind's eye, physical sensations in my body that correspond to problems in their bodies. These impressions help me know who and what to pray for and how to pray.

I do not imply that I have an infallible "hotline" to God, that I always hear his voice and follow his leading. But my point is that I am open to God, listening to him, and confident that he wants to lead us (John 14:26; 16:13–15).

2. *Seeing.* Spiritual eyesight enables us to recognize and work with God in the healing process. As we hear God's voice and pray for people, the Holy Spirit comes on them. When this happens there are emotional and physical phenomena in the person being prayed for that indicate to us the Spirit is present.

Some of these phenomena are obvious: weeping, cries, prolonged and exuberant expressions of praise, shaking, trembling, calmness, bodily writhing and distortions, falling over (sometimes referred to as "being slain in the Spirit"), laughter, or jumping. Other phenomena are more subtle: slight trembling, fluttering of the eyelids, faint perspiring, a sheen on the face, ripples on the skin, or deep breathing. I offer more insights into these phenomena in chapter 12. My point here is that often they indicate the Holy Spirit is manifesting his presence on someone, and that we can learn to recognize what they mean.

3. *Speaking.* It takes time and practice to learn how to pray

and offer words of love, understanding, and assurance to people in need of healing. The best way to learn how to pray for healing is by being around those who know how to pray effectively.

Learning to speak words of love and encouragement is difficult for people who come from families in which verbal love and physical affection were not communicated appropriately. Usually they need practical training in how to honor and respect others, with particular emphasis on developing Christian speech patterns.

In the Bible many people are healed through a command. For example, Jesus rebuked Peter's mother-in-law's fever, and it went away (Luke 4:38–39); after Jesus had put his fingers in the deaf and dumb man's ears and spit on his tongue he looked to heaven and said, "Be opened!" (Mark 7:32–35); and Jesus commanded the paralytic at the pool of Bethesda, "Get up! Pick up your mat and walk" (John 5:8). Shortly after Pentecost Peter healed a crippled beggar by saying, "In the name of Jesus Christ of Nazareth, walk" (Acts 3:6), and he raised Tabitha from the dead when he said, "Tabitha, get up" (Acts 9:40). This is frequently referred to in Christian literature as a "word of command," a word spoken with the authority of the kingdom of God and through which great power for healing is released.

I have witnessed or heard about many instances in which God led someone to command a disease to leave and the person was instantly healed. This happened to my wife, Carol, before she knew about words of command. In 1982 a woman approached her after one of our Sunday morning services, asking her to pray for a skin condition (eczema) that covered most of her body. Through the spiritual gift of the discernment of spirits, Carol sensed the condition was caused by an evil spirit. As Carol talked, anger rose up inside of her, culminating in her yelling loudly at the evil spirit, "Knock it off!" The woman's itching stopped immediately, and she was healed at that moment. She has not suffered from eczema since that day.

Sometimes Jesus spoke a simple declaration and the person was healed. In John 4:46–50, a nobleman twice begged Jesus to come and heal his son. Finally Jesus said, "You may go. Your son will live." In Acts 9:32–35, Peter said to Aeneas the paralytic, "Aeneas, Jesus Christ heals you. Get up and take care of your mat." After Paul had gone to the dead man Eutychus and thrown his arms around him, he said, "Don't be alarmed. He's alive!" (Acts 20:7–12).

There are also prayers of petition. In Mark 7:32–35, the healing of the deaf and dumb man, Jesus "looked up to heaven and with a deep sigh he said to him, 'Ephphatha!' (which means, 'Be opened!')." The fact that Jesus looked up to heaven indicates some kind of petition. In Acts 9:36–43, Peter got on his knees beside the dead woman Tabitha and prayed. Only after he had prayed did he say, full of faith, "Tabitha, get up!"

Finally, sometimes healing comes after someone receives instruction to do a specific act and he or she obeys. In John 9:1–7, Jesus placed mud that he had made with his spit on the eyes of a man, then told him, "Go wash in the Pool of Siloam." The man obeyed and was healed.

Another important speaking skill is learning how to offer a healing apologetic, one that raises faith in those being prayed for. Frequently people say to me, "I want to be healed, but I have difficulty believing that God will heal me." I usually respond by informally teaching them about divine healing. For example, I tell them about the Syrophoenician woman to whom Jesus told that healing was the "children's bread" (Mark 7:27). I ask them, "Are you a child of God?"

"Oh, I have never heard it that way before."

"Well, if you are a child of God, Jesus has prepared healing for you."

I then explain about how the Syrophoenician woman kept pressing Jesus for her daughter's healing, and eventually Jesus recognized her faith and healed her daughter. So, though the Syrophoenician woman was not an Israelite, Jesus still healed her daughter. How much more is he ready to give healing to children of the new covenant. Explanations like this help people to understand healing and raise their faith for healing.

We also need to explain to people why we are praying as we are and why they are experiencing phenomena such as those I described above in the second point (shaking, falling, and so on). This reassures them that God is working, and through this understanding their faith increases.

Another important practice is knowing how to offer words of compassion and comfort when someone is not healed. Many people, when not immediately healed, suffer from frustration and rejection. Divine healing is concerned about the person and not just the condition. Because of this, if we pray for them appropriately we have a basis for a loving and ongoing relationship. I say, "I love you and God loves you very much, and I feel very badly that you were not healed instantly. Maybe you will be healed when prayed for next time. Allow me to pray for you again, okay?" I also encourage them with God's admonition that we ask again and again, that we persevere in seeking him and his kingdom. When they say they have been seeking God again and again, I tell them that is the way the Lord works sometimes before he heals.

Finally, follow-up instructions are very important for those who are healed. If they are seeing a physician or psychologist, I encourage them to tell him or her about their healing. Sometimes their healing is partial, and they still need medical care. Another type of advice is more pastoral in nature. They should be encouraged to have regular involvement in a Christian body in which people receive pastoral care and support. Some people's problems have complex spiritual, psychological, and physical causes, so they need follow-up counseling by a pastor or trained counselor. Many of these people receive healing only to see their condition return again within a few days or weeks, because they did not change their life-styles.

4. *Touching.* A woman who had been bleeding for twelve years was healed instantly when she touched Jesus' cloak. What is remarkable about this healing is that Jesus did not see

her touch his cloak (they were in a crowd), but he sensed "power had gone out from him" (Mark 5:30). In Gennesaret the people "brought all their sick to him [Jesus] and begged him to let the sick just touch the edge of his cloak, and all who touched him were healed" (Matt. 14:35–36).

In the New Testament the laying on of hands was observed in healing the sick (Mark 1:41; 6:5; 16:18; Luke 4:40; Acts 28:8), blessing (Matt. 19:13–15; Mark 10:16), ordaining or commissioning (Acts 6:6; 13:3; 1 Tim. 5:22), and the imparting of spiritual gifts (Acts 8:17, 19.6, 1 Tim. 4:14; 2 Tim. 1:6). When praying for the sick, Jesus usually both touched them and commanded the illness to leave (Matt. 8:1–3; Mark 7:32–35; Luke 4:38–39; 7:12–15; see also Acts 3:1–5; 20:7–12).

In 1983 I had an experience in Göteborg, Sweden, that illustrates the power of touch. I was speaking (with the aid of an interpreter) at a four-day healing conference in a Baptist church. There were three hundred people in attendance, and for the first two days they were quite reserved, not demonstrating much of a response to my teaching. On the third day of the conference I sensed God wanted to heal a woman in the audience who had cancer in her left breast. I said, "I believe God wants to heal a woman who has cancer in the left breast."

Immediately a lady in the balcony stood up and said that she had been interceding and fasting several days for a woman in San Francisco who had cancer in her left breast. Her appeal was eloquent and compelling, but I sensed that the woman for whom I had the word of knowledge was in the audience. So I said, "This is not what the Lord is doing at this moment." I then said, "This woman is in the room now. Only this morning she was released from the hospital. She is sixty years old [I cannot remember her exact age today], and she is seated directly in front of me and slightly to the right."

In response, a woman in a dark, full-length wool coat stood up and said in Swedish, "It's me, it's me." I asked her to come forward for prayer, and as she did I asked for volunteers to pray for her.

Three men from the first row came forward, two standing behind the woman and one in front of her. I asked the woman if she would mind folding her hands over her breast and allow one of the men to put his hands on her hands. She agreed to do it. (I ask permission to lay hands on people to show respect for their personhood.) The men behind her placed their hands on her shoulders. Then I stepped back and told them to wait for me to pray.

But before the interpreter could give them my instructions, I felt a faith command welling up in me and I yelled in English, "Be healed in the name of Jesus." Hardly had the words left my mouth when the power of God came down on all four people; they began shaking and were knocked off their feet to the floor! It was as though the healing power of God went into the woman and out into the three men, or vice versa. The interpreter was so overwhelmed that she began speaking to me in Swedish and to the audience in English! All four rose weeping and praising God. The woman later reported her healing.

In this chapter I have described the guiding principles, values, and practices of an integrated model of healing. In the next chapter I describe programs, personnel, and spiritual gifts.

# 10. An Integrated Model of Healing: Programs and Personnel

Programs are like the rooms and corridors in a building. Each room is designed with a specific purpose in mind—a dining room for eating, a bedroom for sleeping, a bathroom for personal hygiene, and so on. A room's usefulness is always determined by how it contributes to fulfilling the purpose of the building. Programs serve the same purpose in the integrated healing model.

Programs by themselves can be misleading. I frequently receive letters and phone calls from pastoral leaders who say, "Last year I visited your church for a week and returned home and started doing all the things that you do—healing seminars, time for prayer for the sick in all of our meetings, prayer teams, and midweek kinship meetings. But I have not gotten the results that you get. Why?" In part the answer is that they have instituted programs without building a solid base of principles, values, and practices. Usually these leaders themselves have not fully understood our healing values and priorities.

There are several ways in which people may receive healing prayer at the Anaheim Vineyard Christian Fellowship. I have already mentioned that at every general gathering room is left for healing prayer, and a key element in our midweek kinship meetings is prayer for healing. Also, some of the kinship groups send their people out door-to-door to pray for the sick and share the gospel. Each member of our pastoral staff is available at least one day a week for counseling appointments that often include healing prayer. Also, if a need arises for someone at a local hospital, a pastor will go. Trained healing teams are available at the church five days per week. People phone and make appointments to meet with a team. This program is quite successful. During 1986 thirty-two percent of all people prayed for were completely healed, while overall eighty-six percent showed evidence of some significant healing. (We keep detailed histories of people who enter this program.) Our goal is to have healing teams available morning, noon, and night throughout the week. Training programs are the key for raising up healing teams. People are trained through special healing seminars or courses that we offer in a weekly training center. Over three thousand people are enrolled in our weekly training center, which offers dozens of courses covering many themes and topics.

I could write much more about our programs, but they may change tomorrow, depending on the needs of people around us. Principles and values remain constant; programs change. In fact, most cultures are quite different from southern California, which means that most programs for divine healing should probably be different from ours. That is why copying our programs may produce disappointing results. Our principles and values are transferrable—not our programs.

## PERSONNEL

Personnel include people who minister healing (practitioners) and those who train others. Two qualifications must be met by any believers who would practice healing. First, they must have faith for healing. This faith need not be great or perfect; God will use the little that they have, causing it to grow over time. The second qualification is receptivity, an openness to God's healing power.

Notice I did not mention spiritual maturity as a qualification. The spiritual gifts are not given only to mature people; they are given to willing people. In fact, some of the most dramatic healings I have seen came at the hands of new Christians. I do not imply that character is irrelevant to divine healing. The influence of a person's character acts as a multiplying factor in his or her ministry—increasing or decreasing the effects of healing gifts, depending on the practitioner's faithfulness. Still, any Christian—young or old, mature or immature—may be used by God to heal the sick.

Sometimes the spiritual gift of healing is confused with a natural talent for healing. Some people have the ability to encourage and build up others. They have warm temperaments; they are affable and kind toward others. Usually they are sensitive and understanding in such a way that healing, especially healing of broken relationships, seems to flow from them. A warm personality is something the Lord can use in reconciliation and other types of inner healing, but the key element in divine healing is the gift of the Spirit. No single personality type is better than another for practicing divine healing. Practitioners of divine healing may be kind and sensitive, but these natural talents are less important than depending entirely on the gifts of the Spirit, trusting God for healing, and learning how to pray for the sick.

Practitioners of divine healing do not see themselves as the source of healing. The primary source of divine healing is the Holy Spirit and his gifts (1 Cor. 12:11; Heb. 2:4). The recipients of the gifts are the people of God, the body of Christ. When we receive the Holy Spirit, we gain access to all the gifts that we need to advance the kingdom of God (Acts 1:5; 2:4; 11:15–16). The gifts are manifestations of God's grace: "Each one should use whatever gift he has received to serve others, faithfully administering God's grace in its various forms" (1 Pet. 4:10).

There is a difference between possessing the gift of healing and being used by God at a special time and occasion to heal someone. Many people teach that each person has one or two gifts in his or her possession. Christians are encouraged to "discover their gift," with the implication that only a few are called to ministries like divine healing.[1] I believe this teaching—that all Christians possess only one or two gifts and are limited to functioning only in those gifts—is erroneous, for reasons that I discuss below.

In 1 Corinthians 12:4–7 Paul writes about this topic. He says:

There are different kinds of gifts, but the same Spirit. There are different kinds of service, but the same Lord. There are different kinds of working, but the same God works all of them in all men. Now to each one the manifestation of the Spirit is given for the common good.

The Greek word translated "different kinds," *diaireseis*, suggests two dimensions of distribution of the spiritual gifts. There are both a variety of spiritual gifts and a diversity of their assignments in the body of Christ.

A key to interpretation is understanding that the general distribution of the gifts is to the church *corporately*. That is, the gifts are not primarily given to the individual but to the whole body and for the building up of the whole body. This is also a key for understanding the entire section of 1 Corinthians 11:17–14:40, which is perhaps the most definitive teaching on the gifts in the New Testament. Twelve times in this section Paul, by emphasizing the corporate nature and activity of the church, reminds the readers that the spiritual gifts are given *to the body* (11:17, 18, 20, 33, 34; 14:4, 5, 19, 23, 26, 28, 33–34).

Understanding that Paul is speaking of gifts functioning when the body meets resolves what appears to be contradictory advice. For example, in passages like 1 Corinthians 12:30 Paul asks, "Do all speak in tongues?"—implying that all do not. Yet in the next verse he says, "But eagerly desire the greater gifts"—implying the reader should be dissatisfied with only one or two gifts. Later in 1 Corinthians 14:5 Paul says, "I would like every one of you to speak in tongues."

The key is that when the body meets not all should practice the gifts at the same time; that would create chaos. All may at different times experience any of the gifts during general gatherings.

Thus there is a specific distribution of the gifts to individuals that comes on occasions of specific need. That is, the gifts are given in a specific situation for use of the individual for the blessing of others. This means any individual Christian may pray for the sick, but in the congregation he or she should exercise prayer in good order and for the common good.

Most Christians usually exercise one or two gifts—teaching, administration, hospitality, prayer, and so on—but every now and again they exercise a gift they do not usually have. I call that a specific distribution, an anointing for that moment to do a task. In 1 Corinthians 12:7, where Paul says that "the manifestation of the Spirit is given for the common good," the Greek term *phanerōsis*, translated "manifestation," means appearances. That is, the spiritual gifts are appearances of the Spirit, they are the times and ways in which he appears among men and women. The Holy Spirit appears among people, anointing Christians with gifts to meet specific needs. The gifts of healing often come to Christians like that.

Spiritual gifts are given for the common good and in order to glorify God, and they are received in order to be given away. I never speak about "my gift"; instead I talk about the gift God has given me to give away. In fact, through the process of giving away gifts, the gifts are enriched and strengthened.

I remember the first time God gave me the spiritual gift of words of knowledge—facts and information that could only be known supernaturally concerning specific occasions, persons, or things. I could name the secrets of people's hearts. It was an enjoyable gift to have, and since no one else in the church had it, feelings of pride swelled up in me.

Then God told me that I needed to give the gift away; that

is, I needed to lay hands on others and pray that they too receive the gift. I would simply pray, "Lord, please give these persons words of knowledge," and most people received words of knowledge. But Satan began whispering to me, telling me that if I continued to give the gift away I would lose it. So I stopped praying for others to receive the gift, and for the next four months I did not receive one word of knowledge. Finally I went to some friends and asked them to pray for me, and I received words of knowledge again. The next day I realized how the devil had deceived me, and so I redoubled my efforts to pray for others to receive the gift.

Everyone is called to pray for the sick, and a few are given special gifts for it. Some who have the gift are also effective trainers of others to pray for the sick. The gift of healing—and related gifts—develop in individuals according to the following process.

1. *Task.* An analogy may be drawn between praying for the sick and evangelism. Everybody in the body of Christ is called to the task of telling others about the kingdom of God, but some people have the gift of evangelism. Evangelists are very effective: they evangelize with great skill and ability, and they reap bountiful harvests. Some people who are not evangelists are called to do the work of an evangelist, as was true of Timothy (2 Tim. 4:5).

Divine healing works in a similar way: we all are called to the task of praying for the sick, though we acknowledge that there are a few people with special, prolonged anointings for healing (1 Cor. 12:9). For those who do not have an ongoing ministry of healing, there are occasional anointings. This is especially true for parents or church elders, who are given special authority and power to pray for their children and parishioners.

In 1 Corinthians 12:8–9, 11 it says,

To one there is given through the Spirit the message of wisdom, to another the message of knowledge by means of the same Spirit, to another faith by the same Spirit, to another gifts of healing by that one Spirit. . . . All these are the work of one and the same Spirit, and he gives them to each one, just as he determines.

Here is another key to divine healing: God may choose to work through us unexpectedly, even though we do not normally have the healing gift. So we should be open to his anointing us at any time. When faith is exercised and God anoints, divine healing follows.

The Greek noun translated "gifts" (*charismata*) in 1 Corinthians 12:9 has been translated as "gracelets" by Dr. Russell Spittler, professor of theology at Fuller Theological Seminary. "Gracelets" imply occasional manifestations or anointings of gifts for specific purposes and for the good of the congregation. The 1 Corinthians 12:9 passage says that God gives "gifts of healing." In the Greek both "gifts" and "healing" are plural. There are many kinds of illnesses, so there are many healing gracelets.

There are other gracelets besides healing that are commonly used in divine healing. I call one group the gracelets of discernment: a word of wisdom, a word of knowledge, and the discerning of spirits (1 Cor. 12:8, 10). These are gifts of supernatural insights; one "sees" things as God sees them.

A word of wisdom is God revealing his wisdom or insight into a specific situation. Words of wisdom are especially helpful in counseling situations, and they are often given with a Scripture passage.

A word of knowledge is God revealing facts about a situation concerning which the person had no previous knowledge.[2] An example of this is God giving someone exact details of a person's life, to reveal sin, warn and provide safety, reveal thoughts, provide healing, or provide instructions.

The discerning of spirits is the supernatural capacity to judge whether the motivating factor in a person is human, divine, or demonic. It is the supernatural insight into the source of spiritual activity. This last gift is especially important for knowing how to pray accurately for a person's healing.

The gracelets of discernment are experienced through a variety of means:

- Inspirations—floods of thoughts, with specific facts, describing situations;
- Dreams and visions—pictures in the mind's eye; these pictures may include faces, words, situations;
- Impressions—a deep knowing in one's spirit; sometimes a word at the beginning of a sentence triggers a cluster of impressions;
- Scripture verses—passages that trigger insight for a particular situation; and
- Pains in the body—pains or sensations that may correspond to the illness in the person being prayed for.

Another group is called gracelets of power: faith, miracles, and gifts of healing.

The gift of faith is a mysterious surge of confidence in God that arises within a person faced with an insurmountable situation or need. It provides supernatural certainty and assurance that God is about to act through a word or action. The wonderful thing about the gift of faith is that it wells up in me when I least expect it and when I most need it.

Miracles are events in which people and things are visibly and beneficially affected by God's power. The Greek word from which we translate "miracles" is *dunamis*, which means "power." The greatest miracle, that which took the most power, was Christ's resurrection (1 Cor. 15:43–44).

The gracelets of power are experienced in these ways:

- Anointing—a sudden infusion of power, usually felt as a tingling, heat, or a supernatural confidence;
- Detachment—a sensation that something beyond oneself is happening, an awareness of the Holy Spirit's presence and working;

- Words of faith—words that come to people unexpectedly before they say them;
- Dreams and visions—a picture of a miracle or healing may come to one's mind, and then when the circumstance arises, the person prays with boldness; and
- Impressions—these thoughts come as a calm and confident knowing that God will heal or work a miracle; usually I receive these impressions in prayer before I am about to minister.

Sometimes several spiritual gifts work together in healing clusters. The following letter illustrates how a word of knowledge, discernment of spirits, and word of command were instrumental in healing a woman:

June 12, 1986

Dear John:

Here's an account of a sister in our community, Mary [not her real name], who was healed at our healing clinic. During a healing clinic we were having words of knowledge given by different people who were there. One of the women in the community stood up and said that she believed that there was a women with dark hair that had lupus, and that the Lord wanted to heal her. To my surprise one of the women who I knew in the community, with dark hair, stood up and said that she had it. The woman who had received the word of knowledge, Kay, went and prayed with her, along with a few other people. During the time that she prayed over Mary, Kay sensed the Lord tell her that she should tell the "stinking dog" to get out of Mary. At this time, Kay exercised her authority and commanded the "stinking dog" to leave Mary in the name of Jesus. She then saw the image of a wolf slinking down along the aisles of the chairs that were set up nearby, and it left Mary. A few weeks later Mary went to her doctor who had been treating her over the past twelve years for lupus, and to his surprise he found no traces of the lupus. In fact, he couldn't understand it and thought that he had perhaps misdiagnosed the whole thing, based on the fact that there were no traces left in her body. He said it wasn't a matter of remission because there would still be some kind of trace within her. Mary asked if she was healed and he said, "Yeah, you're healed." It was interesting also to find out from Kay that, when she called the disease a "stinking dog" and saw a wolf leaving, she had no idea that lupus is commonly known as the "wolf disease." Well, praise God! . . .

Your brother in Christ,
Dave Nodar
The Lamb of God
Baltimore, Maryland

2. *Ministry.* When divine healing became a regular part of church life in the Vineyard Christian Fellowship, I noticed a few people who over a period of time were especially effective in praying for the sick. They had the gift of healing and, because they were part of a church that regularly prayed for the sick, they had a ministry of healing (see 1 Cor. 12:27–31). Some with a healing ministry were effective in praying for those with physical problems, while others were effective in praying for the demonized or people suffering from the effects of past hurts. For example, C. Peter Wagner (who is a member of another church) is very effective in lengthening legs. Frequently people ask him to pray for their short legs and related back problems. He is almost a hundred percent successful in his prayers.

Some people who have a ministry of healing train others to pray for the sick. The most effective trainers or equippers of the saints are pastors, though not all who are trainers necessarily hold an office in the local church. Recently I went to England and taught about healing. Over three hundred men and women who have a ministry of healing from the United States accompanied me. At the end of each session these "team" members, as I called them, went out into the crowds to pray. Others watched them, learning how to pray from their example. Trainers must be analytical enough to communicate to others a model of divine healing. Of course, they should also be able to pray effectively for the sick, which means having a ministry of healing. This is because the best way for someone to learn how to pray for the sick is by watching another do it. Trainers are also empowered to pass on divine healing to others. Frequently God uses the prayers and laying on of hands of trainers to anoint others for healing. Not everyone is empowered to pray over others and see them anointed for healing.

The most effective way to train people to pray for the sick is through a logical, step-by-step procedure. The method I have developed is the topic of the last two chapters.

# 11. A Healing Procedure: Interview, Diagnosis, and Prayer Selection

Several biblical healing methods can aid Christians in praying for the sick. I developed a procedure through trial and error that I call "five steps to healing prayer." Each element of the five steps is based on Jesus' method of praying for the sick, though in Scripture these steps are not presented in a systematic and chronological fashion. So the application of scriptural truth, not merely the pattern of my personal experience, is the basis for this method.

Each step attempts to answer a question about the sick person's condition: what is the condition? What is its cause? How should I pray for it? When should I stop praying? What should the person do to stay healed? These steps are quite practical and simple to follow. In one conference session most people learn enough to start praying for the sick *immediately*. In other words, this method helps people to know where to start and when to stop in praying for the sick.

The five-step procedure may be used any time and in any place: in hotels, at neighbor's homes, on airplanes, at the office, and, of course, in church gatherings. I have been in casual conversations with people, even with complete strangers, who mention some physical condition, and I ask, "May I pray for you?" Rarely do they decline healing prayer, even if they are not Christians. I then confidently pray for them by following the five-step method.

I usually try to find a quiet and private place to pray for people. This not only protects people from potential embarrassment but also helps them to be more open and honest about their needs, especially when the cause of their condition is serious sin. In large gatherings this means going off to a corner, a separate prayer room, or a private office.

The five steps are:
*Step One:* the interview
*Step Two:* the diagnostic decision
*Step Three:* the prayer selection
*Step Four:* the prayer engagement
*Step Five:* post-prayer directions

In this chapter and the next I describe each of these steps.


## STEP ONE: THE INTERVIEW

The first step in healing prayer is the interview. *The interview answers the question, "Where does it hurt?"* I ask, "What do you want me to pray for?" Then I listen to the answer on two levels: the natural and the supernatural. On a natural level I evaluate the answer in light of my biblical knowledge, what I know about the person, and my past experience in praying for similar problems in other people. This is not a medical interview in which we probe for a technical, medical history. A medical history is important for medical treatments, but not for praying for people's healing. The Holy Spirit is the doctor and the cure; he does not need our technical knowledge to heal. Besides, detailed medical discussions usually only delay healing prayer.


## STEP TWO: THE DIAGNOSTIC DECISION

The second step in the healing procedure is making a diagnostic decision, that is, identifying and clarifying the root of the person's problem. *The diagnostic decision answers the question, "Why does this person have this condition?"* This is a crucial step in the healing procedure, because it determines the type of prayer needed to bring healing.

In fact, this procedure overlaps with the first step. While I am interviewing the person, on a supernatural level I ask God for insight into the ultimate cause of the condition. These insights usually come to me through words of knowledge, words of wisdom, and distinguishing of spirits. Only infrequently do people know the true root of their problem. When they do, the Holy Spirit confirms in my heart that their analysis is correct.

I always have the attitude that it is easier to ask questions than think I must receive words of knowledge. But sometimes God reveals that what the person for whom I am praying thinks his or her need is is not correct.

For example, two years ago Kevin Springer prayed for a woman who had severe back pain. During the interview Jane (not her real name) said that her injury was caused by a physical mishap several years before. But from her response Kevin suspected that something other than physical damage was the source of her back pain. After a short and fruitless time of prayer, Jane turned to return to her seat, discouraged because her back still hurt—this was yet another failed attempt at divine healing for her.

As she turned, Kevin received a specific insight from God into her back problem: that it was related to a poor relationship with her mother. This came to him as a thought: "Her mother. Her mother. There is a problem between Jane and her mother." Because of this insight, he called her back for further prayer.

When the woman returned, Kevin asked her if she were having problems relating to her mother. He said, "Even though you said that you had injured your back in an accident, I believe the Lord is saying that somehow your back problem is also related to a problem that you are having with your mother. What do you think about that?" She confirmed problems that went back to her childhood, though at first she did not make any connection between her back and her mother.

At that point Kevin decided that in fact the healing of Jane's back was related to the healing of her relationship with her mother, and that inner healing was needed before physical healing could happen. After helping her to extend forgiveness to her mother and to receive forgiveness for her sin, Kevin again prayed for her back. This time she was healed instantly. A year later Jane wrote Kevin to confirm that her back remained healed.

Root causes may be quite complex, as Jane's story illustrates. Symptoms in one area of our lives may be caused by problems in several other areas. The following examples illustrate the complex interrelationships among the physical, spiritual, emotional, and social parts of our lives.

Once I was asked to pray for a woman with arthritis. I asked her, "How is your marriage?" She answered, "I am estranged from my husband. Three years ago he left me with six children." I said, "Well, there is a possibility that your feelings about all of that have been buried in resentment and bitterness and that is what is causing this condition. How do you feel about that?" She said, "I don't think so." So I said, "Well, let's just pray about that and see what God does, okay?"

As I began to pray the Holy Spirit came on the woman and penetrated to the deepest part of her heart. She was able to see her bitterness and resentment toward her husband. She forgave him and then received healing prayer for her arthritis. She said she was healed. Several months later she confirmed that she remained healed. In this instance, physical sickness was caused by harboring resentment.

I have also prayed for men and women who are unable to sustain healthy relationships because they have been hurt by a marriage partner. They are incapable of receiving or giving love, even with fellow Christians. This is an example of social problems caused by emotional hurt that came from sin, sin either done by them or against them.

I frequently encounter demons that cause fear and as a result create emotional problems that result in physical problems. An example of this was a woman whose fear—caused by a demon—made her insecure with her husband, which contributed to her problem of feeling like a failure as a wife. These factors in turn caused barrenness. Once the demon was cast out of her life, she was able to love her husband more freely and conceive a child. In this instance, an emotional problem was caused by demonic influence and resulted in a physical problem.

Sometimes I pray for people who, as a result of events surrounding an accident or a serious operation, have suffered from pain or paralysis for years. In some instances there are no longer physical causes for their conditions, although in other instances the physical causes remain.

Accidents and operations affect people emotionally, spiritually, and, of course, physically. These people are vulnerable to suggestions that may become self-fulfilling prophecies, with disastrous effects for their health. Usually around the time of an operation or accident a well-intentioned doctor says, "Your problems are such and such, and you could suffer in such and such a way for the rest of your life." The doctor is convinced the patient cannot get better, which becomes an obstacle to the patient's healing. This happens in two ways.

First, the doctor points out the situation in a way that convinces the patient that he or she will not get better. Doctors need to be candid with their patients; I do not fault them for this. But sometimes their diagnosis results in a word that holds people back from experiencing full health. Doctors wield great authority and influence over their patients; their words have the spiritual power to bless or curse. Folks suffering under these burdens tell me, "The doctor said I probably would never walk again, and that was ten years ago, so it must be true." I tell them, "Well, let's see if Jesus wants to change your condition anyway." I then pray to break the power of the doctor's words.

A second way that doctors may unintentionally create obstacles to healing is by informing patients of their odds for recovery.

They say something like, "Based on statistical studies of cases similar to yours, you have a fifty percent chance that you will again suffer the effects of the disease within one year." This causes people to think of themselves as an impersonal number in a universal game of Russian roulette—not as children of God, living under his grace. In these instances, doctors eliminate God, though they do not tell patients directly that they will not be healed.

So well-intended words from doctors may create formidable obstacles to healing. In many instances the Holy Spirit heals the physical damage only after the power of the doctor's words is broken.

I have prayed for wife beaters who, I discovered through the interview process, were themselves beaten by a father, uncle, or mother. In almost every instance an evil spirit came on them as children. More than once, when I went to cast the evil spirit out of them, the spirit said, "This one is mine! I've had him since he was a young boy." Frequently the men will remember specific boyhood experiences that changed their lives for the worse. (Demons are liars, so they cannot be trusted. But they have said this in so many instances that I believe they probably do gain access to boys and girls who are victims of abuse.) I am not implying that all wife beaters or child abusers are demonized, but I am saying that some are, and there is a relationship between demonization and this type of abusive behavior. In this instance, psychological problems are caused by social conditions and demonic influence.

I could add many other examples to this list, but these are sufficient to illustrate the need to correctly diagnose the cause of a person's condition before actually praying for him or her.

When I first describe the range of causes for illnesses (the list is almost limitless), most people think they are unable to discern these causes. They look at me and say, "It is easy for you. Look at all your experience. It has taken you years to learn how to understand these things." I admit that I have grown in my ability to diagnose these problems over the years, but I have grown mostly in sensitivity to the Holy Spirit's leading and insights, not in an academic understanding of human psychology or medicine. This is not to imply that growing in psychological or medical understanding works against divine healing. The Holy Spirit is the one who leads us through the diagnostic step. He walks with us, accompanying us through the process. But in the end, the burden for healing is on him, not us.

## STEP THREE: THE PRAYER SELECTION

The third step of the healing procedure is prayer selection. *This step answers the question, "What kind of prayer is needed to help this person?"* What lies behind this question is an even more fundamental question: what does God want to do at this particular time for this person? While I assume that God wants to heal, I do not assume that God wants to heal at the exact instant in which I am praying for someone. So I ask, "Lord, do you want to heal right now?"

A secret to healing prayer is that it comes from God having already touched our spirits; it is agreement with God about his will. This is in part what it means to receive an anointing for healing prayer in a specific situation.

An anointing is a knowing in the deepest part of our hearts that God wants to heal someone. "This is the confidence we have in approaching God: *that if we ask anything according to his will, he hears us,*" the apostle John writes. "And if we know that he hears us—whatever we ask—we know that we have what we asked of him" (1 John 5:14–15). The agent of our confidence is the Holy Spirit. He not only comes on us and shows us the will of the Father, but he also comes on the person for whom we are praying and brings healing.

James Robison received the following letter, dated March 17, 1984, from a Texas woman:

Dear Brother James:

For the past few days I have been compelled by the Lord to write and share with you what the Lord did for me at the Bible conference in January. I must be obedient.

Last August, after ten years of marriage and one precious adopted son, the Lord began to renew in me the desire to bear a child. First, he confirmed to me by his word that this was his will in 1 Timothy 5:14. Then the Lord told me to go to my pastor for prayer and his blessing through 1 Samuel 1:17: "Eli answered [Hannah], 'Go in peace, and may the God of Israel grant you what you have asked of him.'"

*At this point, faith began to grow within me, even though several months passed before my faith was answered.*

In January of this year, we went to Dallas for the Bible conference. We were unable to attend every session; in fact, we did not even attend the last two days because of our vacation schedule. We were present, however, when John Wimber ministered the word in healing on Thursday. As he was calling out physical conditions for which the body was to pray, I literally felt the energizing power of God enter my body and I knew I was healed of barrenness, even though Brother Wimber had not called out my condition for prayer.

In the next few days, God graciously gave me evidence of the change which had taken place in my body. The Lord began to fill me afresh with confidence in his promise and in himself. I was able to confess with boldness what God had done and was doing in my life in a way that was totally new to me.

Then, faith became sight. On March 8, 1984, two days before my thirtieth birthday, we learned that I was indeed pregnant for the first time in my life. Needless to say, the "hallelujahs" have not stopped yet, for our God is truly a great God, and only he has the power to create life in a barren womb.

In the Name of Jesus,
Mrs. P

Mrs. P. had heard the Lord speak, so she had confidence for her healing. She simply cooperated in faith with what God said was true about her. But there was more to her story. One week after mailing this letter to James Robison, Mrs. P. began running a fever of between 102 and 105 degrees every day for a week. Her fever was soon joined by excruciating neck and shoulder pain. She was seven weeks pregnant. After she was hospitalized, the doctors diagnosed her as having two viruses, one of which usually caused multiple birth defects, including heart disease, blindness, and microcephaly. She wrote me a letter describing what happened next:

Dear Brother Wimber:

. . . Needless to say, I was devastated. I sought God relentlessly for the next several months, begging him to tell me that my baby was all right. But all he said was, "Do you trust me?" So, I held on to "Though he slay me, yet will I trust him," and my place was in him rather than the assurance of my baby's well-being. (By the way, the Lord said, "no" to all tests, including a routine ultrasound, until I was eight months pregnant.)

Early in October, about three weeks before my due date, the Lord spoke to me during my morning quiet time. By then, I had stopped asking for a "sign" about the baby, so I was surprised when he said, "If you ask me for bread, will I give you a stone?" He confirmed that word through my husband, and from that moment on I knew the baby was fine.

Two weeks later, I began bleeding in the doctor's office during a vaginal exam. The doctor suspected placenta previa, so back to the hospital we went for an emergency ultrasound. Everything was fine in the placenta, however, and my doctor was greatly relieved to learn from the ultrasound that the baby's head size was normal.

Five days later [our baby] was born: nine pounds of health and an astonishment to all the doctors involved.

Praise Him!
Mrs. P.

There are many ways in which we may pray for healing. I have already mentioned several different kinds of prayers used in divine healing—prayers of petition and intercession, words of command, and so on. These different types of healing prayers fall into two categories, petitions directed toward God and words that we receive from God and speak to a condition or demon.

*Prayer directed toward God.* I always ask God about how I should intercede for a sick person. Remember, the key to answered prayer is praying according to God's will. If we believe that he hears us and cares about our needs, we may with confidence approach him and ask how we should pray. Sometimes, even when I have a clear understanding of the cause of a condition, I am not sure about how to pray specifically. In these instances I pray in my mind, "Lord, I know you want to heal this person. Please show me how to pray for him." I then pray quietly in tongues, during which time frequently (though not always) God indicates how he wants me to pray for the person.

Why do I pray in tongues? Praying in tongues for me is like putting up my spiritual antenna: my spiritual receptivity increases. In 1 Corinthians 14:4 it says, "He who speaks in a tongue edifies himself." That describes my experience. As I speak in tongues I edify myself; I build up my faith and spiritual sensitivity.

This practice raises another question: can a person who does not speak in tongues pray effectively for the sick? I do not know why not. Certainly there is no place in Scripture that links effective prayer for the sick with speaking in tongues. Yet, though I acknowledge this, everyone I have met who is effective in healing prayer speaks in tongues.

Usually God directs me to pray for the sick with intercessory prayers. The Latin word from which we get our English word "intercession" is *intercedo*, which means "to go (or pass) between." When we intercede for people's healing, we have a deep concern for them. We stand between them and God, making request for their healing. The most effective intercessory prayers are simple and straightforward: "Lord, please heal Robert of his condition."

Sometimes I ask the persons for whom I am praying to pray for their own healing. I do this for two reasons. First, if they have faith for healing, they may be healed as a result of their own prayers. This is the best kind of healing, because they know that God—not me or any other human—healed them! Second, if they pray without faith (for example, "God, I don't know if you want to heal me, but . . . "), then I know I need to bring instruction about faith and prayer for divine healing. On many occasions Jesus asked people about their faith. He would ask them, "Do you believe that I am able to do this?" He was seeking to elicit from them a response of faith. It pleased him to have them ask for healing. The classic example of this is found in Mark 9:14–32, where Jesus heals a boy with an evil spirit. After Jesus taught the crowd about faith for healing, the boy's father exclaimed, "I do believe; help me overcome my unbelief!" (v. 24). Jesus then cast out the demon.

*Words from God.* Sometimes I sense God telling me to speak a word of command when praying for divine healing. The words—usually a very short sentence—come out before I consciously form them. Words of command come with a burst of faith. I feel the confidence and power of God rise in my heart and release it through my speech. Typically I will lay hands near the afflicted area and say, "I break the power of this condition in the name of Jesus," or, "Stop it!" These prayers are very short and very effective.

I do not understand how the word of command works, but I can describe what my experience has been. In some instances I speak directly to evil spirits, commanding them to leave. In other instances I seem to be speaking to the condition itself. My hands usually tingle and are warm, and I feel something like electricity come out of them when I speak a word of command. I have come to associate feelings like tingling and heat with an anointing of the Holy Spirit on me for healing. Other examples of sensations associated with an anointing for healing include pain or heat in my body in an area that corresponds to where the person I am praying for hurts. When I pray for the person my pain disappears.

Recently I received a letter from two Swedes in which they described their experiences with words of command:

> We have experienced visions functioning in divine healing. We now sometimes see [spiritually] where in a person's body the sickness is located. At other times we see a dark shadow outside of the body at the spot of the sickness. We sometimes are seeing insects, or larger animals like birds of prey, crocodiles, snakes, etc., being located either inside or outside of the body. . . . After having prayed [a word of command] we sometimes see a kind of light over the person . . . just as the evil animal has disappeared. Several times we have seen something like a bright hand touching the sick spot.

Despite my lack of clarity about what actually takes place through a word of command, it is certainly biblical, for Jesus frequently healed through it.

The word of pronouncement is similar to a word of command, only instead of speaking to the condition I announce that a healing is done. With a word of command there is a buildup of power and sensations of tingling and heat accompanied by a sense of encounter; with the word of pronouncement there is an accompanying feeling of supernatural peace, a sense that the battle is over. I usually say, "The Lord has healed you," then offer some follow-up instructions to help ensure the person maintains his or her healing.

Occasionally a word of pronouncement is linked with a prophetic insight. In these instances I suddenly know that the condition will be healed not at that time but sometime in the near future, say, within six days. I tell the person, "I sense that your condition will be healed completely within six days." I then pray that God will fulfill his word.

A third type of authoritative word involves what Scripture calls a prayer of rebuke in which demons are cast out or their power is broken. In a prayer of rebuke we break demons' hold on a person, contain their power, and eliminate their presence.

Rebuking an evil spirit is similar to a word of command. In Mark 9:25, it says; "When Jesus saw that a crowd was running to the scene, he rebuked the evil spirit. 'You deaf and mute spirit,' he said, 'I command you, come out of him and never enter him again.'" Here the simple command is directed toward the evil spirit. I usually say, "In the name of Jesus, I rebuke you, evil spirit. You have no part in Jane's life."

Prayers of agreement are quite effective. In Matthew 18:19–20, Jesus taught, "I tell you that if two of you on earth agree about anything you ask for, it will be done for you by my Father in heaven. For where two or three come together in my name, there am I with them." The key phrase in this passage is "where two or three come together *in my name*." The prayer of agreement has been improperly interpreted as meaning we may agree on anything and it will be done. Instead, it is agreement and belief with other Christians about what the Father has already determined his will to be (see John 5:19). In other words, it is watching for what the Father is doing, then believing him to fulfill it. Another aspect of the prayer of agreement is agreeing with others to actually do what he directs.

The prayer selection is a critical step in the healing procedure. But even if we are not confident about the correct way to pray when we begin, when we actually pray the Holy Spirit frequently confirms or gives new direction. That is what makes the next step, the prayer engagement, the most complex and exciting part of divine healing.

# 12. A Healing Procedure: Prayer Engagement, Phenomena, and Post-Prayer Direction

## STEP FOUR: THE PRAYER ENGAGEMENT

The fourth step of the healing procedure is prayer engagement. *This step answers the question, "How effective are our prayers?"* The prayer engagement consists of prayer, laying on of hands, and, when needed, further interviewing. The way we pray is determined by our diagnostic decision and prayer selection. This step, the most complex in the healing procedure, requires most of this chapter to describe.

I usually lay hands on people when I pray for them. When someone suffers from a physical affliction I try to put my hand near the location of their hurt or suffering. (In the case of a woman with a more intimate malady like breast cancer or an ovarian cyst, I ask her husband or another woman to place his or her hands near the area in need; I then place my hands on theirs. Or, if I am alone with a woman, I ask her to cross her hands over the afflicted area and I place my hands on hers. It is important to treat people with respect so they may maintain their dignity.)

People have asked me about why many Vineyard Christian Fellowship healing team members extend their hands without actually touching the person they are praying for. My answer is that sometimes circumstances create strange customs, and here is the history of this one.

The Anaheim Vineyard Christian Fellowship met in a high-school gymnasium without air conditioning until 1983. During the summers (and on occasion, the winters), temperatures outside were in the 90s, even rising above 100 degrees Fahrenheit; inside the packed gymnasium it was warmer. Under these hot and sticky conditions, only one member of the team would touch the person who needed healing prayer, while other team members put their hands close without actually touching. In 1983 we moved into a building with central air-conditioning, but I noticed people continued putting their hands close without touching when praying for others' healing! People from other denominations and other parts of the world who have attended our healing seminars have also picked up this way of praying.

I do not think there is anything wrong with praying with extended hands not touching the person, especially if one team member does lay hands on the sick person. Still, it is humorous that thousands of people all over the world have learned to pray this way just because years ago we met in a hot and humid gymnasium.

After laying on hands, I pray aloud that the Holy Spirit come and minister to the person. My prayers are quite simple: "Holy Spirit, I invite you to come on this person and release your healing power," or "Holy Spirit, come and show us how to pray," or, more succinctly, "Holy Spirit, come."

People respond to the power of the Holy Spirit in ways that are not always predictable. These "manifestations," or phenomena that occur among people in response to God's power and truth, vary in form: falling over, shaking, sobbing, laughing, screaming out—the list of unusual emotional and physical phenomena is quite long. Some of these phenomena represent horror and aversion to personal sin or sin done against the person. Other manifestations—extreme to be sure—are demonic; they are power encounters in the person between the kingdom of God (the Holy Spirit) and the kingdom of Satan (evil spirits). In many instances people are experiencing the joy and grace of God in a new way and their emotions reflect this newfound peace in relationship with God.

These sorts of spiritual phenomena have frequently been associated with revivals, and they have always raised questions in some Christians' minds. During the Great Awakening of 1726–56, men like Jonathan Edwards, John Wesley, and George Whitefield all witnessed manifestations of excessive emotional and unusual physical states in people for whom they prayed, and these leaders also suffered criticism from other Christians for it.

Sometimes the critics came too close to God's action and suffered the consequences. John Wesley described the bewilderment of an indignant Quaker in his journal entry dated May 1, 1769:

A Quaker, who stood by, was not a little displeased at the dissimulation of these creatures, and was biting his lips and knitting his brows, when he dropped down as thunderstruck. The agony he was in was even terrible to behold. We besought God not to lay folly to his charge. And he soon lifted up his head and cried aloud, "Now I know thou art a prophet of the Lord."[1]

Nonetheless, these responses raise many questions in the minds of sincerely inquiring people. Are the manifestations required in order to get healed? Or, are these responses merely psychologically induced? Could these responses be coming from evil spirits? Don't some people react this way to attract attention to themselves?

I do not question the fact that Satan can and does counterfeit genuine Christian experience, and that psychological suggestion can change people's behavior. Jonathan Edwards acknowledges this possibility: "But as the influences of the true Spirit abounded, so counterfeits did also abound: the devil was abundant in mimicking, both the ordinary and the extraordinary influences of the Spirit."[2] Yet I have seen too many people who had no prior knowledge or experience of these phenomena begin to shake, cry, or fall over when the power of the Holy Spirit came on them. Later they claimed it was one of the most significant and encouraging experiences of their lives!

There were no explanations for their unusual responses other than that God's power or truth touched them. Of course, I have also seen groups where the expected behavior of the ones being prayed for was that they fall over. This was nothing more than learned behavior, religion at its worst.

Perhaps the reason for concern lies behind a misunderstanding about how God works, specifically the idea that emotional and physical reactions, especially where people appear to lose self-control, are contrary to peace and good order. This is an old complaint: commenting on the eighteenth-century New England revival, Jonathan Edwards says, "Some object to it as great confusion, when there is a number together . . . making a noise; and say, God cannot be the author of it, because he is the God of order, not of confusion."[3]

My response to this concern is that Jesus *is* the God of peace and order, but the process of gaining that sometimes means disorder. C. S. Lewis, in his *Chronicles of Narnia*, alludes to this characteristic of God when describing his imaginary Christ figure: "Aslan is not a tame lion." God, Lewis seems to say, is neither predictable nor controllable.

I am not claiming that these physical manifestations are a necessary means or necessary accompaniment of the Holy Spirit's action. Rather I am saying that often they do in fact accompany what the Holy Spirit is doing. However, it should not be surprising that such physical phenomena accompany the healing of deep inner turmoil, reception of forgiveness for grievous sin, and the remembrance of painful experiences. Divine healing involves a process of profound and fundamental change in people. Is it not reasonable that physical reactions should accompany these changes? If our culture were less restrained than it is, these sorts of phenomena would draw far less attention and concern. In fact, this appears to be the case in many Third World countries.

Also notice that these physical phenomena accompany profound healings or spiritual renewals; they are not normally associated with healthy Christians' every day lives. People who have these manifestations and continue in the power of the Holy Spirit should not expect to experience more and more bizarre forms of behavior. The purpose of healing is to produce healthy people who can live life wholly for God.

When I travel I am frequently asked if the weekly meetings of the Anaheim Vineyard Christian Fellowship are a cacophony of bizarre physical manifestations of the Holy Spirit. My answer is "No, though there is some of this from time to time, as we have visitors in need of healing." In fact, far more physical manifestations occur at healing seminars because many of the people are there because they are in need of healing.

Scripture is full of examples of people who, in response to the power of the Holy Spirit, fall over, shake, act drunk, and laugh or sob. I list below the more common types of manifestations and indicate where similar responses are found in Scripture.[4]

*Shaking and trembling,* which may or may not be associated with fear. This may be of varying severity and involve only a part (for example, an arm or leg) or the whole body. Perspiration, deeper breathing, and an increased pulse rate may accompany it. Commonly it is a gentle trembling associated with a quiet sense of joy and peace, and as such it differs from the type of hyperventilation associated with anxiety. But trembling can also be a shaking of extreme violence. I have seen people thrown to the floor and their shaking continue for several hours; they may then have periodic episodes of shaking for days afterwards. The more peaceful type of shaking is usually associated with the empowering of the Holy Spirit for renewal and ministry. The more violent shaking is sometimes the Holy Spirit encountering an evil spirit or unearthing some serious, unrepented sin or hurt.

Scriptural examples of trembling and shaking are numerous. Trembling frequently accompanied the fear of God (Gen. 42:28; Exod. 19:16; Ezra 9:4; Pss. 2:11; 119:120). The prophets usually trembled when they came into God's presence (Isa. 66:5; Jer.

5:22; 23:9; Dan. 10:10–11). In the New Testament, trembling was a common phenomenon (Matt. 28:4; Mark 5:33; Luke 8:47; Acts 7:32; 16:29; 1 Cor. 2:3; 2 Cor. 7:15; Phil. 2:12; Heb. 12:21).

*Falling over* (or "being slain in the Spirit," as it is referred to by Pentecostals). Church history and contemporary experience contain many examples of people falling over and lying supine or prone for several hours. Most people are aware of a sense of calm and feel a sublime indifference to their circumstances. Commonly, no aftereffects are noted, either good or bad. Occasionally this state continues for twelve to forty-eight hours, in which case profound spiritual changes have been said to follow.

The most dramatic falls are those sustained by pastors and ministers, some of whom appear to be thrown by the Spirit on their faces, left prone, and sometimes seen to bang their heads rhythmically on the ground for an hour or so. (Curiously no physical damage or headaches seem to follow the head banging.) The changes following this experience may also be profound. Their ministry is infused with new power and effectiveness.

I received the following letter from a Friends pastor in Idaho in August 1984:

Dear Pastor John,

I have wanted to write to you concerning the Signs and Wonders conference. I found the conference to be the most significant experience of my Christian life apart from my initial acceptance of Christ.

Monday night of the conference I received the gift of tongues [and] was slain in the Spirit (an experience which I had dismissed as theologically impossible). . . . Tuesday and Wednesday proved to be as much, if not more, of a blessing. Thursday was a day of reckoning as God dealt with me. In a vision that was at first terrifying and depressing, God showed me the fruits of my labor as a church planting pastor. As I had operated almost entirely in the energy of my soul, the picture was very bleak. The fact that I had no previous experience of the working of the Spirit was a very lame excuse to the Lord. God, in his mercy, showed me in the same vision what could happen. . . . [He then describes the vision.]

I spent most of Thursday in desolation. I wept harder than I ever have, was terribly depressed (a totally alien response to my personality), and despaired for my life. That night, the Lord tested my faith. Would I worship him in spite of my condition? I did, and as we sang the words, "Oh Lord, have mercy on me, and heal me," our loving Father did just that. Praise his beautiful name! As I lay on the floor weeping, this time with joy, he healed me of some longstanding emotional and spiritual disfigurements.

All day Friday was a powerful day of anointing as God began to use me. The joy of my salvation returned and the visions of ministry here in northern Idaho came. . . .

Since coming home, God has proven himself strong, and our body has undergone a radical transformation. Gifts, blessings, anointings, and ministries are multiplying. We have also been greatly humbled and there has been an incredible amount of repentance, forgiveness and healing of relationships. . . .

Had you not been willing to spell faith "r-i-s-k" I would be herding a flock of dead sheep. Operating in this realm hasn't been easy, nor is it always fun, but it is beautiful and it is right and I praise God I'm part of it.

God's fullest blessings upon you,
Pastor K.T.

On the other hand, far from trying to produce falling, I encourage people who feel like they are going to fall over to sit down, because I want to talk with them during the prayer time. Falling over in itself is of no value if not accompanied by a deeper understanding of God's holiness and grace.

Scriptural examples of people falling over under the power of God include Daniel (twice—Dan. 8:17, 10:8–9), Paul at his conversion (Acts 9:4), the soldiers at Jesus' arrest (John 18:6), the guards at the tomb (Matt. 28:4), and John on the island of Patmos (Rev. 1:17). Twice when Ezekiel saw the glory of God he fell on his face (Ezek. 1:28, 3:23). There are also instances of people being thrown to the ground by demons when they came into the presence of Christ (Mark 9:20).

*Drunkenness.* Often a state of mind and body resembling intoxication occurs. People may be euphoric, usually following a new appreciation of God's grace, a new sense of the wonder of his pardon. They feel "heavy," may not be able to rise, need assistance in walking, or else they are uncoordinated in their gait, stumbling awkwardly, and slurred in their speech. Paul's words contrasting drunkenness with being filled with the Spirit may have more significance than might at first appear (Eph. 5:18). Usually such a state is associated with a fresh allegiance to the Lord. Scriptural examples of "drunkenness" with the Holy Spirit include Hannah (1 Sam. 1:12–17) and Pentecost (Acts 2:13, 15).

Fr. John Bertolucci, a powerful Catholic evangelist from the University of Steubenville, Steubenville, Ohio, told my coauthor a remarkable story of praying for a young man at the latter's ordination. Actually, the story began a day earlier:

On a Sunday in March of 1985 I attended a meeting in which Doug Gavrilides, a lay evangelist who ministers mostly in Central and South America, explained how the Holy Spirit had come on him when John Wimber prayed over him. I had known Doug for many years, and it was obvious to me that his life had been radically affected; God's power and anointing were on him in a new way. What I found interesting about what he said was that John had prayed, "May the Holy Spirit and the kingdom of God come on you and consume you." In Catholic teaching, the prayers "May the Holy Spirit come and purify us" and "Thy Kingdom come" are used interchangeably. I was touched by what Doug said, but even more moved by the power of God that was in his life.

The next day I attended a Day of Recollection at a seminary. I spent the day with students and faculty, and, coming off of my experience with Doug, I felt the presence of God on me in a special way. The day culminated in the ordination of a deacon. The local bishop presided over the liturgy. I had preached the homily at the service, and was participating with other priests in the ordination. The liturgy called for the candidate to lie prostrate in the middle of the assembly, with those present praying the litany of the saints, which is petition for global intercession. While we were praying I harkened back to Doug's sharing the previous day and felt God was telling me to pray for the candidate. In the Catholic tradition we feel silent prayers without touching a person can be effective. That was the only appropriate way for me to pray at that time. So I fixed my gaze on him and prayed, "Lord, let your kingdom come on him." To my amazement he began shaking! This was quite unusual in an ordination setting.

Later, following a celebration dinner, the young deacon asked to speak with me. He said that while he was lying prostrate on the floor he had one of the most profound spiritual experiences of his life. He said that for years he had suffered from migraine headaches—they were so serious that his superiors had considered withholding ordination until they were healed. Because of the excitement and anticipation of the ordination, he was suffering from headaches. But during the litany of the saints, something remarkable happened. He said, "I felt a tremendous power come over me. Then something left me, followed by something coming into me. I felt drunk through the rest of the service. And all of my migraine symptoms left me. I was healed! I feel better than I have ever felt in my life."

Several weeks later Doug Gavrilides and Fr. Michael Scanlan returned from a John Wimber healing seminar to the Holy Spirit Monastery in Steubenville (I am a member of this monastery). On a Saturday night they told 12 or 13 of us about how the Holy Spirit had worked in healing and renewing people during the seminar. So our Superior asked them, "Well, why don't you pray for us?" When they invited the Holy Spirit to come, one brother immediately broke into laughter, and soon we were all laughing. Then I came under what I can describe only as the glory of God—I was knocked to the floor and felt drunk. When I tried to stand up, I couldn't. I cried out, "Lord, I'm an intelligent man, but I can't get up!" Since this happened to me I have experienced a greater awareness of God's presence and a new anointing of his power.

*Bodily writhing and distortions.* These come in many forms, including jumping up and down (I call this "pogo-sticking"), contracting arms and hands and making them clawlike, contorting the face, stiffening the body, and so on. I believe that some of these movements indicate conflict over a particular sin, sometimes a sexual sin. Violent convulsing movements, especially when associated with hissing, indicate demonization. Scriptural examples include the demonized man in the Capernaum synagogue (Mark 1:21–26), the healing of a boy with an evil spirit (Mark 9:26), and the Gerasene demoniac (Luke 8:28).

*Laughing and sobbing.* Some people erupt into giggling and laughter, which may continue for hours and episodically for days. Sobbing comes the same way—I know of one man, Blaine Cook, who sobbed episodically for three months. Usually laughter and sobbing indicate the need for emotional healing. In some instances they are the emotional response to experiencing God's holiness (sobbing) or grace (laughter) in a new way.

Scriptural examples of laughing and sobbing include Abraham (Gen. 17:17), Sarah (Gen. 21:6), and Israel's weeping at Ezra's reading of the Law (Neh. 8:9). Proverbs 14:13 says, "Even in laughter the heart may ache. . . . "

*Prolonged and exhuberant expressions of praise.* Many times people will begin praising God and not stop for hours. Their personal prayer practices are altered for the better. In many instances this is associated with receiving the gift of tongues and indicates a fresh anointing with the power of the Holy Spirit.

I would need several pages to list all of the scriptural examples of prolonged praise. Instead, I will only list a few of the New Testament examples: the Magnificat (Luke 1:46–55), Zechariah's song (Luke 1:64, 68–79), the healed paralytic (Luke 5:25), the Samaritan healed of leprosy (Luke 17:15), and the crippled beggar (Acts 3:8–10).

I expect skepticism regarding such extreme emotional and physical responses, even from Christians. But for those who experience God's healing power, these experiences are life-changing.

Tom Rabaut, from Ann Arbor, Michigan, describes how his skepticism was overcome during one of my healing conferences:

When I started hearing about the new ways in which the Holy Spirit is working among us, I was very skeptical. My attitude was, "Why do we have to have such an emphasis on physical manifestations?" I also suspected that those people who were responding in a physical way to the presence of the Holy Spirit (by trembling or falling or laughing, for example) were people who were predisposed to being somewhat weird. So I wasn't very enthusiastic when I walked into the arena where the healing conference was to be held. "I really don't want to be here," I told my wife. I own a business and considered myself too busy to sit and listen to talks for three days.

As soon as the conference began though, my heart was being moved; I was seeing attitudes I needed to change, sins I needed to repent of. In one of the first sessions, I began to tremble as I experienced the presence of God, and then I started shaking and sobbing. At that point, everyone who was experiencing an anointing was asked to come up front so that the whole assembly could see many different types of physical manifestations. That's the last thing in the world I wanted to do! Yet I knew that, for me, stepping forward would be an important step, a sign that I wanted to "let go and let God." So I joined the group of "weird" people up front and stood there shaking for half an hour.

"Oh, that was easy for you, Tom," someone said to me later. "You've been in the community drama group and are accustomed to audiences." Well, I *am* confident on stage, but only when I have control. Letting God take over and deal with me while six-thousand people look on isn't something I'm predisposed to!

Yet I didn't care about that, because what God was doing with me was a true renewal and revitalization. He was reaching deep, deep down and healing wounds from past experiences. He was loving me—regardless of who I was, what I had done, where I came from. In a way I don't fully understand, that physical manifestation opened me up to a whole new dimension of God's love. I was so refreshed by the conference that I wouldn't leave the arena each day till it was time to go home to bed—not even for meals. I was spending my time praying with other people and getting prayed with. And as I did that, God seemed to be infusing in me his heart for wounded individuals.

Because of what God did with me at the conference, I've become more spiritually aware of the wounds that others have experienced and have tried to minister God's love to them, as God ministered it to me. I've fallen in love with the Lord and with his word in a way I'd never experienced before. Sometimes while I go about my business, doing the most ordinary tasks, I have to stop and wipe away the tears: what I'm experiencing is God's tender mercy.

Perhaps there are many of us who are skeptical, like I was. But I think that God means to "zap" all of us. And once we let God take over, we'll never be the same![5]

These phenomena are obvious, but other phenomena of the Holy Spirit are more subtle. Often the Holy Spirit comes on people and they do not recognize it. They might experience slight trembling, fluttering of the eyelids, deep breathing, or faint perspiring, much like slight nervousness or the result of too much coffee. Sometimes they feel a weight on their chest or a "heaviness" in the air. Usually this indicates the presence of the Holy Spirit, the first signs of his coming to minister. I have learned to recognize these traits and ask the people if they are experiencing them. If they are feeling these things, I encourage them to open their hearts more fully to God. And I ask the Holy Spirit to continue to pour his life out on the person. I pray, "More of your power, Lord. More!"

One final caveat: the work of the Holy Spirit is more internal than external, more concerned with heart attitudes than outer actions. In many instances when I pray for someone *nothing* external appears to happen to them, and yet the healing power of God is at work in them.

This was brought home to me recently when I heard of an Episcopal priest from the Midwest United States who invited the Holy Spirit to come on his congregation during a Eucharist liturgy. (From a fellow priest he had heard wonderful stories of God's shaking people at the core of their beings, resulting in many healings and renewal.) So he explained the healing power of God to the people, then asked that God pour out his Spirit.

He waited—five minutes, ten minutes—and the congregation sat stony-faced and impassive. He was embarrassed and felt foolish. Finally he finished the liturgy and released the people. He could not leave the church fast enough.

But something had happened. Over the next two months people streamed into his office telling him of God's work in their lives. Some were healed, many more renewed. Eventually he tried inviting the Holy Spirit again, this time with dramatic manifestations—people fell over, shook, and were healed. But who is to say that this was any more significant than the first time he prayed?

Several conclusions may be drawn from this brief survey. First, we should not be surprised by how the Holy Spirit manifests himself to people. Second, unusual emotional and physical phenomena are common in Scripture, church history, and today. Third, these experiences do not ensure healing; healing is an internal work of the Holy Spirit. Finally, we do not pray over people for these experiences; we pray for God's power to come and heal them.

I have described in detail many of the physical manifestations of the Holy Spirit to help people recognize the presence and power of the Holy Spirit when we pray for healing. Why? Because when we recognize God's healing power is on the person for whom we are praying, we are able to bless his presence and pray for more power. This is a fundamental principle for effective healing prayer: honor what the Lord is doing, and usually he will do more.

Also, when we recognize the Holy Spirit is on people, we can help them to understand and cooperate with his work in their lives. Some people do not realize that God may manifest himself in these ways, so they become passive or frightened, unable to receive their healing. When I am unsure about what the Holy Spirit is doing I ask questions. "Do you feel anything now? A warmth or tingling?" "Is God speaking to you?" Some people have so little faith for healing that even when the Holy Spirit manifests himself powerfully, they do not believe that he is healing. I encourage them not to be afraid and to open their hearts to God and receive his healing power. I pray for a while, then talk with them, then pray again. Usually this goes on for over an hour, in some instances even longer.

Many people are insensitive to their own bodies. They fail to understand that certain phenomena are caused by the Holy Spirit.

Several years ago I talked about divine healing with a group of about ten theology students from Germany. When we had finished our discussion they expressed serious doubts about everything I had said. So I suggested that we try an experiment: we would invite the Holy Spirit to come right then and minister healing and renewal. They chuckled and said, "Sure, why not?" Much to their surprise, most of them experienced the power of God.

During the prayer time I could tell that the Holy Spirit was particularly strong on one young man who was tall and stood erect. I asked him, "Do you feel anything?" He answered, "No, nothing." So I said, "That's strange, because I believe the Holy Spirit is on you. Why don't you sit down?" He answered, "I can't sit down. I can't move. I don't feel anything, and I can't move." He was confused about what was going on—he believed that God does not work that way. I continued to pray for him, stopping occasionally to explain what God was doing. As he understood what the Holy Spirit was doing, he opened his heart fully to God's power and was healed of inner hurts.

Taking time to ask questions during the prayer engagement step may also indicate the root cause is different from what was initially thought. For example, it is not unusual to determine during the diagnostic step that a person needs inner healing, then during the prayer engagement discover they also need deliverance from an evil spirit.

As I wrote in Part II, there are four areas that divine healing may be applied to: the spirit, the effects of past hurts, the body, and demonization. Each of these requires a different application of healing prayer. (Below I describe in greater detail the prayer engagement—the fourth—step for each of these areas.) It is important to note that most people have problems in at least two of them. For example, sometimes I start praying for people's past hurts, which opens up the need to pray for a physical problem, and then suddenly, I discover a demon! I used to think, "How complex can this get?" Then the Lord reminded me that human beings *are* complex—after all, we have been made in God's image—but the Holy Spirit is capable of sorting out all of our problems.

*The spirit.* Most spiritual problems are caused by unconfessed sin and unbelief. When the need for healing of the spirit is diagnosed I take the following steps.

First, I ask the persons to agree with God about their sin. I ask, "Do you agree that this is sin? Do you agree that you need to deal with it before God? Will you pray and tell God that? I will agree with you about it." If the individuals do not know how to pray, I help them. If they are unwilling to pray, I talk with them about what sin is and how it kills people. (If they still refuse to pray, I tell them that I have nothing to offer them.)

Then I help the persons experience God's forgiveness through the ministry of proclaiming them forgiven. I base this practice on authority given in John 20:23: "If you forgive anyone his sins, they are forgiven; if you do not forgive them, they are not forgiven." I say, "In the name of Jesus Christ I forgive your sins." When I pray this prayer I also ask the Holy Spirit to apply his forgiveness to the deepest part of their hearts: "Lord, help this person to receive the experience of forgiveness." Then I stand back and pray for them quietly. Only the Holy Spirit can apply forgiveness at the deepest level of their beings, where they have been held captive to guilt and shame. This experience, described by many as an overwhelming sense of forgiveness, is usually associated with what looks like ripples of energy and heat coming over their bodies.

After this I ask them, "How do you feel?" My goal is that they acknowledge their forgiveness and confirm and secure God's victory. After this I pray again, giving thanks to God for setting the captives free. In some cases, such as with stealing or some other form of personal harm against another, restitution or apology is called for. For this I give specific counsel and emphasize their need to talk with their pastor about any further actions that may be required.

I also teach them about the process of renewing their forgiveness, in which forgiveness penetrates to a deeper level of their lives. Satan will attempt to rob them of their newly experienced forgiveness by sending feelings of unforgiveness that they may mistake for actual unforgiveness. They will be tempted to once again take on the guilt of their sin, especially if they have not fully accepted Christ's forgiveness. I tell them, "When those feelings come it is like a bird coming to roost. Just shrug it off in the name of Jesus. It doesn't belong to you. Over a period of time your emotional reactions will conform to Christ's truth."

*The effects of past hurts.* People who suffer from the effects of bad memories, either from personal sin or being sinned against, need to receive and extend God's forgiveness and receive God's healing power to free them from bondage to their past hurts. Most people need help to understand how their past hurts affect them. The following, a composite sketch taken from several similar incidents, is a typical interaction with a man who as a child was abused by his mother and now suffers from cancer:

I ask, "How do you feel about your mother now? I think that a natural feeling would be bitterness and anger."

He responds, "I don't feel that way because I am a Christian."

Now I am sure that this is the root of his emotional and spiritual problems, so I say, "Are you sure? I sense that you do feel that way, though you cannot describe these feelings very well." On rare occasions I get tough and say, "You are lying to yourself when you say you don't feel that way. You are angry toward your mother for what she did, and that is why you are sick."

"How do you know that I am angry toward my mother?"

"You are still hurting every time the subject comes up. If you were free there would be no pain. But the pain is still there, so let's get rid of it."

My goal in confronting him is to get him to acknowledge and be willing to deal with his anger and bitterness. My second goal is for him to be released from bondage to his anger and bitterness. I do this by getting him to forgive his mother.

Extending forgiveness to those who have sinned against us is difficult for many people, because they also have been unforgiving toward God for allowing the circumstances in the first place. Typically a person asks, "Why did Jesus let that happen to me? Why did he put me in such a horrible family?"

After waiting a while for his anger to subside, I say, "I want you to understand that the hurt happened to Jesus when it happened to you. He was there with you, so he knows the pain." Most people do not realize that Jesus is a victim too, that at the cross he suffered every sinful deed that has ever been committed.

"Oh, you mean he was with me, and he felt bad about it too?"

"Yes," I say, "so let's give it up to God. Let's let him wash you free from the contamination of this sin—both that you committed and that was committed against you—so you'll never have to feel hurt about it again." Then I lead him through a prayer in which he extends forgiveness to his mother and repents and receives forgiveness for his own sinful attitudes.

Sometimes when I invite the Holy Spirit on the persons, they remember things that happened years before and that they had forgotten. In some instances the hurt involved in these memories contributes to bizarre phenomena. (I remember praying for one man who as a boy had been deeply hurt by his father. When I invited the Holy Spirit to come and minister to him, he was thrown to the ground and started howling like a dog. His pain was palpable.) As these kinds of painful memories arise, I encourage the persons to understand that Jesus was with them through it all and that now they may extend forgiveness. In other words, I reinterpret their experience in the light of God's purpose.

In many instances I have to take authority over problems that have been passed on to children from their parents. Exodus 20:5 says, "I, the Lord your God, am a jealous God, punishing the children for the sin of the fathers to the third and fourth generation of those who hate me, but showing love to a thousand generations of those who love me and keep my commandments" (see also Exod. 34:7). Alcoholism is a good example of this type of problem. Children of alcoholics have a seventy percent chance of becoming alcoholics themselves. When I encounter adult children of alcoholics (even if they are not practicing alcoholics), I pray to break the power of influence of alcoholism that comes from being raised in an alcoholic home. I say, "I break the power of alcoholism in the name of Jesus, and I release you from the sins of your parents." That is a powerful prayer. Through it I have seen people who struggled with alcoholism and other compulsions like pornography and homosexuality freed from their bondage.

For those who suffered from compulsive sexual sin that had its roots in the sins of their parents, I speak healing to that area. For example, if a person has struggled with a sexual sin, I say, "Lord, I ask that you bring healing and wholeness to this person's genital organs. Cleanse the organs with the power of your blood." On several occasions they reported later that almost all remembrance of or desire for that sin was wiped away, and their sexual orientation became right and appropriate.

Some people are in bondage to certain sins because they have practiced them for so long. They are out of control and compulsive, doing the very things that they hate. Usually they do not understand why they commit them and are frustrated and depressed about their lack of self-control. For example, I have prayed for many men and women who cannot resist getting involved in affairs, even though they know they are wrong, self-destructive, and destructive to others.

I believe God has given us the power to break these bondages. In Matthew 16:19 Jesus told the disciples, "I will give you the keys of the kingdom of heaven; whatever you bind on earth will be bound in heaven, and whatever you loose on earth will be loosed in heaven." This authority that Christ has given us is not authority to determine, but to announce, guilt or innocence. That is what I do, announce God's truth, when

I pray over someone who is held captive to the desire to commit fornication or adultery.

The principle of dedicating parts of the body to the Lord also applies to breaking bondages. Sometimes a residue of the effects of a person's wrongdoing remains in the parts of his or her body that were used in the service of evil. This residue must be dealt with for complete healing. I have seen people who had been promiscuous have their sexual organs prayed over, that they might be cleansed and set aside for holiness. While we prayed their bodies flinched and trembled, as though the Holy Spirit was cleansing them. The result was complete freedom from past sins and a joy and confidence about their sexuality.

Occasionally I must break emotional ties people have with other people. For example, former lovers frequently exert emotional influence in people's lives for years after the affairs have ended. I have also observed people who once were involved in cult groups or under abusive leaders struggle for years with fear and anger. In many of these cases they are released from their fear and anger when I break the soul tie with their former partner, group, or leader.

*The body.* I always lay hands on or near the afflicted area of the body as I pray. The prayers, as I have already noted, may vary greatly: intercession, words of command, words of pronouncement, even getting the person himself or herself to pray.

Frequently I speak to the condition itself. For example, several years ago I prayed for a young woman with a scoliosis of the spine. She was wearing a T-shirt, so when I looked at her back I could see that it was severely deformed, with a two-inch variance from the middle to the top. I stood behind her and spoke to the spine: "In the name of Jesus, I command you to straighten." Then I went up the spine, placing my hand on each vertebra and watching them move back in place. I said, "That one, Lord, straighten that one!" and another vertebra would move. As I prayed the woman felt heat all over her body (she began to perspire), and she experienced what she later described as a state of ecstacy. She looked drunk. By the end of our prayer time, her back had only a half-inch variance.

I watch closely for manifestations of the Holy Spirit on the person for whom I am praying. For this reason I do not close my eyes when I pray. When I see the different types of spiritual phenomena I described early in this chapter, I point out to the person what I see, and I ask him or her about what is being experienced. "How are you feeling? What is going on?" Occasionally I will see nothing happening, but when I ask if they are experiencing anything they say, "Yes. I have never experienced God in this way before." Then I find out they have been healed.

In some cases I offer an explanation for what is happening to them. Once I was praying for someone and nothing appeared to be happening. The man looked strained. So I asked him, "What is wrong?" He said, "My head irritates me. It is tingling over the top." We had been praying for his stomach, yet his head was tingling. I thought, "Lord, you blew it. You sent healing to the wrong place." But then I decided, "Well, Lord, if that is what you are doing, I will bless it." So I laid hands on his head and began blessing God for his healing work, and the man's stomach was healed.

*Demonization.* Of all the different types of healing, prayer for the demonized is best done in a private setting. It may require hours of prayer and several follow-up sessions to cast demons out of severely demonized people.

Prayer for the severely demonized is best accomplished in teams of two to five people. There should be a clearly defined leader; the others should lend prayer support and provide some counsel. I usually place people to either side of the demonized person and tell them to pray. On occasion I have asked someone to record what happens, to write down the demons' functions and relationships so that we have a basis for later evaluating whether all the demons are gone or not. If the session goes on for a long time, I find it helpful to change the team members' positions to keep their concentration sharp.

Frequently Christians misdiagnose psychological disorders as severe demonization. I never call anything a demon until I have actually talked with it. I use several criteria to assess whether I am talking with a demon. For example, demonized persons undergo major personality changes when the demon speaks through them (Mark 5:1–5). Their eyes also indicate the presence of a demon. They may roll back and flutter, or the whole pupil may disappear so that all I can see is the white part of the eyes. Sometimes the eyes operate independently of one another or become very still and covered by what appears to be a film. They may also dilate to such an extent that all I can see is the pupil.

Other common physical manifestations suggest the presence of a demon. I have seen nostrils flair, lips purse, teeth appear to grow (though they were not actually growing), the throat enlarge, and the body puff up. I have seen persons fall to the floor and slither and hiss like snakes. I have heard all kinds of animal noises—barking, bellowing, roaring. I have witnessed people excreting foul-smelling fluids out of openings in their bodies. Many of these manifestations happen only in the severely demonized, but when they happen there is no question about the presence of a demon.

When I know that I am dealing with a demon, I command its attention by looking straight into the demonized person's eyes and saying, "Look at me!" I then command the demons to tell me their names (see Mark 9:25). I say, "In the name of Jesus, I command you, spirit, tell me your name."

Evil spirits do not want to tell their names, because sometimes their names reveal what they do to people. They will say, "Why do I have to tell you my name?" or, "I don't want to tell you my name," or, "I don't have a name." They will say anything to avoid telling who they are. When they begin speaking like this, I say, "Stop that! Now, tell me your name."

A special word of caution is in order here: I only command demons to identify themselves when a person is out of control, when it seems obvious to me that an evil spirit is speaking through the person I am praying for. At no time do I encourage the person I am praying for to give up control to the evil spirit.

When they do tell me a name, it is usually in a language that I cannot understand. For example, recently one told me its name was Kimutu. I then asked, "What does it mean?" Again, it resisted but finally said, "Pain." This made sense; I was praying for a man who had pain in his neck and head. I immediately commanded the demon to leave: "In the name of Jesus, I command you to leave this person." The man was healed.

Sometimes I ask a demon for more details about what it does. For example, if one says that its name is "Fear," I might ask, "What do you make this person afraid of?" When I ask the person later if that particular fear was a problem, usually he or she says that it is one of the biggest obstacles to living a full Christian life.

Demons enjoy talking to distract me from casting them out. My response is always the same: I silence them (Mark 1:34). Sometimes they try to bargain with me, saying, "Let's do such and such." I respond, "Be silent. I don't bargain. You must go!" They may be very religious, very "spiritual." For example, they may prophesy, speak in tongues, even quote Scripture. They will argue, sometimes quite persuasively. They will pretend not to be demons. Sometimes they shriek to draw attention to themselves. Again, in all these instances I silence them and cast them out.

In most instances, the demonized persons are not aware they have demons until I pray with them. Then they appear to become frightened, and the demons threaten them. "When I get you away from here," the demons say, "I am going to kill you." When I suspect this is happening, I silence the demon and then gain the attention of the person for whom I am praying. When I am sure that I am talking with the person and not the demon, I explain that they have nothing to fear because Christ is stronger than any demon. I then ask them, to the best of their ability, to cooperate with Jesus in the casting out of the demon.

The expulsion of demons is a form of power encounter in which the kingdom of Satan is driven out by the kingdom of God.[6] It is never easy. It is a test of faith that requires concentration, perseverance, and God's anointing. The expulsion comes through commanding the demon to go: "I command you in the name of Jesus to come out." But saying these words does not automatically ensure that the demon will leave. Jesus indicated that some demons are more difficult to expel than others (Mark 9:29). They require greater faith and prayer.

The evil spirit's leaving is frequently accompanied by some reaction in the severely demonized person: falling down, crying out, moaning, deep exhaling, foul odors—all of which are then followed by an unusual peace (Mark 9:26). But demons have many hiding tactics to lead me to believe they have left when they haven't. For example, just because someone is thrown to the ground and shrieks when I command a spirit to leave does not mean the spirit has left. I usually get down on my knees and look into the person's eyes, then say, "If there is a spirit in there, I command you to manifest."

Another method for identifying evil spirits is to pray for various parts of the body, asking that the Holy Spirit consecrate them (see Rom. 12:1-2). I pray, "In the name of Jesus I consecrate the feet, ankles, [and so on, through the entire body] to the Lord. I consecrate these parts according to Romans 12:1-2." Sometimes I will get to a certain part of the body and the person will react in some way. For example, his or her eyes may open and roll back. When this happens I stop what I am doing and begin the process of demon expulsion again: identify, silence, and cast out.

Occasionally I encounter an obstinate demon, one that will not respond to my commands. For these I have found it helpful to step back and say, "Jesus, here is a demon of hell that is standing against you and your church. You take care of it." Then shrieking will usually follow, for they are afraid of Jesus and the Holy Spirit.

After I expulse demons my goal is to see the person be fully restored so the demons will not return (Matt. 9:25; see also

12:43–45). Only Jesus can fill a void created by the departing spirits, so I interview the person to make sure that he or she has a sincere relationship with Christ. If the individual does not, I preach the gospel and then invite him or her to pray with me to receive Christ. In most instances I must lead persons in prayers in which they renounce the occult or some other form of spiritualistic involvement. In many instances inner healing and the giving up of sin will also be called for. Then I pray that the Holy Spirit will come and fill them completely.

Instances of mild demonization are far more common than those of severe demonization—and far easier to pray for. By "mildly demonized" I mean people who are prone to periodic attack from evil spirits in certain areas of their lives, like sexual temptations or temptations to steal or lie. Usually I ask if they have problems in these areas, and if they say that they do I will cast the demon away with a simple word of command: "In the name of Jesus, I command you evil spirit to leave." Then I minister to the need for forgiveness, repentance, and filling of the Holy Spirit.

Because divine healing is a process, knowing when to stop praying is very important. When I first began praying for the sick, I thought that in each session I should pray for someone until he or she was healed. In some instances the sessions went on for hours, and even then the person was rarely healed. I soon began to ask the question, "When should I stop praying?"

I use several criteria for knowing when to end the time of prayer in Step Four. The most common way is when the Holy Spirit indicates that it is over, usually by withdrawing his power. I see that the person for whom I am praying is not responding to my prayers and I notice the senses associated with healing prayer that I experience—tingling in the hands, warmth, a supernatural peace—are withdrawn. Sometimes the persons who are being prayed for indicate that the prayer time is over, that they have received what they came for. Also, when I cannot think of anything else to pray for or when I have prayed for everything and it seems that I have not gained any ground, I stop. In this last instance, I encourage the person to come back at a later time for more prayer.

## STEP FIVE

The last step in the healing procedure is the post-prayer directions. *The post-prayer directions answer the questions, "What should this person do to remain healed?" and "What should this person do if he or she was not healed?"* When people are not healed I reassure them that God loves them and encourage them to seek more prayer. Usually this means directing them to a prayer team or kinship group in which they may receive longer-term prayer.

I instruct those who are healed to sin no more and no longer follow the ways of the flesh (see John 8:11). This involves a variety of practical advice, determined by the problem, that includes advice about Scripture reading and study, prayer, and works of righteousness. The key to maintaining these spiritual disciplines and living free of sin, though, is living within the context of overall pastoral care. The preparation, ministry, and follow-up necessary for divine healing can take place only where there is sufficient commitment, responsibility, and accountability among Christians. This means involvement in a church congregation and usually involvement in some form of small group in which relationships of support and challenge nurture faith and righteousness.

# Epilogue

One of the Protestant Reformation's key contributions to the church was a recovery of the centrality of the Bible in the Christian life. The Reformers perceived the need for objective criteria to judge all matters of faith and practice, and they looked to the Old and New Testaments to fill that need. They also taught that all Christians are called to submit their faith and practice directly to Scripture. In recent years Roman Catholics too have discovered a new appreciation for personal Scripture study, acknowledging that the power of God is released through his word.

I believe that if the Old and New Testaments are going to be a source of constant reforming power in the church, the doctrine and practice of divine healing must be brought into contact with the Scriptures. That was a fundamental presupposition in this book, an approach, I pray, that has increased your understanding and practice of healing.

If we are serious about the Reformation doctrine—an idea found in Scripture—that the church reformed is always reforming, we must make room for growth in practices like divine healing in the modern church. Divine healing was undeniably a part of Christ's ministry and something that he expected the church to experience. So though we may never fully understand divine healing, nevertheless we must actually pray for the sick.

There remain many unanswered or unanswerable questions regarding divine healing. Why don't we always experience healing when we pray for it? Why are some people healed and others, especially good people, not healed? Why are some people only partially healed? Why has divine healing alternately diminished and peaked throughout the history of the church? Will we ever definitely answer whether God allows sickness? What is the relationship between sickness and sanctification? Why are some people more effective than others at praying for the sick? I have offered answers to all of these questions, though I acknowledge that at best they are only partial explanations. Much more could and should be written about these topics by men and women more qualified than myself.

But I do not believe we need *exhaustive* answers to these questions and others like them to start praying for the sick now. The key word in this sentence is "exhaustive," for faith without any understanding of its object and content is worthless. Yet I am convinced that sometimes Christians' demands for exhaustive knowledge are excuses for not believing in and acting on what they do know. I do not mean to imply that the questions are unimportant, nor that it is wrong to add knowledge to our faith. But even now, while acknowledging that I will never exhaustively understand divine healing, I am satisfied to act on what I know now, confident that I will know more fully in the future. To paraphrase Blaise Pascal, "I believe, therefore I will know . . . eventually."

My prayer for you, readers, is that with regard to divine healing you be content with "see[ing] but a poor reflection as in a mirror" and with "know[ing] in part," because the day will come when you "shall know fully" (1 Cor. 13:12). Because of the fullness of the kingdom of God that is coming, we may confidently live with the portion that we have now.

# Appendix A: Glossary of Terms

**animism:** the belief that all objects in the material world are inhabited by souls or spirits.

**bondage:** subjection or slavery to some sort of compulsion, restriction, or restraint in a certain area of life. In Christ we have the power to break the power of that bondage and set the person free. The roots of these bondages may be spiritual, psychological, or physical.

**deliverance:** setting a person free from a bondage, usually from demonic influence.

**demonization:** to be influenced, afflicted, or tormented in some way by demonic power.

**discerning of spirits:** a supernatural capacity to judge whether the motivating factor in a person is human, divine, or demonic (1 Cor. 12:10).

**divine healing:** healing by direct intervention of the one and only true God, the living and personal God revealed in Scripture and in particular in Jesus Christ.

**exorcism:** prayer for deliverance from evil spirits.

**expulsion:** the casting out and driving away of demons.

**faith healing:** healing that is attributed to a person's faith, not Jesus.

**gift of faith:** a mysterious surge of confidence in God that arises within a person faced with an insurmountable situation or need. It gives that person a certainty and assurance that

God is about to act through a word or action (1 Cor. 12:9; 13:2).

**gracelets:** occasional manifestations or anointings of gifts for specific purposes and for the good of the congregation.

**holistic medicine:** a secular healing movement influenced by Eastern religions and the occult that is at odds with historic Christianity (*see also* "New Age Movement").

**inherited demons:** demons that are passed from parents to children.

**inner healing:** a process in which the Holy Spirit brings forgiveness of sins and emotional renewal to people suffering from damaged minds, wills, and emotions.

**interpretation of tongues:** the God-given ability to interpret tongues spoken in an assembly, making the message intelligable to those present (1 Cor. 12:10).

**kinds of tongues:** spirit-inspired speaking (*glossolalia*) in which the conscious mind plays no part. It is speaking in a language (whether earthly or angelic) that is not learned by the speaker (1 Cor. 12:10, 28).

**miracle healing:** any healing that is supernatural, which may include healings by God, Satan, and demons.

**miracles:** events in which people and things are visibly and beneficially affected by God's power working through an individual (1 Cor. 12:10, 19).

**New Age movement:** a large and diverse group of organizations, religious groups, publications, and individuals influenced by Eastern religious thought and the occult, and who in turn are influencing Western culture and many Christians. Most members of the New Age movement believe in monism (the idea that all is one), pantheism (the idea that all is god), enlightenment (the idea that humans must realize that they are god), syncretism (the idea that all religions are one), and cosmic evolution (the idea that this age is heading toward a "new age" of consciousness and unity).

**point of contact:** the doing of some act, such as touching something, which quickens and releases faith, causing healing to take place. The phrase was popularized by Oral Roberts.

**prayer of rebuke:** a prayer in which demons are cast out or their power is broken (Mark 9:25).

**prayer of agreement:** a prayer in which two or more people discern God's will and in faith act on it. A prayer of agreement is not arbitrarily agreeing on something and expecting God to do it automatically.

**prophecy:** declaring the heartthrob of God to his church for the purpose of edification. It is not a skill, aptitude, or talent. It is the actual speaking forth of words given by the Spirit of God (1 Cor. 12:10, 28; Rom. 12:6).

**psychiatric:** relating to emotional, mental, or behavioral disorders.

**psychic:** that part of man that is sensitive to spiritual or supernatural forces, either of God or the devil.

**supernatural healing:** a scientifically inexplicable miracle that may be divine healing but also may have its source in Satan or demons.

**word of command:** a powerful and effective prayer in which the speaker commands, in a short sentence, an evil spirit or disease to leave a person.

**word of knowledge:** a spiritual gift through which God reveals facts about a situation for which a person had no previous knowledge (1 Cor. 12:8).

**word of pronouncement:** a powerful and effective prayer in which the speaker announces a healing is complete or will be complete at some time in the near future.

**word of wisdom:** a spiritual gift through which God reveals his wisdom or insight into a specific situation (1 Cor. 12:8).

**worldview:** a set of presuppositions or assumptions that we hold consciously or subconsciously about the basic makeup of the world and that powerfully affects how we understand and relate to the world.

# Appendix B: Healing Those in Hospitals

Hospitals are perhaps the most difficult places in which to pray for healing. I believe the reason for this is that hospitals, though committed to healing, are often under the authority of those who may oppose divine healing (see Rom. 13:1–7). Physicians, of course, are committed to a scientific approach to healing, which can be influenced by materialism and rationalism. This orientation, intentionally and unintentionally, mitigates against the practice of divine healing. So we must learn to honor their authority while not giving up our authority to heal.

I pray for the sick in hospitals in the same way I pray for them in other settings. But to deal effectively with the unique hospital environment, special personal preparation is required. I liken this preparation to putting on the proper uniform and equipment of a soldier. Here is a summary of the preparation I always go through at home:

1. I read Scripture and remind myself of who Jesus is and what he has done. He is the mighty God, able to heal (Isa. 9:6). He is the compassionate God, willing to heal (Mark 1:41). He gave his life to make us whole (1 Pet. 2:24). He conquered evil and is now reigning over all authorities and powers (Eph. 1:20–23).

2. I read Scripture and remind myself of who I am in Christ. I am God's child and servant (1 John 3:1). I am righteous and worthy in Christ (2 Cor. 5:21). I am seated with Christ in heavenly places (Eph. 2:4–6). I am God's co-worker (2 Cor. 6:1).

3. I read Scripture and remind myself of my authority and mission to heal. I have been sent just as Jesus was sent (John 20:21). I have been commissioned to heal (Matt. 10:7–9). I have been empowered to heal (Acts 1:8).

4. I empty myself of natural considerations, fears, presumptions, and preoccupations. I can do nothing in myself (John 5:19–20; 15:5). If anyone is healed in the hospital it is because Jesus does it. I ask God what he wants to do and where I fit into his plans.

When I arrive at the hospital I follow my normal, five-step procedure for divine healing. However, there are certain aspects of that procedure that require particular emphasis. I usually do the following:

1. I invite the Holy Spirit for guidance and discernment when I first arrive in the hospital room.

2. I am especially careful to look for a healing environment. I ask myself, "What is the atmosphere in here like? Full of death? Suspicion? Fear? Despair?" On several occasions I have had to ask people to leave, usually relatives who have no faith for healing. I rebuke any evil spirits that I sense might be present, which has a dramatic affect on the room's atmosphere. Also, people are quite susceptible to the influence of evil spirits during times of serious illness. As a result I am sensitive to the possibility of their need for deliverance.

3. I concentrate on what God is telling me to do, not on the patient's condition. Just the sight of a very ill person—the physical deterioration, machines, needles, and hospital personnel—can dampen my faith. When I concentrate on the patient, I can become overwhelmed by the idea of the impossibility of healing. But when my attention is given to God, I am confident that he can heal.

4. I ask God to help me to show a special love for the patient. I especially try to touch the person, to communicate to him or her God's love and my love through holding hands or touching a shoulder.

5. I read Scripture aloud, which releases faith for healing in the patient and in me.

6. I pray aloud, asking for God's mercy and faith for healing. And I encourage the patient to pray aloud with me.

# Appendix C: Healing in the Old Testament

**GENESIS**
20:17

**EXODUS**
4:6–7
15:26
21:18–19
23:25

**LEVITICUS**
13:1–46
14:1–32
15:1–33
16:29–30

**NUMBERS**
12:1–15
16:41–50
21:4–9

**DEUTERONOMY**
7:15
32:39

**JOSHUA**
5:8

**1 SAMUEL**
6:3
16:14–23
25:6

**1 KINGS**
13:4–6
17:17–24

**2 KINGS**
2:19–22
4:8–37
5:1–14
13:21
20:1–11

**2 CHRONICLES**
7:14
20:9
28:15
30:20
32:24–26

**JOB**
5:18

**PSALMS**
6:2
30:2
32:3–5
34:19–20
38:3, 7
41:4
55:18
103:1–5
107:17–20
147:3

**PROVERBS**
3:8
4:22
12:18
13:17
15:4, 30
16:24

**ECCLESIASTES**
3:3

**ISAIAH**
6:10
19:22
30:26
32:3–4
33:24
35:5–6
38:1–8, 16
53:5
57:18–19
58:6–8
61:1

**JEREMIAH**
3:22
8:15, 22
14:19
17:14
30:12–17
33:6
46:11
51:8–9

**LAMENTATIONS**
2:13

**EZEKIEL**
30:21
34:4, 16
47:12

**DANIEL**
4:34, 36

**HOSEA**
5:13
6:1
7:1
11:3
14:4

**NAHUM**
3:19

**ZECHARIAH**
11:16

**MALACHI**
4:2

# Appendix D

## AN OVERVIEW OF THE HEALING MINISTRY OF JESUS

| # | DESCRIPTION | MATT. | MARK | LUKE | JOHN | |
|---|---|---|---|---|---|---|
| 1. | Man with un-clean spirit | | 1:23–25 | 4:33–35 | | A B |
| 2. | Peter's mother-in-law | 8:14–15 | 1:30–31 | 4:38–39 | | B C D |
| 3. | Multitudes | 8:16–17 | 1:32–34 | 4:40–41 | | A B C E |
| 4. | Many demons | | 1:39 | | | A F |
| 5. | Leper | 8:2–4 | 1:40–42 | 5:12–13 | | B C G H |
| 6. | Paralytic | 9:2–7 | 2:3–5 | 5:17–25 | | B E |
| 7. | Man with with-ered hand | 12:9–13 | 3:1–5 | 6:6–10 | | B G |
| 8. | Multitudes | 12:15–16 | 3:10–11 | | | A |
| 9. | Gerasenes demoniac | 8:28–32 | 5:1–13 | 8:26–33 | | A B |
| 10. | Jairus's daughter | 9:18–19; 23–25 | 5:22–24; 35–43 | 8:41–42; 49–56 | | B C E |
| 11. | Woman with is-sue of blood | 9:20–22 | 5:25–34 | 8:43–48 | | G I |
| 12. | A few sick people | 13:58 | 6:5–6 | | | C |
| 13. | Multitudes | 14:34–36 | 6:55–56 | | | E I |
| 14. | Syro-phoehnician's daughter | 15:22–28 | 7:24–30 | | | A D E |
| 15. | Deaf and dumb man | | 7:32–35 | | | B C D |
| 16. | Blind man | | 8:22–26 | | | B C D |
| 17. | Child with evil spirit | 17:14–18 | 9:14–27 | 9:38–43 | | A B C E |
| 18. | Blind Bartimaeus | 20:30–34 | 10:46–52 | 18:35–43 | | B C G H |
| 19. | Centurion's servant | 8:5–13 | | 7:2–10 | | D E |
| 20. | Two blind men | 9:27–30 | | | | B C G |
| 21. | Dumb demoniac | 9:32–33 | | | | A |

| # | DESCRIPTION | MATT. | MARK | LUKE | JOHN | |
|---|---|---|---|---|---|---|
| 22. | Blind & dumb demoniac | 12:22 | | 11:14 | | A |
| 23. | Multitudes | 4:23 | | 6:17–19 | | F J |
| 24. | Multitudes | 9:35 | | | | F J |
| 25. | Multitudes | 11:4–5 | | 7:21 | | F J |
| 26. | Multitudes | 14:14 | | 9:11 | 6:2 | H |
| 27. | Great multitudes | 15:30 | | | | F J |
| 28. | Great multitudes | 19:2 | | | | |
| 29. | Blind & lame in Temple | 21:14 | | | | |
| 30. | Widow's son | | | 7:11–15 | | B H |
| 31. | Mary Magdalene & others | | | 8:2 | | A |
| 32. | Crippled woman | | | 13:10–13 | | B C |
| 33. | Man with dropsy | | | 14:1–4 | | C |
| 34. | Ten lepers | | | 17:11–19 | | B F G |
| 35. | Servant's ear | | | 22:49–51 | | B |
| 36. | Multitudes | | 5:15 | | | |
| 37. | Various persons | | | 13:32 | | A |
| 38. | Nobleman's son | | | | 4:46–53 | B E |
| 39. | Invalid | | | | 5:2–9 | B G |
| 40. | Man born blind | | | | 9:1–7 | B C |
| 41. | Lazarus | | | | 11:1–44 | B |

A. Drove out demons
B. Word spoken
C. Touched by Jesus
D. Prayer of another
E. Faith of another

F. Preaching of Jesus
G. The person's faith
H. Jesus moved by compassion
I. Person touches Jesus
J. Teaching of Jesus

# Appendix E

## THE HEALING MINISTRY OF THE DISCIPLES

| Description | Matthew | Mark | Luke | Acts |
|---|---|---|---|---|
| 1. Jesus' Ministry Described | 11:2–6 | | 7:18–23 | |
| 2. The Twelve Sent | 10:1–11:1 | 3:13–19 | 9:1–11 | |
| 3. The Seventy-two Sent | | | 10:1–24 | |
| 4. Disciples Attempt to Cast Out Demons | 17:14–21 | 9:14–29 | 9:37–45 | |
| 5. Power to Bind & Loose | 16:13–20 | | | |
| 6. Great Commission | 28:16–20 | 16:14–20 | 24:44–53 | 1:1–11 |
| 7. Jesus Ministry Described | | | | 2:22 |
| 8. Signs & Wonders at Apostles' Hands | | | | 2:42–47 |
| 9. Healing of Lame Beggar | | | | 3:1–4:22 |
| 10. Prayer for Confidence & Healing Signs | | | | 4:23–31 |
| 11. Signs & Wonders at Apostles' Hands | | | | 5:12–16 |
| 12. Ministry of Stephen | | | | 6:8–15 |
| 13. Ministry of Philip | | | | 8:4–13 |
| 14. Ananias and Saul | | | | 9:10–19 |
| 15. Peter Heals Aeneas (Lydda) | | | | 9:32–35 |
| 16. Peter Heals Dorcas (Joppa) | | | | 9:36–43 |
| 17. The Ministry of Jesus | | | | 10:34–41 |
| 18. Magician Struck Blind by Paul | | | | 13:4–12 |
| 19. Paul & Barnabas in Iconium | | | | 14:1–7 |
| 20. Lame Man at Lystra | | | | 14:8–18 |
| 21. Paul Raised at Lystra | | | | 14:19–20 |
| 22. Slave Girl at Philippi | | | | 16:16–40 |
| 23. Paul at Ephesus | | | | 19:8–20 |
| 24. Eutychus Raised from the Dead | | | | 20:7–12 |
| 25. Paul Recalls Ananias | | | | 22:12–21 |
| 26. Paul on Malta | | | | 28:1–10 |
| 27. Galatians 3:5 | | | | |
| 28. Hebrews 2:4 | | | | |

# Appendix F

## Signs and Wonders in Sheffield: A Social Anthropologist's Analysis of Words of Knowledge, Manifestations of the Spirit, and the Effectiveness of Divine Healing

By Dr. David C. Lewis Religious Experience Research Project, Nottingham University, Alister Hardy Research Centre, Oxford

There is a woman here whose name begins with L. . . . She is thirty-two years old, has had a throat condition for eight years, and has taken medicine for it but it hasn't helped her.

There is a woman with a grumbling appendix, and I don't know if she knows it or not but she is pregnant too!

There is a young man here, about thirty-five years old, with a lot of problems in his marriage. He lives in the Midlands. He has been thinking this week about leaving his wife but the Lord wants you to stay and be reconciled with your problems. Do not leave your wife.

The above are just three examples, each spoken by a different person, among the literally dozens of so-called words of knowledge uttered at a conference on Signs and Wonders and Church Growth held at Sheffield City Hall, October 28–31, 1985. Over twenty-eight hundred participants packed the building each day, most of them Anglicans. Most of the others were from nonconformist denominations, but it is also likely that there were Roman Catholics, as there were at a similar conference in London in 1984.[1] John Wimber, the principal speaker, stressed the need for breaking down such divisions and each delegate was given on registration a book on healing written by Francis MacNutt.[2] Whatever their denomination, the delegates came to learn through practical training how to develop for themselves healing ministries in their own churches.

As a social anthropologist, I tried to study what was going on at this conference by using the standard anthropological techniques of participant observation and in-depth interviews. Normally anthropologists study a small community over a long period of time, but in this case I had a large crowd to study for only a few days. Between sessions I would talk to those around me about their experiences, under the circumstances a very natural topic of conversation. My informants were therefore normally without some of the inhibitions that sometimes interfere with "formal" interviews when the informant knows the answers will be recorded; most of my informants were unaware of my purpose in asking such questions until later in the conversation. Attempting to make sense of such reports and of my own observations of what was going on demands a consideration of theories from anthropology, sociology, psychology, and even parapsychology as well as the theological explanations given by the informants themselves. How to fit these different models of explanation together became a far greater task than I had at first anticipated.

## Words of Knowledge

The words of knowledge mentioned above pose one of the more difficult problems for rational explanation. There was no way in which most of the medical conditions mentioned could have been ascertained in advance. Delegates to the conference came from all over the country and when registering for it had supplied details only of their names and addresses. About equal proportions of men and women attended and the age spread also seemed representative of the adult population in general. While there was an overrepresentation of professional clergy, the majority of delegates were lay people who had specially taken time off work to attend the conference. Most were white and middle-class, probably reflecting the composition of the churches interested in the conference: until the last twenty or thirty years the phenomena seen at this conference were confined largely to black and working-class Pentecostal churches, but through this conference (and similar ones during the previous two weeks in Brighton and London as well as one in London in 1984) some of the mainline denominations had also begun to develop healing ministries using these words of knowledge.

The conferences represent a further development in what has been called the "charismatic renewal" in such denominations. The late Canon David Watson of St. Michael-le-Belfry church in York was one of the Anglican leaders of this renewal movement. It was his friendship with John Wimber that eventually led to these conferences being held in England. Wimber was the principal speaker at the conference but an Anglican bishop, David Pytches (formerly the bishop of an Anglican diocese in South America and at present minister of St. Andrew's church in Chorleywood, Hertfordshire) led one of the afternoon workshops each day. Both Wimber and Pytches had brought with them teams of assistants who had already gone through training in these ministries. During most sessions the assistants were the ones who prayed with those who asked for healing in response to a word of knowledge, while Wimber remained at the front giving a commentary on what was happening.

The words of knowledge in themselves generated faith and an expectancy of healing on the part of both the "healers" and the "healed." If, as they believe, God has given a word of knowledge about a person's condition, then they can expect God to heal that condition, whatever it might be. Their model is that of Jesus himself, who said, "The Son . . . can do only what he sees his Father doing" (John 5:19); therefore if the Father has given a word of knowledge they see that as evidence of "what the Father is doing." A further extension of their theology is that Jesus taught his disciples how to heal the sick, cast out demons, and so on; therefore if the church today is the "body of Christ" then Christians today ought to be able to do the same.

The question then arises whether these words of knowledge, healings, and other related phenomena can be explained by means of an alternative, nontheistic model. An obvious hypothesis is that the words of knowledge come from some form of ESP such as telepathy or clairvoyance. Some of them are reminiscent of messages given at spiritualist meetings in which a medium or clairvoyant says there is someone present with such-and-such an illness, perhaps on occasion indicating the general area of the room in which the person is sitting. The methods by which the knowledge is said to come are similar too: they include phenomena such as mental pictures, very strong impressions—"one just knows without a shadow of doubt"—and experiencing a pain in one's own body one knows "is not really one's own pain" (but which identified the location of the other's pain). Relatively rarely one "sees" words (invisible to others) written out over a person's body or in the air. According to Blaine Cook, one of Wimber's assistants, the words can even in his experience involve medical terms like "Osgood-Slatter's disease," a term previously unknown to him, his career having been in the local civil service, not in medicine. However, there are also several important differences between what I observed at Sheffield and the reports of spiritualist meetings.

The first of these differences involves the level of specificity of some of the words of knowledge (as illustrated by the first quotation at the beginning of this appendix), which seems to exceed the level of specificity of most apparently similar phenomena reported from elsewhere.[5] Sometimes at Sheffield it seemed as if supplementary words of knowledge came if the person did not identify himself or herself right away, as illustrated by the following series from John Wimber:

Someone with cracked ribs—fell last winter on snow or ice and the ribs haven't healed properly. The left foot slipped. It hurts right through the left side...[Pause]. It was February this year, on slushy, icy stuff—hit hard on the ground . . . [Longer pause]. Your name is George.

A second area of difference from what has been reported from spiritualist meetings concerns the possibilities of fraud. It is known that many spiritualist healers go around a regular circuit of meetings and so are likely to build up knowledge about the regular congregation in each place.[4] However, the very fact that Wimber and his team had come from the United States and had no control over those who would apply to attend the conferences after reading about them in popular Christian magazines lends a greater credence to the authenticity of their claims.

Compared also with the practices of mediums or psychics who are consulted on a one-to-one basis, there is the absence of any use of personal objects like necklaces as so-called inductors through which the medium seeks to ascertain knowledge about another person. Claims by Wimber and his colleagues that these words of knowledge operate also at an individual level—not only in large meetings—are less easy to check up on because of the very nature of the situation. Moreover, the words of knowledge themselves are not predictable in terms of when or how they might come, so it is impossible to provide an experimental situation for testing the one-to-one words of knowledge. (Even in the large meetings their numbers can vary considerably.) Being unable to observe such one-to-one encounters for myself, I can only refer to accounts such as one described in Wimber's book *Power Evangelism*. In it he describes how he saw the word "adultery" on the forehead of a fellow passenger in an airplane, followed by a revelation of the name of the man's mistress. When Wimber asked this stranger if that name meant anything to him and explained that God was the one who had revealed this information, the man rapidly broke down in sobs of remorse which culminated in his conversion.[5]

## Statistical Probability

These same facts also make it difficult to attribute these words of knowledge to statistical probability. Certainly if the one-to-one cases can be verified (as they presumably could by independent corroboration from the man in question and those who knew him), then we are dealing with a completely different level of probability than that which mentions a common ailment among a crowd of almost three thousand people. While there were many such "generalized" words of knowledge uttered at Sheffield, particularly by those who were trying out for the first time a word they thought they had received, some of the more specific ones are very difficult to dismiss in terms of probability theories.

The woman whose name began with "L" exemplifies this well. I was able to interview her the next day in person. Her name is Linda. Linda said that as soon as Wimber began to speak—even though he was not too sure of the name—she felt God speaking to her in her heart that it was her. As the other details were given, she became convinced of it and went down from the balcony where she had been sitting to the stage at the front. Hers was also the only case I came across in which the word of knowledge was not one hundred percent accurate, in that she will not be thirty-two until April this year. (Wimber also admitted in public his uncertainty about her name, thinking it was something like "Lorma" or "Lerman" but being certain that it began with "L.") In Linda's case we can estimate that if there were about 1500 women present at the conference and if there are about 20 common initials of women's names (excluding initials like X, Z, or Q) then about 75 women might have been expected to fit the first two specifications. If most of those present were aged between twenty and sixty—but Wimber did have a discrepancy of one year (or a few months) in this detail—then we could allow 13 age brackets of three years each, allowing for an error of one year on either side. This brings us down to about six possible women. It is difficult to estimate the total "universe" of possible organs, especially as left and right sides may be specified or details such as "fifth cervical disc" and so on may be included. Doctors or those with medical training might be able to list hundreds of different parts of the body, but for the present purposes let us take a very conservative figure and assume there are only 30 principal organs or parts. Even with a choice of only 30 bodily areas, we are down to 0.2 people who would fit these criteria by chance alone. Then there is the detail of "eight years," which is considerably longer than the average length of time for a throat illness to persist in a woman of this age. If we take an arbitrary figure of one in 50 throat conditions lasting as long as eight years then we find that on the basis of chance alone 0.004 people in this crowd might be expected to have such a combination of traits. In other words, even by using very conservative figures such as a choice of only 30 organs in the body, the crowd would have to have been 250 times larger than it actually was for just one person to have had such a combination of characteristics through chance alone.

The fact that for virtually all the words of knowledge someone present was willing to be identified as having the illness mentioned shows that the words themselves were regarded as accurate, at least subjectively. There is still a difference between a person who considers himself or herself to have arthritis and the person whose arthritic condition is diagnosed as such by a medical doctor, although those whom I interviewed about claimed healings were all those who had received medical diagnoses previously.

One case in which I had prior evidence of a condition involved a nurse whom I had interviewed in a different context the previous week. A question about her attitudes toward children had led her to tell me that she had endometriosis (tumors in her uterus), which had prevented conception, a personal detail this couple had confided to only one other person in their church. Owing to their work, she and her husband had to take turns to go to Sheffield on different days, but the wife was present for an afternoon workshop on physical healing when Blaine Cook had a word of knowledge about endometriosis—using the specialist medical term that the nurse had told me the previous week. When she gasped in amazement at this—and as far as I could tell no one else claimed it—Cook prayed that God would give her the child she was wanting so much. This appeared to be an auxiliary word of knowledge, but in the circumstances a logical inference from her condition could not be ruled out. This mention of endometriosis was the twenty-first word of knowledge out of a total of thirty-five during that afternoon's workshop alone.

Four afternoon workshops on different topics were being conducted simultaneously in different halls, reducing the numbers involved in any particular one. This particular workshop was combined that afternoon with another one, so we might guess that attendance at it would have been around 1500, of whom half might be expected to be women. Out of 750 or so women one having endometriosis in conceivably attributable to a lucky guess through statistics alone. However, this was actually among the less specific cases mentioned that afternoon; examples of some of the other thirty-four given out by Blaine Cook are as follows (in all these cases someone acknowledged having such a condition):

An ear condition—infection—with a lot of fluid in the ear so that when you wake up there is fluid even on the pillow [acknowledged by a woman on the right].

A woman with a cyst on the left ovary—have real severe pain about six or seven days before you have your menstrual cycle [acknowledged by a woman on the left; Cook then asked for a woman nearby to lay a hand on the left side of the woman in question and to pray for her].

The left foot—a fungus on the bottom which comes up between the last three toes to the top of the foot [a man on the balcony].

Thirty-nine people with heart conditions or high blood pressure [they were asked to stand and raise their hands so that those around them could pray for them].

[A little later Cook announced:] Also someone with a prolapsed heart valve who didn't come forward [a man on the right then identified himself].

Abscessed tooth, lower jaw, second molar [a woman on the right].

Fifth cervical disc damaged in the neck [a woman on the right].

And a gentleman with the same condition [I was unable to see if anyone acknowledged this one as by then so many people were standing up and praying in groups for those who had already identified themselves].

Bruised right heel bone. Hit too hard on something and bruised very badly [a man on the left at the back].

Someone planning to get a root canal seen to on one of teeth in upper right side of mouth—just about to go for tests [a woman on the right].

These examples are among the more specific and detailed ones for which I was able to see people identify themselves as having such conditions. Three other conditions were mentioned in which Cook suggested the person in question should "tap someone on the shoulder and ask them to pray for you" instead of identifying themselves in public: these were for a fungal condition on the anus, vaginal herpes, and an infection in the right breast causing a discharge out of the right nipple. Cook appeared embarrassed by this last mentioned condition, commenting, "Oh boy, why does he do it to me?!"

## Telepathy

Cook, Wimber, and all the others having words of knowledge attribute them to divine revelation, but on the surface a more "natural" explanation might be telepathy. Telepathy has a rather dubious status within orthodox science, however, so scientifically controlled tests of telepathy and related phenomena (clairvoyance, etc.) are relatively few. When such tests are conducted, they limit the number of possible choices to a known, predetermined set to calculate the statistical probabilities of random guesses. Subjects are asked to tell which card has been chosen or to predict which light will flash out of a limited possible set. The results of hundreds of such series are then tabulated and analyzed for statistical significance. If five correct guesses out of a hundred are attributable to chance, then as the proportion of correct answers rises, the probability of the results being due to chance becomes correspondingly less and less. For most experiments the accuracy level is well below one hundred percent, even if statistically significant, but certain individuals with practice do manage to obtain scores that are very highly significant.[6] It appears that practice does lead to marked improvements in accuracy both in such scientific tests and in what I observed at Sheffield, insofar as the most detailed words of knowledge containing specific facts about a person's age, name, or unusual condition were spoken by those with longer experience of this phenomenon and more generalized statements such as "a dull pain over the right eye between the eye and ear," "gallstones," "irregular heartbeat," or "pain in the left foot" were given by those who had never previously had a word of knowledge but here were encouraged to pray and ask God for one.

Outside of controlled scientific experimental conditions, there are occasional reports of close relatives, spouses, or good friends finding that they are thinking about the same thing at the same time and wondering if it were due to telepathy. It is difficult to assess the scientific status of such experiences because of unanswered questions about whether or not a common stimulus might have channeled thoughts along parallel lines. Even if such reports of telepathy can be verified, however, they still seem to be confined to those with close ongoing relationships. The phenomena observed in Sheffield involved such knowledge being picked up by strangers across a crowded auditorium; the people had no previous contact with each other and the knowledge claimed was about personal details that are not normally discernible even if they had spoken face to face. The very fact that some of those having the more detailed words of knowledge had recently arrived from the United States means that if some form of telepathy were involved, it was of a different nature from what is reported between people with existing close ties.

Our knowledge of telepathy and similar phenomena is still in the rudimentary stages, so even if the Sheffield phenomena are of a different kind than that reported between close friends or relatives, it does not mean that it is not still explicable in terms of a telepathy hypothesis. It simply means that our knowledge is extended further or that new dimensions to the psi factor need to be considered. Our conventional model of telepathy tends to see it as a kind of "radio" with a transmitter and one or more receivers, but some of the Sheffield phenomena suggest that this model is also inadequate for certain details. These are the cases when a word of knowledge includes details of how many people have a particular illness, such as "three people with dyslexia" or "thirty nine people with heart conditions or high blood pressure." On the first evening Wimber had a word of knowledge involving the numbers "four" and "one" in association with the word "barren" but was unsure if they meant "14" or "41." He asked those unable to have children, whether male or female, to come forward and line up in front of the stage. Some bunched up together and merged on the steps with a few others who had come forward in response to other words of knowledge so I was unsure of my own counting, but it was within two of the number "41," which Wimber arrived at from his better vantage point of the stage. (Although one of those to go forward was the husband of the woman with endometriosis, he slipped away quietly back to his seat without being prayed for or revealing his wife's condition because he decided after going forward that the problem was not his but his wife's. Therefore there could have been no report on the woman's condition to Blaine Cook who had the word of knowledge about endometriosis three days later.)

The significance of specific numbers mentioned like "three," "39" or "41" is that in a radio analogy one would have to imagine a radio being able to identify how many stations were broadcasting the message on several different bands. It is as if the range of possible wave lengths were rapidly scanned, all those broadcasting the same message were identified, and the number of different transmitters counted. This is a much more sophisticated model than one of a single transmitter and one or more receivers of a single message, so that the radio analogy becomes strained when it comes to the question of multiple "transmitters" and counting each one separately.[7]

## When the Spirit Comes

Through words of knowledge various people were identified as the ones God wanted to heal and they were then prayed over by those around them (or, at the beginning of the conference, by the team members who came with Wimber and Pytches). The power to heal is attributed to the Holy Spirit and at the beginning of each so-called clinic session all those present were invited to "wait for" the Holy Spirit to come upon them. Wimber would pray briefly for the Holy Spirit to "come," then stand at the front while everyone waited quietly, usually standing and often in a position in which the hands were upturned and held out in front as if the persons were in the act of receiving. Some even stood with their hands clasped together behind their backs as if unwilling to participate in what was going on around them. Wimber at the front cracked jokes like "Now don't get religious on me" but soon began to cry out "Let it come" as he saw some of the physical manifestations of the Holy Spirit's presence. These ranged from a kind of beatific stillness and quietness settling over a person to the opposite extreme of falling over and lying on the floor. In between there were phenomena such as the shaking of one or both hands, laughing, crying, or a stiffening of the body. Such phenomena have been reported in Christian religious history from at least the time of Wesley onwards, although the biblical reference to the disciples appearing as if drunk on the day of Pentecost might be taken as evidence of similar phenomena in the first-century church.[8]

Most Methodists would be suspicious of such modern phenomena occurring in Methodist churches even if such things occurred at the time of Wesley, and modern Quakers no longer manifest the quaking that gave them their name, but it appears that people of many different denominations at Sheffield experienced such phenomena sometimes involuntarily. During the very first clinic session a forty-five-year-old woman found her right hand was shaking while all those around her were sitting without any visible manifestations. She tried to stop her hand from shaking by holding it with her other one until both began to shake so violently that her behavior became obvious to those around her. She had not expected such behavior and it was not until the third day that Cook explained their interpretation of these physical manifestations. There had been no previous suggestion that such phenomena were to be expected, so this women and others like her tried to suppress such phenomena when they occurred during the first clinic. In subsequent sessions there may have been more expectancy of seeing such behavior, so the element of psychological suggestion cannot be ruled out for later meetings even if it is difficult to account for phenomena at the first clinic by such theory.

During the physical healing workshops on the third day Cook explained that they regard these manifestations as being partly due to an "overload" of the nervous system, particularly for phenomena like hands shaking. One twenty-nine-year-old man was genuinely surprised to be told half an hour later that during a certain time of prayer his hand had been shaking violently. This incident would indicate that the autonomic nervous system or the motor parts of the brain could be involved without any consciousness of what is happening in the body. Phenomena such as a stiffening up are attributed to inner conflict between the Holy Spirit and personal sins or other barriers. Some cases of people screaming out are attributed usually to the release of suppressed hurts from the past but may occasionally be attributed to the expulsion of demonic forces. Those who screamed seemed mainly to be women. I interviewed two of them—one of them the wife of an Anglican curate—and they both testified that they would never normally scream like that in public but found themselves doing so as the Holy Spirit brought to the surface various past hurts. It is difficult to explain such "unconventional" behavior by a standard "crowd conformity" model.

The behavior of a few individuals who screamed out or of the man who suddenly began to grunt and growl and needed to be held down by several of those around him (attributed by those there as evidence of a demon manifesting itself) might be regarded as a form of mass hysteria were it not for the fact that relatively few people actually manifest such symptoms. More people have symptoms such as shaking hands, weeping, or stiffening but during any one clinic the numbers of individuals actually manifesting such signs are still a minority. Those around them either watch or participate in praying for such people, but I would estimate that rarely would more than one in ten of the audience be the focus of such attention during any one clinic. By the end of the four days most people had experienced something, but there were still some who wanted to experience some special manifestation and had not done so. (A few seemed to attempt to mimic phenomena like hands shaking, but their attempts were obviously artificial and they were told to stop it by the more experienced team members.)

From the outside such behavior might easily be attributable to emotionalism, but it is then surprising to find that when interviewed about their experiences afterward a relatively high number reported a sense of detachment from the proceedings and inner calm or peace. Emotions are obviously involved but not to the degree that the behavior could be labeled "emotionalism" alone and left at that. This sense of detachment from one's physical body, almost like being a spectator, even applies to those who manifest quite extreme behavior like screaming. One twenty-four-year-old woman, for example, began to have a vision of Jesus, first of his arms and later of his body but his facial features were still unclear. She tried to clear her mind of any faces she knew well, such as her father's, so as not to project such features on to the vision in her mind's eye. She felt that "Satan was saying to [her] that it was not real." As she struggled to put her arms out to hold onto Jesus, she felt a severe pain right across her stomach as if some forces were trying to prevent her from reaching Jesus. The severity of the pains caused her to scream out, but despite these experiences she nevertheless felt somehow detached from her body, conscious of what was happening but not seeming to be really "in" it or part of it. During the experience her arms and legs became numb and it took about half an hour for sensation to return to them afterward.

In several cases there appeared to be a progression from "strong" to "mild" manifestations during the conference. Those who near the beginning felt that past hurts were being dealt with or found themselves stiffening up as if an inner conflict were taking place—what Wimber terms a "power encounter" as the Holy Spirit confronts forms of resistance—were by the end of the week exhibiting less dramatic symptoms such as expressions of joy or rapture. Those who at the beginning manifested hand shaking or tingling in the hands were usually those who saw these symptoms as evidence of a call to some kind of a healing ministry and who were often praying over other people by the end of the week. Sometimes the "shaking hand syndrome" occurred again while they were praying over others but sometimes not. It would appear as if the forms these phenomena take in different people may depend on individual factors as diverse as one's personal needs, personality, and even physiological makeup; the hand that shakes more or begins to shake first is often the hand one writes with, whether right or left.[9]

Occasionally people fall over onto the floor or feel they have to sit down in a chair. Different reasons are given for this but all involve a sense of feeling overwhelmed. (Wimber uses the word "overwhelm"; he says that the Greek word from which we get the word "baptism" means "overwhelmed" more than simply "dipped," and he therefore interprets some of these experiences as evidence of an "overwhelming" ["baptism"] in the Holy Spirit.) A twenty-three-year-old girl described how first her legs began to shake violently, then calmed down, and then it "came again with my hands shaking as well." Eventually her hands stopped and only her legs shook, but by that time she had become unable to stand and had fallen first to her seat and then flat onto the floor where she "lay for quite a while, feeling totally at peace." When she was afterwards helped back to a sitting position she "felt as if I just wanted to sit there for an hour or so and allow his Spirit to continue to be with me and flow through me, just being at peace." She felt God had been "filling" her with "his love." Others also described similar experiences in terms of "love," "joy," or "peace," although one girl described her experience of what appeared to me like ecstasy as "joy alternating with deep-seated pains and hurts from the past: joy then pain then joy then pain. . . . "

It appeared as if some of the more extreme emotional feelings were experienced more by women than men, and in particular more by younger women than older ones. However, older people also felt the "overwhelming" so that they fell over, though I know of more female than male cases of this. Some described their experiences in terms of "a great, heavy weight knocking me over" or "a heavy weight or pressure on the chest so that I had to sit down." The mention of "weight" is particularly interesting because it was not a feature mentioned by Wimber or the other speakers, so the fact that several people mentioned such a "weight" could not be attributed to suggestion. Wimber had mentioned the idea of "waves," saying that sometimes the Holy Spirit suddenly comes in an engulfing wave but more often comes in "waves" of ever-increasing intensity; first a few people becoming "engaged" by the Spirit, then more and more.

I find such experience particularly interesting because of their similarities with the report of an experience by a Baptist minister who, while praying by himself thirty years ago, experienced "waves" of God's love that eventually became so intense "I had to ask God to stop it" after an unknown period of time, which he guessed might have been up to an hour or more.[10] So far his experience has never been repeated but his clearest impressions in retrospect were of "waves" and "weight." The similarities of language and the context of Christian prayer indicate that his experience seems very similar to that reported by some people at Sheffield—but from a sociological perspective it is extremely significant that such experiences can occur also in an individual, private context and apparently without being expected or humanly initiated.

The Healing Process

Words of knowledge were often used at Sheffield to identify people to be prayed for, but sometimes general categories of people were invited to stand for prayer, as on the final evening when there was a special prayer for ministers and church leaders. In the latter case prayer was of a more general nature—for God's "blessing," "strength," "courage," or whatever—whereas prayers for healing tended to involve more specific procedures. First, the person was interviewed about the illness and its relevant details, then a diagnosis was made about it, whether its origin was "natural" or "supernatural," then the approapriate kind of prayer was selected, which was followed by another time of prayer that was punctuated by further questioning and feedback from the person being prayed for. Finally some general counsel might be given after the prayer time.

Each case is different but the following description illustrates some of the common features (words of knowledge, interview, and prayer). It took place during the first afternoon workshop on physical healing, which was lead by one of Wimber's team, John McClure, a pastor from Newport Beach, California. He had arrived in Sheffield from London that morning to discover that he was to lead that workshop the same afternoon. Two days previously he had awakened at 5:00 A.M. in his hotel room in London and found he had a blockage or constriction in his windpipe. It was such a severe constriction that he thought he was dying, but in his subsequent account he reported that he "had to rebuke the enemy and it left me." Then "the Lord told me that there would be someone like this to be healed" when he came to Sheffield. Therefore at the first workshop he said that there was somebody with a recent difficulty in breathing; McClure did not know if it was asthmatic or phlegm, only that the windpipe was narrow.

A woman then came forward and McClure interviewed her, asking how long she had had the condition and what her precise problems with it had been. She said that at the age of six weeks she had had eczema and then since the age of two had had asthma. It had improved subsequently but "in the last six months I had been getting a lot of phlegm in the throat, very tight and constricting." McClure commented that he sensed "the enemy wants to terrify you and even try to kill you through this." He then prayed along the lines of, "May the kingdom of God come upon you. . . I speak to the lungs in Jesus' name, 'Be cleared.' . . . I speak to the breathing apparatus in Jesus' name, 'Be cleared.' . . . Be cleared in Jesus' name."

After this McClure interviewed the woman further, stressing that he wanted her to be truthful about whether or not she could feel any change at all. She replied that she did feel cleared and could no longer hear her own breathing. McClure confirmed that at the beginning he had been able to hear the woman's breathing "but not now." The woman then returned to her seat, her final comment being that she felt she "could run a mile"!

Cases like this in which an instantaneous change of some kind is reported are not the rule by any means. Many others report either gradual change or no change at all. Wimber himself cites figures from studies conducted in the United States in which thirty percent of people report some measure of healing after the first session of prayer, an additional ten percent after the second session, and over seventy percent by the time they have been prayed for ten times. They rationalize such results by pointing out that Jesus himself once prayed twice for a blind man, and even some of Paul's friends seem to have experienced prolonged illnesses. Nevertheless the fact that a considerable proportion of people do claim some measure of healing raises the question of how the healing actually works.

Many of the physical phenomena already described as physiological symptoms of the presence of the Holy Spirit bear remarkable similarities to trancelike states. This is not surprising in view of the kind of concentration involved if one has a vision of Jesus of the kind mentioned earlier, because the physiological condition that is likely to accompany the concentration involved in such a vision is most likely one that resembles a trance. However, the very fact that these states do resemble hypnotic trances raises the question of whether or not what is actually happening is a form of hypnosis. Empirically it is very difficult to answer this because the same results might be produced from quite different stimuli, just as a suntan can be produced by the "natural" rays of the sun or by the "artificial" device of an ultraviolet lamp. The problem is compounded by similarities of result, because genuine healings can take place under hypnosis in the same way as are reported as answers to prayer. The very environment of having a group of people around one praying and expressing concern may provide a form of therapy in itself. In a context in which people are open to suggestion and are expecting genuine results as well as have a confidence both in God and in the healing team, the element of suggestion is likely to be strong.

However, this theory does not in itself account for all the range of phenomena actually manifested at Sheffield. It does not account for the accuracy of some of the words of knowledge (and those receiving the words of knowledge are not in trancelike states when they receive the information) and neither does it account for behavior such as that recorded in the following account:

Sarah is a twenty-three-year-old woman who deliberately sat separately from her best friend, Lynne, in order to avoid being influenced by Lynne or her husband within the overall crowd. At first Sarah was rather "put off by seeing so many white, middle-class Christians" at the conference and was a little skeptical on that account because she is particularly concerned for the poor, working-class, and immigrant groups among whom she had been working. During one of the clinics, however, Sarah glanced over to the section where Lynne was being prayed for. Suddenly "in a split second, with no time to even think about Lynne or feel compassion for her I found myself doubled up in a severe *emotional*—not physical—pain as I felt myself experiencing all the pain and hurt Lynne had been through in her life." Immediately Sarah dashed "like a banshee" out along the corridor and in to where Lynne was, threw herself at her friend's feet and cried out "I'm really hurting for you." Sarah's pain then disappeared and at the same time the resistance in Lynne which those praying for her had been finding also seemed to melt away. Shortly afterwards one of those praying asked Lynne, "Did your father leave you when you were eleven years old?" an idea which had come to his mind and was then verified as true. They then prayed for emotional healing for Lynne and for "healing of her memories."

Behavior such as Sarah's would need to be explained by some other form of psychological mechanism such as an extremely deep and sudden empathy rather than by any reference to trance states. It is interesting that she bore a kind of vicarious pain for her friend and that some of the words of knowledge come as forms of pain that "one knows are not one's own pain." Such experiences seem to be particularly appropriate in a context where everyone believes in Christ's vicarious suffering on their behalf. Moreover they see themselves as belonging to a group that in the New Testament is compared to a body with many organs in which "if one part suffers, every part suffers with it; if one part is honored, every part rejoices with it" (1 Cor. 12:26).

## THE EFFECTIVENESS OF HEALING

The whole purpose of the conference was to train Christians in healing ministries and the acid test of such healing is whether or not it actually works. However, when I tried to follow up afterwards with those who received prayer for healing, it became clear that there were too many problematic questions involved to enable a clear verdict to be made. In the first place, it is extremely difficult to check up on medical reports before and after the conference because such reports are not always available. Even when they are available, there is still a possibility of the doctor having made a wrong diagnosis or of having made a tentative diagnosis when the full range of information was unavailable. For some illnesses it is quite likely that the person would have recovered anyway through "natural" processes of healing even if he or she thinks that such processes were miraculously speeded up in Sheffield. In other cases physical symptoms might have psychosomatic causes and when the psychosomatic roots were dealt with the physical symptoms disappeared. Other cases might involve a temporary alleviation of a condition, but there is then the question of whether or not a later relapse might occur. This is particularly pertinent to the case of a woman with multiple sclerosis who walked from her wheelchair supported on either side at first because of her wobbly knees; after prayer specifically for her knees by someone who had also once been a cripple she found herself able the next day to walk around for about forty-five minutes with straight legs.

Another problem in following up reports of healing is that because so many people were being prayed for simultaneously, I could not observe each case in detail and so could not confirm for myself accounts such as that of a man's clubfoot changing its shape towards a more normal one within the space of about fifteen minutes.

Owing to these difficulties in assessing the effectiveness of such prayers, I leave this question open and conclude with two accounts of those who claimed healings during the conference itself:[11]

Linda, the one with the throat problem, went on to the platform where Wimber interviewed her. The whole audience could hear her croaky voice through the microphone. After a relatively brief time of prayer Wimber asked her how she felt. She said she felt about the same, but even as she spoke her voice sounded clear. Wimber asked her to count and it was when she reached "three" that she herself realized that her voice had cleared. When I interviewed her the next day she said that all the symptoms had gone except that she could feel a small warm patch of heat on her throat where she believed therapy was still continuing.

Ginny is thirty-one years old; ten years ago she had begun to suffer a degeneration in her lower spine. Medical doctors had said she would eventually end up in a wheelchair but as a measure to alleviate the degeneration had inserted two metal pins into one of her vertebrae in January 1985. By September the specialist could confirm that the bone had grown over the pins. Ginny at first had to wear a plaster cast which was later replaced by a metal-reinforced corset to keep her back rigid. She claimed that it was medically impossible for her to bend her back, but after prayer during the conference she found she was able to bend down virtually to touch her toes. After this she went up onto the stage, bent down several times, and then lifted up the front of her jumper to display the corset while explaining what had happened to her. Apparently it was only when I interviewed her the next day that she realized that in order for her to demonstrate her healing the metal reinforcements in the corset must have become temporarily flexible too. She described with evident joy how for the first time in many months she had been able to bend over a washbasin to wash her hair and perform other routine tasks and she herself remained curious about what happened to the metal pins in her back.

# Notes

## INTRODUCTION

1. This verse is found in the so-called longer ending of Mark's Gospel, which many scholars do not consider original. But we note that, first, it is the form of Mark accepted as canonical by the church through the centuries, even if it was a later edition and, second, it witnesses at the very least to what the early church believed Jesus had said.

## CHAPTER 1

1. This understanding of the gifts of tongues and interpretation would be challenged by some Christians. My purpose here is only to tell our story, why we withdrew from charismatic movement at that time. The merits of Carol's thinking about tongues and interpretation at that time are a secondary issue.
2. See my extensive notes on holistic medicine in Chapter 4, Note 4. Also see Douglas R. Groothuis, *Unmasking the New Age* (Downers Grove, IL: InterVarsity, 1986), chap. 3.
3. J. Sidlow Baxter, *Divine Healing of the Body* (Grand Rapids, MI: Zondervan, 1979), 18–25.
4. Ibid., 23.
5. Linda Coleman, "Christian Healing: Is It Real?" in *SCP [Spiritual Counterfeits Project] Journal* (August 1978): 42.
6. A. J. Krailsheimer, trans., *Pascal Pensees* (New York: Penguin, 1966), 255, Pensee 735.
7. For a fuller explanation of the influences of worldviews, see our earlier book, *Power Evangelism* (San Francisco: Harper & Row, 1986), chap. 5.
8. For example, see John W. Beardslee III, ed. and trans., *Reformed Dogmatics* (Grand Rapids, MI: Baker, 1977), 141. This section on miracles is taken from the *Compendium of Christian Theology*, an admirable summary of Reformed theology, by the seventeenth-century Reformed scholar Johannes Wollebius of Basel.
9. John T. McNeill, ed., Ford Lewis Battles, trans., *Calvin: Institutes of the Christian Religion*, The Library of Christian Classics, vol. 21 (Philadelphia Westminster, 1973), 1, 467, (4.19.18).
10. Jaroslav Pelikan, ed., *Luther's Works*, vol. 24 (Philadelphia: Fortress, 1961) 367. Luther also said, "How often has it happened and still does, that devils have been driven out in the name of Christ; also that by calling on

his Name in prayer the sick have been healed!" Quoted in J. Sidlow Baxter, *Divine Healing of the Body* (Grand Rapids, MI: Zondervan, 1979), 76.

11. Francis MacNutt, *Healing* (Notre Dame, IN: Ave Maria, 1974), 13.
12. C. I. Scofield, ed., *The New Scofield Reference Bible* (New York: Oxford University Press, 1967), 1207, annotation to Acts 28:8. For the dispensationalist teaching on divine healing, see Wade Bogg, *Faith Healing and the Christian Faith* (Richmond, VA: John Knox, 1956).
13. Wimber and Springer, *Power Evangelism*, 89–90, 119–121; also see Charles Hodge, *Systematic Theology*, vol. 1 (Grand Rapids, MI: Eerdmans, 1975), 636.
14. C. S. Lewis, *The Problem of Pain* (New York: Macmillan, 1940), 93.
15. This argument assumes Paul's "thorn in the flesh," what he called "a messenger of Satan," was physical illness. In 2 Corinthians 12:7–10 it does not state clearly that it was physical; in fact, a more likely interpretation is that Paul's thorn was lifelong opposition from some single, perpetually aggravating person. The term "thorn" is used three times in the Old Testament (Num. 33:55—"thorns in your sides"; Josh. 23:13—"thorns in your eyes"; Judg. 2:3—"thorns in your sides"); in each instance it refers to the opposition of other people—never sickness. Second, after calling his "thorn in the flesh" a "messenger of Satan" that he three times "pleaded with the Lord to take away" (2 Cor. 12:8), Paul boasts about his weaknesses and delights in "insults, in hardships, in persecutions, in difficulties" (v. 10). Why no mention of illness? Finally, the entire Letter of 2 Corinthians is a defense against those who were challenging both Paul's personal integrity and his authority as an apostle. All three of these reasons indicate Paul's "thorn in the flesh" was most likely opposition from other people.
16. Albert Camus, *The Plague* (New York: Vintage Books, 1972). Note: Camus was not a Christian, but there are Christians who hold to his "Christian" understanding of suffering.
17. Questions about the extent and kind of abuse Christians should submit to are not dealt with here. Paul is speaking of the typical social, emotional, and verbal abuse that Christians encounter. Certainly he would not endorse passively accepting severe abuses like spouse beating or severe harassment in the workplace in a culture where we can change jobs and have legal options—though Christians should not be surprised when these abuses happen. Nevertheless, some of the abuse in the New Testament included being tortured to death (Heb. 11:35–38). Regarding slaves and masters, Paul was not endorsing the institution of slavery, as some have erroneously assumed. His concern was to make the best of an institution that could not be changed at that time.
18. Kathryn Kuhlman, *I Believe in Miracles* (Englewood Cliffs, NJ: Prentice-Hall, 1962), 8.
19. Having said this, I do not endorse all the various contemporary models and methods of divine healing. Sometimes God heals *in spite* of our weird models. In Part III I introduce what I call an "integrated model" of healing, one many Christians find easy to understand and accept and one from which they have learned to pray over people effectively.

## CHAPTER 2

1. There are cases where God delivered a righteous individual although he punished the group. Examples are Lot (Gen. 19:1–29; 2 Pet. 2:7) and Ebed-Melech (Jer. 38:7–13; 39:15–18).

2. The following Old Testament passages are examples of judgment for disobedience:
   Numbers 11:1–35—Complaint about adverse conditions
   Numbers 12:1–16—Miriam and Aaron complain about Moses
   Numbers 16:41–50—Complaint after Korah's rebellion
   1 Samuel 5:1–6:21—The ark of God
   2 Samuel 24:1–25—David's census
   2 Kings 5:15–27—Gehazi's greed
   The following Old Testament passages are examples of reward for repentance or obedience:
   Exodus 12:1–51—The Passover
   Numbers 22:4–9—Bronze serpent
   Deuteronomy 7:1–16—Health and prosperity promised
   2 Kings 5:1–14—Naaman healed
   2 Kings 20:1–11—Hezekiah's recovery

3. Meredith G. Kline, *By Oath Consigned* (Grand Rapids, MI: Eerdmans, 1968), 21.

4. C. F. Keil and F. Delitzsch, *Commentary on the Old Testament,* vol. 1 (Grand Rapids, MI: Eerdmans, 1973), 59.

5. See also Morton T. Kelsey, *Healing & Christianity* (New York: Harper & Row, 1973), 33–45.

6. Werner Foerster, "Sōzō," *Theological Dictionary of the New Testament,* vol. 8: 990.

7. John Wilkinson, *Health and Healing* (Edinburgh: Handsel, 1980), 33.

8. Ibid., 31.

9. Ibid., 33.

10. Rarely does God bring suffering on the righteous in the New Testament. Even in the Old Testament the fact that God is said to send illness is probably because Satan is not yet mentioned. For example, in 2 Samuel 24 God is said to tempt David, while a different account of the same incident, found in 1 Chronicles 21, says Satan tempted David. As Satan is revealed, we see things formerly attributed to God attributed to him. This is also true in the intertestamental literature and the Dead Sea Scrolls (for example, see the *Manual of Discipline* [1QS 13]).

11. Wilkinson, *Health and Healing,* 19–20.

12. Alexander Roberts and James Donaldson, eds., *The Ante-Nicene Fathers,* vol. 1, *Against Heresies* (Grand Rapids, MI: Eerdmans, 1973), 409.

13. For more on this subject, see John Wimber with Kevin Springer, *Power Evangelism* (San Francisco: Harper & Row, 1986).

## CHAPTER 3

1. Ralph C. Martin, *Hungry for God* (London: Collins Fontana, 1976).
2. Francis MacNutt, *Healing* (Notre Dame, IN: Ave Maria, 1974).

## CHAPTER 4

1. J. Gresham Machen, *The Christian View of Man* (London: The Banner of Truth Trust, 1937), 144–48.
2. Hans Walter Wolff, *Anthropology of the Old Testament* (Philadelphia: Fortress, 1974).
3. G. C. Berkouwer, *Man: The Image of God* (Grand Rapids, MI: Eerdmans, 1962), 47.
4. What I have written about divine healing and the whole person must not be confused with "holistic healing," a secular movement that is influenced by Eastern religions and the occult. At first glance there is a similarity between holistic healing and Christian healing, because holistic healing does emphasize that the human being is a union of body, mind, and spirit. But the similarity between the two ends there, for holistic medicine offers philosophical and spiritual solutions that are at odds with historic Christianity.

    Brooks Alexander, in an article entitled "Holistic Health from the Inside" (*SCP Journal* [August 1978]: 4) writes:

    What is holistic health? The general public probably identifies holistic medicine as the resort to unusual methods of treatment, such as acupuncture or psychic healing. This is true partly because the media have (naturally) seized upon the most striking and visible features of the phenomenon in their effort to define it. . . .

    Alexander goes on to quote from the article "What is Holistic Health?" by Richard B. Miles, published in the holistic movement publication *Holistic Health Review* (Fall 1977: 4):

    Holistic health is a point of view about the Universe, about human life in the Universe, and about how one finds this extra something in life . . . the joy of creativity, the knowing of consciousness, the fulfillment of self-actualization. . . .

    The basic assumption of holistic health views the Universe as a friendly and supportive place. . . . Harmony and resonance are the result of vibrations which enjoy one another. Within the assumption of a friendly Universe . . . [the] creative intention, emerging from within the individual, leads each person to . . .

    —stand in communion with a benevolent Universe;
    —seek a personal knowledge of the inner vision and spirit of the Higher Self (God within) through creative intuition and imagination;
    —perceive and interpret through a fearless and clear mind exercising intellectual autonomy and integrity . . .

Alexander concludes:

In this brief statement, we can see several clearly identifiable points of classic occult philosophy. . . . The religious point of view embodied in the holistic movement is an integral part of the occult/mystical worldview that is making a coordinated thrust into every aspect of our cultural consciousness. It is not a fad, it will not go away, and it is fundamentally hostile to biblical Christianity.

Also see Paul Reisser, M.D., Teri K. Reisser, and John Weldon, *The Holistic Healers* (Downers Grove, IL: InterVarsity, 1983), 14–49. The authors describe "ten articles of faith in the new medicine":

Precept 1: The whole is greater than the sum of its parts.
Precept 2: Health is more than disease.
Precept 3: Individuals are ultimately responsible for their own health or disease.
Precept 4: Natural forms of healing are preferable to drugs and surgery.
Precept 5: Any method of promoting health or preventing disease has the potential for being holistic.
Precept 6: Health implies evolution.
Precept 7: To understand health and disease, we need an alternative model, one that is based primarily on energy rather than matter.
Precept 8: Death is the final stage of growth.
Precept 9: The thinking and practices of many ancient civilizations are a rich storehouse of knowledge for healthy living.
Precept 10: Holistic health practices must be integrated into the mainstream of life and health care through influencing public policy.

The authors go on to point out that in the New Consciousness (or New Age) movement the concept of "universal energy" is the basis of all existence "in much of holistic health," and that "it appears under a variety of aliases, such as universal life energy, vital forces, Ch'i, prana, bioplasma, para-electricity, and animal magnetism." Behind these concepts, the authors note, are "four basic ideas which form the cornerstone of most Eastern mysticism and occult metaphysics." These ideas, so antithetical to Christianity, are:

1. "All is one" [pantheism].
2. "Man is a divine being."
3. "The purpose of life is to become aware of our divine nature."
4. "Enlightenment leads to the exercise of 'psychospiritual' power."

Because of the occult implications associated with use of the term "energy," I was unsure about using it when describing the phenomena of the Holy Spirit coming on people in divine healing. But I decided in favor of using the term in this book, because so many people use it to describe what they are feeling when the Holy Spirit comes on them, and because in the Eastern Orthodox Christian tradition the term "divine energies" has always been acceptable and not had occult overtones.

Let readers beware that when I use terms like "energy" or "electricity"

I am referring to phenomena that occur when the infinite, personal, triune God of the Bible pours out his Spirit, the Third Person of the Trinity, on people. These are words that people use to describe their experience. Frequently healing accompanies this experience. I do not imply that God is an impersonal force, that human beings are a part of God, or that we will ever become God.

5. Leon Morris, *The Gospel According to John* (Grand Rapids, MI: Eerdmans, 1971), 496.

6. Ibid., 497.

7. Alan Anderson, "How the Mind Heals," *Psychology Today* (December 1982): 51.

8. See O. Carl Simonton, M.D., Stephanie Matthews-Simonton, and James Creighton, *Getting Well Again* (Los Angeles: Tarcher, 1978); and William A. Nolen, M.D., *Healing: A Doctor in Search of a Miracle* (New York: Random House, 1974).

9. *The Sword of the Spirit Newsletter* (January 1986): 6.

10. Paul Reisser, M.D., "Implications of the Holistic Medicine Movement," *SCP Journal* (August 1978): 32.

11. David C. Needham, *Birthright* (Portland, OR: Multnomah, 1979), 88.

12. Martyn Lloyd-Jones, *The Cross* (Westchester, IL: Crossway, 1986), 179.

13. David W. Torrance and Thomas F. Torrance, eds., *Calvin's Commentaries, St. John, 1–10* (Grand Rapids, MI: Eerdmans, 1974), 119.

14. Lloyd-Jones, *The Cross*, 184–195.

15. Needham, *Birthright*, 61.

## CHAPTER 5

1. I am using the term "inner healing" sparingly and judiciously in this chapter, because different authors use it to mean so many different things, many of which I do not agree with. In many instances inner healing is based on secular psychological views of how our personalities are formed and influenced. But where these views contradict the biblical teaching, they must be firmly rejected.

2. David Seamands, *Healing for Damaged Emotions* (Wheaton, IL: Victor, 1981), 7.

3. Michael Scanlan, *Inner Healing* (New York: Paulist Press, 1974), 9.

4. Rita Bennett, *How to Pray for Inner Healing for Yourself and Others* (Old Tappan, NJ: Revell, 1984), 25.

5. Karen Horney, *Our Inner Conflicts* (New York: Norton, 1945).

6. Regarding incest among conservative Christians, Vincent E. Gil, Ph.D., in a paper entitled "In Thy Father's House: Incest in Conservative Christian Homes," presented at the Twenty-eighth Annual Meeting of the Society for the Scientific Study of Sex, San Diego, California, September 19–22, 1985, reports: "Despite strong taboos and religious sanctions against the practice, reports of intrafamilial child sexual abuse have increasingly surfaced from such families." From my experience in recent years, I have

observed an increase in the incidence of women and men raised in Christian families who suffer from the childhood trauma of incest. Whether this indicates a higher incidence of incest or a greater openness to admit to incestuous relationships, I do not know. Paul Vitz, professor of psychology at New York University, in a conversation with my coauthor, Kevin Springer, in June of 1985, said that the incidence of incest in the general population is probably much higher than psychologists thought it to be in the past.

7. Theodore Elliott Dobson, *Inner Healing: God's Great Assurance* (New York: Paulist Press, 1978), 125.
8. Scanlan, *Inner Healing*, 52.
9. Francis MacNutt, *Healing* (Notre Dame, IN: Ave Maria, 1974), 182.
10. Bennett, *How to Pray for Inner Healing*, 26.
11. Agnes Sanford, *The Healing Gifts of the Spirit* (Philadelphia: Trumpet Books, 1966), 48.
12. William Barclay, *The Letters of James and Peter*, rev. ed. (Philadelphia: Westminster, 1976), 46.
13. Scanlan, *Inner Healing*, 17-19.
14. Steve Scott and Brooks Alexander, "Inner Healing," *SCP Journal* (April 1980): 15.
15. Scanlan, *Inner Healing*, 51.
16. Wilder Penfield, "Memory Mechanism," *American Medical Association Archives of Neurology and Psychiatry*, 67 (1952): 178-198.
17. Dobson, *Inner Healing*, 130.
18. Scanlan, *Inner Healing*, 49.
19. Ibid., 28, 49.
20. Even Herod could not have raised such an amount; the total war reparations to Rome in 180 B.C. were only a few hundred talents, and that was a burden to Antiochus III, whose kingdom included Palestine, Babylonia, and Syria.

## CHAPTER 6

1. Randy Frame, "Putting Satan's Work into Perspective," *Christianity Today* (April 18, 1986): 30–32.
2. In the West, we live in an age where belief in the devil and demons is waning while belief in the supernatural appears to be on the rise. On the surface these two trends contradict one another, but actually they help define a more significant cultural trend that is redefining spirituality for many people. Modern belief in the supernatural is losing its Christian roots; movements like Scientology, the Forum (formerly est), Lifespring, Transcendental Meditation, Silva Mind Control, and parapsychology all claim to be based on a mixture of science and metaphysics. I believe these so-called New Age movements are conduits into Western culture for Eastern religious thought, the occult, and direct demonic attack. They introduce people to supernatural experience while denying the source of great spiritual harm: evil spirits. Thus though many men and women are more

open to supernatural encounters, often they are unaware of the danger of encountering Satan and demons.

3. C. S. Lewis, *The Screwtape Letters* (New York: Macmillan, 1971), 32–33.
4. Jeffrey Burton Russell, *Satan and the Early Christian Tradition* (Ithaca, NY: Cornell University Press, 1981), 221. The early church after the close of the canon also believed in the existence of Satan and demons. For example, Cyprian, the Bishop of Carthage (A.D. 250–258), in North Africa, took the demonic world seriously. In his treatise *On the Vanity of Idols*, he described how demons possessed certain Magi of false religions:

These spirits . . . are lurking under the statues and consecrated images: these inspire the breasts of their prophets with their afflatus, animate the fibres of the entrails, direct the flights of birds, rule the lots, give efficiency to oracles, are always mixing up falsehood with truth, for they are both deceived and they deceive; they disturb their life, they disquiet their slumbers; their spirits creeping also into their bodies, secretly terrify their minds, distort their limbs, break their health, excite diseases to force them to worship of themselves, so that when glutted with the steam of the altars and the piles of cattle, they may unloose what they had bound, and so appear to have affected a cure (*The Ante-Nicene Fathers*, vol. 5, Cyprian, *Treatise* 6.7 [Grand Rapids, MI: Eerdmans, 1975] 465).

Tertullian (ca. 160–220), also from Carthage in North Africa, taught that demons were the source of many human problems:

Their business is to corrupt mankind; thus, the spirit of evil was from the very beginning bent upon man's destruction. The demons, therefore, inflict upon men's bodies diseases and other bitter misfortunes, and upon the soul sudden and extraordinary outbursts of violence (Joseph Defferari, ed., *The Fathers of the Church*, vol. 10, Tertullian, *Apology*, [Washington, DC: The Catholic University Press], 69).

Russell, who traced the development of the concept of the devil in Christian thought through the fifth century, concludes that "by [that] time the main lines of the tradition had been established" (*Satan*, 11).

All of the Protestant reformers believed humanity was in a struggle against Satan and demons. For example, John Calvin wrote in his *Institutes of the Christian Religion:*

The fact that the devil is everywhere called God's adversary and ours also ought to fire us to an unceasing struggle against him. . . . If we are minded to affirm Christ's kingdom as we ought, we must wage irreconcilable war with him who is plotting its ruin. . . . In sum, we experience in all of Satan's deeds what Christ testifies concerning him, that "from the beginning he was a murderer . . . and a liar" (John 8:44). For he opposes the truth of God with falsehoods, he obscures the light with darkness, he entangles men's minds in errors, he stirs up hatred, he kindles contentions and combats, everything to the end that he may overturn God's kingdom and plunge men with himself into eternal death. From this it appears that he is in nature depraved, evil, and malicious. For there must be consummate depravity in that disposition which devotes itself to assailing God's glory and man's salvation. This, also, is what John means in his letter, when he writes that "the devil has sinned from the beginning" (1 John 3:8). Indeed, he considers him as the author, leader, and architect of all malice and iniquity (John Calvin, *Institutes of the Christian Religion I*, The Library of Christian Classics, vol. 20 [Philadelphia: Westminster, 1967], 174).

5. Russell, *Satan*, 225.
6. Michael Scanlan and Randall J. Cirner, *Deliverance from Evil Spirits* (Ann Arbor, MI: Servant, 1980), 14.
7. See John Wimber with Kevin Springer, *Power Evangelism* (San Francisco: Harper & Row, 1986), chaps. 1–2.
8. Lewis, *The Screwtape Letters*, vii.
9. Origen, *The Fundamental Doctrines*, in W. A. Jurgens, ed., *The Faith of the Early Fathers* (Collegeville: The Liturgical Press, 1970), 192.
10. Lewis, *The Screwtape Letters*, vii.
11. Scanlan and Cirner, *Deliverance from Evil Spirits*, 30.
12. Merrill F. Unger, *Demons in the World Today* (Wheaton, IL: Tyndale House, 1971), 113.
13. For more detailed criteria for demon possession, see also John L. Nevius, *Demon Possession* (Grand Rapids, MI: Kregel, 1968), 45–59; John Warwick Montgomery, ed., *Demon Possession* (Minneapolis, MN: Bethany House, 1976), 224; Kurt Koch, *Demonology, Past and Present* (Grand Rapids, MI: Kregel, 1973), 136–47; and Unger, *Demons in the World Today*, 102–108. The Roman Catholic Missal mentions four signs by which possession may be recognized:

   1. Knowledge of a language previously unknown;
   2. Knowledge of hidden or secret things;
   3. Demonstration of superhuman strength;
   4. An aversion to the things of God.

14. Montgomery, *Demon Possession*, 225–26.
15. Dom Robert Petitpierre, O.S.B., ed., *Exorcism* (London: SPCK, 1972), 18–19.
16. Scanlan and Cirner, *Deliverance*, 63.
17. Ibid., 64–65.

**CHAPTER 7**

1. See also John Wilkinson, *Health and Healing* (Edinburgh: Handsel, 1980), 21, 85, 103. Wilkinson writes:

   The paucity of specific references to health and healing in the Epistles is of great interest in view of the fact that these writings form over a third of the bulk of the New Testament. Some of them are contemporaneous with events recorded in the Acts, whilst others are not, and it cannot be denied that they reflect a lessened interest in health and healing when compared with that book, as that book in turn reflects a lessened interest in healing when compared with the Gospels. It can be argued that the character of a Letter does not lend itself to the mention of incidents of healing in the same way as a chronicle of events such as we have in the Acts. However, the Pauline Letters frequently deal with problems on which the local Christian communities have sought his advice and since healing is only referred to in passing in them we can only presume that healing was not a problem (p. 103).

J. Sidlow Baxter, in *Divine Healing of the Body* (Grand Rapids, MI: Zondervan, 1979), writes:

What is the first thought which leaps to mind? Is it not the *very small space* given to physical healing [in the Epistles]? In a way, it seems disappointingly small. Let it tell us the comparatively small importance which *God* puts upon it. Let it indicate its comparatively minor place over against the major emphases of the New Testament Letters to Christian believers.

Note that I describe it as a *comparatively* diminutive concern. In itself it is important enough, like various other weighty matters which are given only scant reference in Scripture; but *relatively*, that is, over against the great spiritual and eternal issues which are the heart of the Christian message, it is among the incidentals of lesser concern.

This sparse mention of the subject in the Epistles strikes a sharp contrast with the frequency of miracle healings in the four Gospels and the Acts of the Apostles. And let us be reminded, it is the New Testament *Epistles*, not the Gospels or the Acts, which are specifically addressed to the church as a whole, to local churches, and to individual Christians as such. It is the Epistles which are exclusively the property of the church and which furnish all those teachings which are specifically "church" doctrines and which reveal all the Lord's special provisions for his church and which set the norm for the church's life, fellowship, witness, and experience throughout the present age (p. 157).

I would challenge Baxter on two counts. I agree that the Epistles are addressed to the church, but so are the Gospels of Matthew and John. Matthew is designed as a handbook for the church (hence its topical organization of discourses), and John is likely aimed at strengthening the faith of believers more than bringing unbelievers to faith. Mark is reportedly a compilation of the stories Peter told to the church in Rome. As I have pointed out in the chapter, the Epistles assume the Gospels as basic church teaching. Furthermore, the Epistles are never systematic (even Romans) but are occasioned by problems and issues. Thus they are to a degree hit-and-miss affairs. If the early church did not have a problem with something, the Epistles rarely discuss it. Hence our lack of information about baptism and the Lord's Supper, among other things. In fact, had the Corinthians not had problems, we likely would never have known how Paul's churches celebrated the Lord's Supper. Because of these two factors, the fact that something is rarely discussed in the Epistles bears no relationship to its importance for the church.

Baxter goes on and launches into a Scripture study that concentrates on the five passages in the Epistles in which divine healing is mentioned. Here is his conclusion:

Although much present-day preaching of divine healing is, in my judgment, misfounded on a wrong interpretation of Scripture, there remains nevertheless sufficient evidence in the New Testament that a ministry of divine healing for the body is meant to be still in operation today, at least inside local Christian churches. As we have seen, there is (1) clear promise of such healing in response to faith, (2) a clear inclusion of healing in the Spirit's distribution of "gifts" among believers, (3) clear reference to such healing as being experienced by the Lord's people in those early days of the church. . . . Yes, divine healings are meant for the church today (p. 180).

2. I am especially indebted to Dr. Paul Reisser, a physician from Thousand Oaks, California, whose comments were quite helpful in writing this section. See also Morton T. Kelsey, *Healing and Christianity in Ancient Thought and Modern Times* (New York: Harper & Row, 1973), 69–79. Wilkinson, in *Health and Healing* (p. 24–25), observes these classes of disorders: (1) physical diseases, which include (A) acute disease and (B) chronic disease; and (2) demon possessions, which include (A) disorders in which specific physical manifestations are described and (B) disorders in which no specific physical manifestation is described.

3. Paul Reisser, M.D., "Implications of the Holistic Medicine Movement," *SCP Journal* (August 1978): 33.

4. Notice that no team member encouraged or suggested that D. M. form mental images, or that the images and words that he experienced were in themselves a psychic source of healing power. The occult method of "visualization" was not used here. The healing took place because the Holy Spirit applied God's grace to D. M.'s heart, not because the images and words that he experienced contained power in themselves.

5. Gerald C. Davison and John M. Neale, *Abnormal Psychology: An Experimental Clinical Approach*, 3rd ed., (New York: Wiley, 1982), 70–72. See also James C. Coleman, James N. Butcher, and Robert C. Carson, *Abnormal Psychology and Modern Life*, 7th ed., (Glenview, IL: Scott, Foresman, 1984), 231.

6. Wilkinson, *Health and Healing*, 25.

7. See the end of Note 4, Chapter 4 for comments on my use of the terms "electricity" and "energy."

8. Francis MacNutt, *The Prayer That Heals* (Notre Dame, IN: Ave Maria, 1981), 57–58.

# CHAPTER 8

1. For further explanation, see David Watson, *Fear No Evil* (London: Hodder and Stoughton, 1984), chap. 8; and Edward England, ed., *David Watson, A Portrait by His Friends* (Crowborough: Highland Books, 1985), chap. 12.

2. Timothy's not using wine could have been the cause of his problem. Paul had taken a Nazarite vow and therefore abstained from wine. Perhaps Timothy for that or similar reasons had also abstained. Greeks and Hebrews believed either water or wine alone was unhealthy. An early Greek

source recommends, "Water alone is bad and wine alone is bad, but mixed together [one part wine to two parts water] they are the drink of the gods." So Paul is advising not so much medicine as healthy eating practices.

3. The Greek word translated here "sick" *(asthenounta)* may also be understood as weak in faith (Rom. 4:19), weak in conscience (1 Cor. 8:11), almost sinful (Rom. 5:6; Heb. 4:15), inner poverty (Gal. 4:9), or poverty (Acts 20:35). All translators agree the correct translation in 2 Timothy 4:20 is "sick." See Gustav Stählin, "Asthenēs," *Theological Dictionary of the New Testament*, vol. 1 (Grand Rapids, MI: Eerdmans, 1964), 490–93.

4. Speculation regarding Paul's illness in Galatians 4:13–14 should not be confused with speculation regarding his "thorn in the flesh" in 1 Corinthians 12:7–10. See Chapter 1, note 15 for my discussion of Paul's "thorn in the flesh."

5. Many commentators believe Paul's thorn in the flesh was some form of sickness. Scripture is silent on this point. I do not believe it was sickness. For my arguments, see Chapter 1, footnote 15. For an opposing viewpoint, see John Wilkinson, *Health and Healing* (Edinburgh: Handsel, 1980), chap. 11.

6. Some commentators have said that their sickness was due to personal sin. The commentators claim that, because healing is found in the atonement and applicable to us in the same way as salvation—i.e., immediately and automatically. The only explanation for an illness that is not healed, they deduce, is personal sin, especially from a lack of faith. This is the same explanation that Job's three friends offered for his troubles, and for this they received Job's angry rebuke (Job 13:7).

7. R. A. Torrey, *Divine Healing* (Grand Rapids, MI: Baker, 1974), 53.

8. For examples of those who teach healing is not in the atonement, see Trevor Martin, *Kingdom Healing* (London: Marshalls, 1981); and Gordon D. Fee, *The Disease of the Health and Wealth Gospels* (Costa Mesa, CA: The Word for Today, 1979). For those who teach healing is in the atonement, see John P. Baker, *Salvation and Wholeness: The Biblical Perspectives of Healing* (London: Fountain Trust, 1973); T. J. McCrossan, ed. Roy Hicks and Kenneth E. Hagin, *Bodily Healing and the Atonement* (Tulsa, OK: Faith Library, 1982); and Hugh Jeter, *By His Stripes* (Springfield, MO: Gospel, 1977).

9. J. Sidlow Baxter, *Divine Healing of the Body* (Grand Rapids, MI: Zondervan, 1979), 137.

10. Colin Brown, *That You May Believe*. (Grand Rapids, MI: Eerdmans, 1985), 200.

11. Ibid., 202–203.

12. Baxter, *Divine Healing of the Body*, 133.

13. Donald Gee, *Trophimus I Left Sick* (London: Elim, 1952), 21–22.

14. Ibid., 26.

15. Ibid., 27, 29.

16. Ibid., 27.

17. See John Wimber with Kevin Springer, *Power Evangelism* (San Francisco: Harper & Row, 1986), chap. 1.

18. Ibid., chap. 3.

19. Taken from Samuel Southard, unpublished class notes, Fuller Theological

Seminary, 1984. I am indebted to Samuel Southard for much of my thinking on ministry to the terminally ill and the bereaved.

20. Samuel Southard recommends writing out our prayers for the sick or repeating other people's prayers that have been effective. It is especially helpful to leave a copy of the prayer with those whom we visit. Two excellent sources of prayers are Ernest A. Payne and Stephen F. Winward, ed. *Orders and Prayers for Church Worship* (London: Carey Kingsgate, n.d.); and Catherine Marshall, ed. *The Prayers of Peter Marshall* (New York: McGraw-Hill, n.d.).

## CHAPTER 9

1. In the short summary below I will make a few comments on the practices of different schools of divine healing and mention a few of their leaders. A word of caution about these categories: they are not meant to sharply divide one group from another. In fact, many individuals have practices that fit into more than one movement. I identify five models:

1. *The Pentecostal Model.* Pentecostals were the modern pioneers in divine healing and are the most successful group ministering divine healing in the twentieth century, with over fifty-nine million members in the world today, as reported by David Barrett in *The World Christian Encyclopedia* (London: Oxford University Press, 1982). Healing is ministered primarily through a healing revivalist or evangelist, with most healings taking place at mass meetings. They also place great importance on healing and evangelism, which helps account for their explosive growth during this century. There have been approximately fifty well known Pentecostal healing evangelists in the last seventy years. Key personalities today include Oral Roberts, Kenneth Copeland, and Morris Cerullo.

2. *The liturgical-sacramental model.* This model is practiced mostly in the Anglican and Roman Catholic churches. As the title implies, healing is ministered by priests and through the sacraments—especially the sacraments of the Eucharist, reconciliation, and anointing the sick. The ministry of healing is limited largely to official church meetings. Key leaders are Morris Maddocks, Anglican Bishop of Selby, England, and Father Edward McDonough, a Roman Catholic priest from Roxbury, Massachusetts.

3. *The neo-Pentecostal model.* The leaders of this model see themselves as healers and trainers of healers. There is an emphasis on developing healing teams and not on single healing evangelists. Healing usually takes place in pastoral settings like healing retreats, special conferences, church gatherings, and homes. Prayer is the primary means of healing, so learning how to pray effectively is important. Inner healing often precedes physical healing. Key leaders include Francis MacNutt, Ralph A. DiOrio, Michael Scanlan, and Leanne Payne.

4. *The deliverance-Pentecostal model.* This model places an emphasis on evangelism and deliverance ministry, which is done by an evangelist in healing campaign meetings. The training of others for the deliverance

ministry is limited. Key personalities include Gordon Lindsey, a Pentecostal evangelist during the fifties and sixties, T. L. Osborn, Lester Sumrall, Kenneth Hagin, and Derek Prince.

5. *The psychological-spiritual or inner-healing model.* This model emphasizes the healing of memories, past hurts, resentments, and guilt that are submerged in the subconscious mind. Leaders use words of knowledge, counseling, faith imagination, and role playing in the healing process. Key leaders include Dennis and Matthew Linn, Ruth Carter Stapleton, David Seamands, Barbara Pursey, John Hampsch, and John and Paula Sandford.

Almost every model I studied offered some insight into divine healing, though few of them fully satisfied my concerns for an equipping model. In most instances they were written to convince the reader that God could heal today, and that he did this almost exclusively through a few individuals with the gift of healing. The exceptions to this were the writings of Francis MacNutt, Dennis and Rita Bennett, and Michael Scanlan. But they were not written with evangelical Protestantism in mind, the tradition of which I am a part. These books include Francis MacNutt's *Healing* (Notre Dame, IN: Ave Maria, 1974) and *The Power to Heal* (Notre Dame, IN: Ave Maria, 1977); Michael Scanlan's *Inner Healing* (New York: Paulist Press, 1974); Michael Scanlan and Randall J. Cirner's *Deliverance from Evil Spirits* (Ann Arbor, MI: Servant, 1980); and Rita Bennett's *How to Pray for Inner Healing for Yourself and Others* (Old Tappan, NJ: Revell, 1984). Though I learned much from reading these books, a far greater contribution came from Scripture study and experience.

2. Jackie Pullinger, *Chasing the Dragon* (Ann Arbor, MI: Servant, 1983).

3. John Wilkinson, *Health and Healing* (Edinburgh: Handsel, 1980), 9, 1.

4. This is the topic of our first book, *Power Evangelism* (San Francisco: Harper & Row, 1986).

## CHAPTER 10

1. See Howard A. Snyder and Daniel V. Runyon, *The Divided Flame* (Grand Rapids, MI: Zondervan, 1986), 101–108.

2. For a social anthropologist's view of words of knowledge, see appendix F.

## CHAPTER 12

1. John Wesley, *The Works of John Wesley*, vol. 1 (Peabody, MA: Hendrickson, n.d.), 190.

2. Jonathan Edwards, *The Works of Jonathan Edwards*, vol. 2 (Philadelphia: Banner of Truth, 1975), 260.

3. Ibid., 271.

4. Much of this material comes from John White's unpublished notes, delivered at the *Church Growth Leadership and the Kingdom of God in the '90s* conference in Anaheim, California, February 1986. Used with permission.

5. *The Sword of the Spirit Newsletter* (January 1986): 6–7.
6. John Wimber with Kevin Springer, *Power Evangelism* (San Francisco: Harper & Row, 1986); chap. 2.

## APPENDIX F

Author's note: During the October 1985 Sheffield conference I was not aware that Dr. David C. Lewis was conducting a study. In fact, I had neither personally met nor heard of Dr. Lewis. However, after reading his paper I thought his findings were significant enough to publish in this volume. I would like to thank Dr. Lewis for graciously granting me permission to publish his work.

1. A questionnaire distributed at the 1984 London conference, analyzed by Douglas G. T. McBain of Manna Ministries Trust, London, and by C. E. Fryer, Minister of Ilfracombe Baptist Church, Devon, produced figures showing the self-classified denominational allegiance of respondents as Anglicans (42.5%), Baptists (25.5%), House Churches (16%), Pentecostals (4%), and Evangelicals (3.5%). A residual category (8.5%) was classified in the unpublished report as "Others, including Roman Catholics."
2. Francis MacNutt, *Healing* (Notre Dame, IN: Ave Maria, 1974).
3. A two-part article by Hendrik G. Boerenkamp entitled "A Study of Paranormal Impressions of Psychics" has been published in the *European Journal of Parapsychology*, vol. 5 (1985): 327–71. A group of fourteen psychics or mediums, six male and eight female, was studied (although two dropped out after one series), and the investigation allowed the subjects to operate in their conventional ways at home, using "inductors," and having the usual amount of feedback on their statements provided by the investigators. Each session was tape-recorded. It was concluded that about ten percent of the subjects' statements met the criteria of "no logical explanation" but of these only one out of ten met the criteria of "sufficient degree of correspondence" between statement and reality. However, it was concluded that the one percent incidence of "unexplained" and "true" statements could still be satisfactorily explained by assuming chance coincidence (pp. 365–66).
4. Dr. Alan Gauld, personal communication. Dr. Gauld is the author of *Mediumship and Survival: A Century of Explorations* (London: Heinemann, 1983).
5. John Wimber with Kevin Springer, *Power Evangelism* (London: Hodder and Stoughton, 1985), 44–46; (San Francisco: Harper & Row, 1986), 32–34. This incident is quoted also by David Pytches in his book *Come, Holy Spirit* (London: Hodder and Stoughton, 1985), 101–102.
6. The classic pioneer studies of ESP are those by J. B. Rhine, professor of psychology at Duke University, who was the first to apply statistics to the study of ESP. Details are given in J. B. Rhine, *The Reach of the Mind* (London: Faber and Faber, 1948). Other studies of ESP are detailed in J. B. Rhine and J. G. Pratt, *Parapsychology* (Springfield, IL: Thomas, 1957);

also see S. G. Soal and F. Bateman, *Modern Experiments in Telepathy* (London: Faber and Faber, 1954). Examples of high scores in telepathy trials are 2,923 out of 11,000 trials or 466 out of 1,600 trials, the "intrinsic percentage score" (which adjusted for discrepancies with statistical probability, etc.) in these cases being 8.2 percent and 11.4 percent respectively (Soal and Bateman, p. 313).

It should be noted that ESP subjects—even individuals producing highly significant scores (e.g., 270 out of 950, compared with a chance expectation of 190)—have sooner or later lost their abilities (D. J. West, *Physical Research Today* [Harmondsworth: Penguin Books, Ltd. 1962] pp. 133, 147–48).

7. An analogy between telepathy and radio waves constitutes the title of one of the pioneer studies of telepathy, Upton Sinclair's *Mental Radio* (New York: Collier-Macmillan, 1971). A radio type model is still implicit in popular ideas about telepathy but, because psi phenomena are so little understood, the analogy remains a possible working model that might be discarded as further data come to light.

8. Acts 2:13–16. Details of some of these manifestations as recorded by John Wesley are quoted by Wimber in *Power Evangelism* (British ed., 37; American ed., 25).

9. For this observation on left- and right-handedness I am indebted to Rev. Nigel Wright, the minister of Lytham St. Annes Baptist Church.

10. Rev. Michael Caddick, personal communication. He also informs me that the Hebrew word *kabod*, translated as "glory," has a primary meaning of "weight" or "substance" (as in "a man of substance"). Also see Alan Richardson, ed., *A Theological Word Book of the Bible* (London: S.C.M., 1950), p. 175.

11. Rex Gardner, F.R.C.O.G., is a consultant obstetrician and gynecologist whose presidential address to the Newcastle and Northern Counties Medical Society was published in the *British Medical Journal* (vol. 287 [December 24–31, 1983: 1927–33]) under the title "Miracles of Healing in Anglo-Celtic Northumbria As Recorded by the Venerable Bede and His Contemporaries: A Reappraisal in the Light of Twentieth-Century Experience." He compares miracles attributed to St. Cuthbert of Lindisfarne and his contemporaries with well-documented medical case histories from the twentieth century that resemble in many details those described for the seventh century. However, even in the face of comprehensive and detailed medical evidence and the diagnoses of four medical consultants who remain confident about the accuracy of their diagnoses, those unable to explain a case of a eye being healed after prayer (when conventional medicine was unable to help) then called in doubt the accuracy of the original diagnoses. Gardner concludes that "even in well-documented cases where patients and doctors are available for questioning and medical records can be examined, proof of miraculous cure is probably impossible" (p. 1929).

For such reasons I do not attempt here to delve into the medical aspects of these cures, which are outside my professional competence as a social anthropologist, since medical experts may disagree among themselves about such matters. I can only take the same stance as that of Gardner, whose detailed accounts of seven case histories involving "miraculous" cures are followed by the observation that "no attempt has been made to prove that miracles have occurred, such proof being probably impossible. The adjective 'miraculous' is, however, permissible as a convenient short-hand for an otherwise almost inexplicable healing which occurs after prayer to God and brings honor to the Lord Jesus Christ" (p. 1932).

# Bibliography

Alexander, William Menzies. *Demonic Possession in the New Testament*. Grand Rapids, MI: Baker, 1980.

Bakus, William, and Marie Chapian. *Telling Yourself the Truth*. Minneapolis, MN: Bethany House, 1980.

Baker, John P. *Salvation and Wholeness: The Biblical Perspectives of Healing*. London: Fountain Trust, 1973.

Basham, Don. *Deliver Us from Evil*. Washington Depot, CO: Chosen Books, 1972.

Baxter, J. Sidlow. *Divine Healing of the Body*. Grand Rapids, MI: Zondervan, 1979.

Bayly, Joseph. *The View from a Hearse*. Elgin, IL: Cook, 1977.

Bennett, Dennis and Rita. *Trinity of Man*. Plainfield, NJ: Logos International, 1979.

Bennett, Rita. *How to Pray for Inner Healing for Yourself and Others*. Old Tappan, NJ: Revell, 1984.

Berkouwer, G. C. *Man: The Image of God*. Grand Rapids, MI: Eerdmans, 1962.

Bounds, Edward M. *Satan: His Personality, Power, and Overthrow*. Grand Rapids, MI: Baker, 1972.

Brown, Colin. *That You May Believe*. Grand Rapids, MI: Eerdmans, 1985.

Bubeck, Mark I. *Overcoming the Adversary*. Chicago: Moody, 1984.

Camus, Albert. *The Plague*. New York: Vintage, 1972.

DiOrio, Ralph A. *Called to Heal*. Garden City, NY: Doubleday, 1982.

Dobson, Theodore Elliot. *Inner Healing: God's Great Assurance*. New York: Paulist Press, 1978.

Fast, Reginald. *Heal the Sick*. London: Hodder and Stoughton, 1978.

England, Edward, ed. *David Watson*. Crowborough: Highland Books, 1985.

Fee, Gordon D. *The Disease of the Health and Wealth Gospels*. Costa Mesa, CA: The Word for Today, 1979.

Gee, Donald. *Concerning Spiritual Gifts*. Springfield, MO: Gospel, 1972.

Ghezzi, Bert, and Mark Kinzer. *Emotions as Resources*. Ann Arbor, MI: Servant, 1983.

————. *Facing Your Feelings.* Ann Arbor, MI: Servant, 1983.

Glennon, Jim. *Your Healing Is Within You.* London: Hodder and Stoughton, 1978.

————. *How Can I Find Healing?* London: Hodder and Stoughton, 1984.

Gordon, A.J. *The Ministry of Healing: Miracles of Cure in All Ages.* Harrisburg, PA: Christian Publications, 1882.

Green, Michael. *I Believe in Satan's Downfall.* Grand Rapids, MI: Eerdmans, 1981.

Groothuis, Douglas R. *Unmasking the New Age.* Downers Grove, IL: InterVaristy, 1986.

Hagin, Kenneth E. *Understanding the Anointing.* Tulsa, OK: Faith Library, 1983.

Harper, Michael. *Spiritual Warfare.* Plainfield, NJ: Logos International, 1970.

Jeter, Hugh. *By His Stripes.* Springfield, MO: Gospel, 1977.

Judisch, Douglas. *An Evaluation of Claims to the Charismatic Gifts.* Grand Rapids, MI: Baker, 1978.

Kallas, James. *Jesus and the Power of Satan.* Philadelphia: Westminster, 1968.

————. *The Real Satan.* Minneapolis, MN: Augsburg, 1975.

Kelsey, Morton T. *Christianity as Psychology.* Minneapolis, MN: Augsburg, 1986.

————. *Healing and Christianity in Ancient Thought and Modern Times.* New York: Harper & Row, 1973.

Koch, Kurt E. *Between Christ and Satan.* Grand Rapids, MI: Kregel, 1961.

————. *Charismatic Gifts.* Quebec, Canada: The Association for Christian Evangelism (Quebec), 1975.

————. *Christian Counseling and Occultism.* Translated by Andrew Petter. Grand Rapids, MI: Kregel, 1965.

————. *Demonology, Past and Present.* Grand Rapids, MI: Kregel, 1973.

————. *The Devil's Alphabet.* Grand Rapids, MI: Kregel, n.d.

Krailsheimer, A. J., trans. *Pascal Pensees.* New York: Penguin, 1976.

Kreeft, Peter. *Making Sense Out of Suffering.* Ann Arbor, MI: Servant, 1986.

————. *Occult Bondage and Deliverance.* Grand Rapids, MI: Kregel, n.d.

Kuhlman, Kathryn. *I Believe in Miracles.* Englewood Cliffs, NJ: Prentice-Hall, 1962.

Langton, G. Edward. *Essentials of Demonology.* London: Epworth, 1949.

Lawrence, Roy. *Christian Healing Rediscovered.* Downers Grove, IL: InterVarsity, 1980.

Levitt, Zola, and John Wildon. *Psychic Healing.* Chicago: Moody, 1982.

Lewis, C. S. *The Problem of Pain.* New York: Macmillan, 1974.

Linn, Dennis, and Matthew Linn. *Deliverance Prayer.* New York: Paulist Press, 1981.

———. *Healing Life's Hurts.* New York: Paulist Press, 1978.

Lloyd-Jones, D. Martyn. *The Cross.* Westchester, IL: Crossway, 1986.

———. *Romans.* Grand Rapids, MI: Zondervan, 1976.

Machen, J. Gresham. *The Christian View of Man.* London: The Banner of Truth Trust, 1937.

MacNutt, Francis. *Healing.* Notre Dame, IN: Ave Maria, 1974.

———. *The Power to Heal.* Notre Dame, IN: Ave Maria, 1977.

———. *The Prayer That Heals.* Notre Dame, IN: Ave Maria, 1981.

Maddocks, Morris. *The Christian Healing Ministry.* London: SPCD, 1981.

Martin, George. *Healing: Reflections on the Gospel.* Ann Arbor, MI: Servant, 1977.

Martin, Trevor. *Kingdom Healing.* London: Marshalls, 1981.

McCrossan, T.J. *Bodily Healing and the Atonement.* Edited by Roy Hicks and Kenneth E. Hagin. Tulsa, OK: Faith Library, 1982.

Montgomery, John Warwick, ed. *Demon Possession.* Minneapolis, MN: Bethany House, 1976.

Needham, David C. *Birthright.* Portland, OR: Multnomah, 1983.

Nevius, John L. *Demon Possession.* Grand Rapids, MI: Kregel, 1968.

Newport, John P. *Demons, Demons, Demons.* Nashville, TN: Broadman, 1972.

Nolen, William A. *Healing: A Doctor in Search of a Miracle.* New York: Random House, 1974.

Payne, Leanne. *Real Presence.* Westchester, IL: Crossway, 1979.

Pytches, David. *Come, Holy Spirit.* London: Hodder and Stoughton, 1985.

Reisser, Paul C., Teri K. Reisser, and John Weldon. *The Holistic Healers.* Downers Grove, IL: InterVarsity, 1983.

Roberts, Alexander, and James Donaldson, eds. *The Ante-Nicene Fathers.* Grand Rapids, MI: Eerdmans, 1973.

Russell, Jeffrey Burton. *The Devil: Perceptions of Evil from Antiquity to Primitive Christianity.* Ithica, NY: Cornell University Press, 1977.

———. *Satan and the Early Christian Tradition.* Ithaca, NY: Cornell University Press, 1981.

Sandford, John and Paula. *Healing the Wounded Spirit*. South Plainfield, NJ: Bridge, 1985.

———. *The Transformation of the Inner Man*. South Plainfield, NJ: Bridge, 1982.

Sanford, Agnes. *The Healing Power of the Bible*. Philadelphia: Holman, 1969.

———. *The Healing Light*. New York: Ballantine, 1972.

———. *The Healing Gifts of the Spirit*. Philadelphia: Trumpet, 1966.

Scanlan, Michael. *Inner Healing*. New York: Paulist Press, 1974.

———. *Let the Fire Fall*. Ann Arbor, MI: Servant, 1986.

———. *The Power of Penance, Confession and the Holy Spirit*. Notre Dame, IN: Ave Maria, 1972.

Scanlan, Michael, and Randall J. Cirner. *Deliverance from Evil Spirits*. Ann Arbor, MI: Servant, 1980.

Seamands, David A. *Healing for Damaged Emotions*. Wheaton, IL: Victor, 1981.

———. *Healing of Memories*. Wheaton, IL: Victor, 1985.

———. *Putting Away Childish Things*. Wheaton, IL: Victor, 1982.

Seeberg, Reinhold. *Textbook of the History of Doctrines*. Grand Rapids, MI: Baker, 1964.

Seybold, Klaus, and Ulrich B. Mueller. *Sickness and Healing*. Translated by Douglas W. Stott. Nashville, TN: Abingdon, 1981.

Shiels, W.J. *The Church and Healing*. Oxford: The Ecclesiastical History Society, 1982.

Schlemon, Barbara Leahy. *Healing the Hidden Self*. Notre Dame, IN: Ave Maria, 1982.

Simpson, A. B. *The Gospel of Healing*. Rev. ed. New York: Christian Alliance Publishing, 1955.

Sipley, Richard M. *Understanding Divine Healing*. Wheaton, IL: Victor, 1986.

Snyder, Howard A., and Daniel V. Runyon. *The Divided Flame*. Grand Rapids, MI: Zondervan, 1986.

Stapleton, Ruth Carter. *The Gift of Inner Healing*. Waco, TX: Word, 1976.

Synan, Vinson. *In the Latter Days*. Ann Arbor, MI: Servant, 1984.

Tapscott, Betty. *Inner Healing Through Healing of Memories: God's Gift—Peace of Mind*. Kingwood, TX: Hunter, 1975.

Thomas, W. Ian. *The Saving Life of Christ*. Grand Rapids, MI: Zondervan, 1970.

Torrey, R. A. *Divine Healing*. Grand Rapids, MI: Baker, 1974.

———. *I Talk Back to the Devil*. Harrisburg, PA: Christian Publications, 1972.

Unger, Merrill F. *The Baptizing Work of the Holy Spirit*. Grand Rapids: Zondervan, 1964.

———. *Biblical Demonology*. Wheaton, IL: Scripture Press, 1952.

———. *Demons in the World Today*. Wheaton, IL: Tyndale House, 1971.

———. *What Demons Can Do to Saints*. Chicago: Moody, 1977.

Vitz, Paul. *Psychology As Religion*. Grand Rapids, MI: Eerdmans, 1977.

Wallace, C. H. *Witchcraft in the World Today*. New York: Board, 1967.

Watson, David. *Fear No Evil*. London: Hodder and Stoughton, 1984.

Wilkinson, John. *Health and Healing*. Edinburgh: Handsel, 1980.

Wimber, John, with Kevin Springer. *Power Evangelism*. San Francisco: Harper & Row, 1986.

Wink, Walter. *Naming the Powers: The Language of Power in the New Testament*. Philadelphia: Fortress, 1984.

Wise, Robert L. *Healing of the Past*. Oklahoma City, OK: Presbyterian and Reformed Renewal Ministries International, 1984.

Wolff, Hans Walter. *Anthropology of the Old Testament*. Philadelphia: Fortress, 1974.